AUTHENTIC

CHINESE

CUISINE

FOR THE CONTEMPORARY KITCHEN

Bryanna Clark Grogan

Book Publishing Company
Summertown, Tennessee

Interior art: Kim Trainor
Cover design: Warren Jefferson
Interior Design: Gwynelle Dismukes
              Cynthia Holzapfel

Published in the United States by
Book Publishing Company
P.O. Box 99
Summertown, TN 38483
888-260-8458
www.bookpubco.com

03 02 01 00   1 2 3 4 5 6

Grogan, Bryanna Clark, 1948-
  Authentic Chinese cuisine for the contemporary kitchen / Bryanna Clark Grogan.
      p. cm.
Includes index.
  ISBN 1-57067-101-X (alk. paper)
  1. Cookery, Chinese. I. Title.
  TX724.5.C5 G76 2000
  641.5951--dc21   00-010674

Calculations for the nutritional analyses in this book are based on the average number of servings listed with the recipes and the average amount of an ingredient, if a range is called for. Calculations are rounded up to the nearest gram. If two options for an ingredients are listed, the first one is used. Not included are optional ingredients, serving suggestions, or fat used for frying, unless the amount of fat is specified in the recipe.

Dedication

This book is for my son, Timothy Glenn Clark, who only likes broccoli in a stir-fry and thinks my vegetarian sweet-and-sour is awesome!

Acknowledgements

Thanks to Benjamin Lee, wherever you are, for sharing your mother's recipes and Chinese cooking know-how. And many thanks to my long-suffering editor, Michael Cook, who is so patient and understanding.

Contents

INTRODUCTION

"The earliest Chinese cookery book with measurements, by Madame Wu of Kiangsu, goes back to the Sung Dynasty [A.D. 10th to 13th century]."

From *Chinese Gastronomy* by Hsiang Ju Lin and Tsuifeng Lin, Hastings House, New York, 1969

It's been almost 30 years since Benjamin Lee, a fellow student at Langara College in Vancouver, B.C., began trading Chinese cooking lessons for my home-cooked Italian meals. It was Benjamin who first taught me some of his mother's recipes and techniques and who gave me the courage to really delve into Chinese cooking.

I spent my teen-age years in San Francisco and then moved to Vancouver as a young married woman, so I was exposed to the greatest Chinese shopping and eating on the west coast of North America. In San Francisco we lived in the Marina District, just over the hill from North Beach and Chinatown, with the sights, sounds, and smells of great Chinese cuisine just a short bus ride or a healthy hike away.

We now live near Vancouver and love to visit our favorite Chinese restaurants when we are in town. We are lucky that where we live we can obtain most of the Chinese ingredients we need, but it's still fun to go shopping on Vancouver's Pender St. on a Sunday morning.

The streets are crowded and noisy, filled with families shopping together, friends greeting each other, and shopkeepers extolling the virtues of their produce. There are wide-eyed tourists, expensively dressed Hong Kong businessmen and women, and grandmas carrying fat grandbabies in cloth slings on their backs. And there is so much to choose from! I'm only saved from overspending by the weight of my carrier bags!

In the last eleven years or so, my Chinese cooking has changed since I am now vegan. The Chinese have an ancient Buddhist vegetarian cuisine, which even nonvegetarians frequently enjoy for religious and health reasons. Our favorite Buddhist vegetarian Chinese restaurants in Vancouver, the Bo Jik and the Bo Kong, are always full of Chinese families enjoying the incredibly varied delights of Buddhist temple cuisine.

Chinese cooks have mastered the art of making what they call "Buddha's meats" or "mock meats." I have read one theory that these dishes were developed because the monks did not want to deprive their guests of the flavors they craved. Stella Lau Fessler, author of *Chinese Meatless Cooking*, wrote, "To a Chinese cook, imitating a certain meat dish with nonmeat ingredients is not simply a matter of replacing meat. It is instead an effort to show off the great culinary art of China, to make the impossible possible." I can perhaps put myself in the same category— I enjoy "making the impossible possible"!

Most "mock meats" can stand on their own as delicious foods, reminiscent perhaps of the food they are replacing, but different. I like the taste and texture of Chinese vegetarian "roast duck," both the canned seitan (cooked gluten) variety and the bean curd skin (yuba) variety made in Buddhist restaurants. I also enjoy the other canned braised seitan products made in China—the curried type and the "mock abalone," for instance.

I love trying the "mock meats" and "mock meat" dishes the restaurant chefs prepare, using bean curd skin, tofu, mushrooms, seitan, nuts, and even potatoes. Currently, some Chinese chefs are also using textured soy protein products. I have had some delicious "chicken" dishes made from these products, which are produced especially for the Chinese restaurant trade. It's so much fun to be able to order delicious dim sum, such as stuffed dumplings and spring rolls, and soups (which vegetarians always have to avoid in ordinary restaurants, since the broth is almost always meat or chicken-based) without worrying about the contents! I usually end up taking home cartons of vegetarian dumplings and cold "mock meat" combinations so that we can enjoy them one more time. This also gives me an opportunity to analyze the ingredients and perhaps reproduce them in my own kitchen.

There are many excellent Chinese vegetarian cookbooks available which cover Chinese vegetable cookery (usually with some tofu), but most of them totally avoid the whole subject of "mock meats." I hope to fill that particular void in this book, rather than simply rehash what has gone before. I hope you will enjoy the results as much as my family does.

Of course, there is much more in this book than meat substitutes! Vegetables are the basis of Chinese cuisine, vegetarian or not. Since we are being urged to eat more vegetables than ever before (9 to 11 servings of fruits and vegetables a day, according to many experts), Chinese vegetarian cuisine can provide variety and culinary delight along with nutritional excellence.

Chinese cuisine is vast; the vegetarian recipes alone could fill many volumes. So, necessarily, this book is a collection of my favorite recipes and not an exhaustive compendium of Chinese vegetarian cuisine. I feel confident that this book will complement any other Chinese vegetarian cookbooks you may have. I have tried to provide a balanced selection of recipes, grouped according to cooking technique. I have also included information on ingredients, equipment, and how to plan, cook, and serve a Chinese meal.

The recipes are as authentic as possible, without calling for extremely exotic ingredients that may be hard to find. I have provided suggestions for authentic-tasting substitutes whenever possible. After all, Chinese cooks are nothing if not inventive and have always worked wonders with whatever ingredients were available to them in the far-off countries to which they have emigrated over the years. The most important ingredients have always been fresh, good-quality vegetables.

I have used a few ingredients that are familiar to long-time vegetarians but perhaps not to Chinese cooks, such as nutritional yeast. I feel sure that North American Chinese vegetarian cooks will incorporate some of these Western ingredients into their cuisine over time, just as they have begun to use textured soy protein, and just as Western vegetarians have absorbed so many Chinese ingredients and techniques into their own cooking.

These recipes reflect my own taste preferences; you can adjust them to suit your own. For instance, I am not fond of three very frequently used Chinese canned ingredients—straw mushrooms, baby corn, and bamboo shoots. I find the straw mushrooms slimy textured, the baby corn tasteless, and the odor of the bamboo shoots unpleasant. So I don't use them! I just leave them out or substitute something I do like. (If you like them, by all means slip them into my recipes.) A cook has culinary license to make these kinds of changes!

These recipes are designed by a vegan vegetarian cook for use in a modern North American kitchen. You don't need to purchase special Chinese equipment. I use a few modern shortcuts, but never if it takes away from the authentic taste. I have used far less oil or other fat in most of the recipes than the average Chinese cook, but this is not first-and-foremost a low-fat cookbook. There is even a chapter on deep-frying, but I have given unorthodox alternative instructions for oven-frying, pan-frying, broiling, or grilling wherever possible (unorthodox because Chinese kitchens seldom have ovens).

I hope you will enjoy this culinary adventure as much as I have and continue to explore one of the world's most varied, healthful, and exciting cuisines as the new century unfolds.

Bryanna Clark Grogan

A NOTE ABOUT TERMINOLOGY

The spelling of translated Chinese words varies widely. In addition to the fact that there are different characters for words in Mandarin and Cantonese, there are three main systems for translating Chinese characters into English words—Pinyin, Yale, and Wade-Giles. The older Wade-Giles spellings are more familiar to many of us, but the Pinyin system was officially adopted by the Chinese government in 1979. I have simply chosen the spellings that occur most often or that I like the look of best.

I have used some Japanese words for common Asian ingredients simply because they are now universally accepted in Western cooking terminology. Most people know what "tofu" (the Japanese word) is, but they might not know what "bean curd" or "doufu" is. The same problem applies to yuba (the Japanese word for "bean curd skin," which can also be translated from the Chinese as "bean milk sheets," "pressed tofu," and other confusing things). Seitan is the Japanese word for savory, braised wheat gluten dough. Most Western gluten products are marketed under the name seitan. I have used the word gluten only when discussing or defining gluten products that are not flavored and braised or when describing Chinese commercial products which are labeled gluten.

Chapter I

A SHORT HISTORY OF CHINESE VEGETARIAN CUISINE

The Buddha said:
"One will enjoy longevity
By not killing or harming others.
One will seldom be sick
If one relieves others' worry and grief."
Maharatnakuta Sutra

Vegetarian cooking has a long and honorable history in China. The Chinese have developed a serious vegetarian cuisine from Buddhist and Taoist influences, sometimes referred to as Chinese temple cuisine.

In China there has always been a link between food and health and food and spirituality. The earliest mention of vegetarianism in China was recorded during the Zhou Dynasty (beginning c. 1028 B.C.). There are other references in ancient texts written during the reign of the Han Emperor Ming (58-75 A.D.) predating the introduction of Buddhism into China by several hundred years. The Chinese word for vegetarianism, *zhai*, originally meant abstinence. Over time, Chinese vegetarian cooking has developed into a culinary specialty of great sophistication.

Some scholars insist that the development of vegetarianism in China had more to do with the introduction of many foreign fruits and vegetables during the Han Dynasty (206 B.C.-222 A.D.) than with the introduction of Buddhism. The appearance of bean curd (tofu)

and many other soy products during the Han Dynasty, together with the discovery of making gluten from wheat, further enriched and diversified the developing vegetarian cuisine.

Two Chinese philosophers influenced Chinese life and cuisine. Confucius established civilized Chinese patterns of eating that were practiced and elaborated upon by other Chinese philosophers and intellectuals. These individuals created the art of cooking and appreciating fine cuisine.

Confucius' contemporary Lao-tze taught the Chinese what is now known as Taoism—that leading a natural life of peace, harmony, and happiness is achieved by simplicity, meditation, and tranquility. Good food and good health are closely associated in Taoism. Taoists believe that the plants which are life-giving for animals are also good for humans. Early Taoists influenced Chinese cuisine from its infancy. They explored the medicinal and health-giving properties of plants, herbs, and spices. Although most Taoists do not reject meat, the orthodox belief is that meat is unclean and must be omitted from the diet in order to purify the blood; therefore, many Chinese health cures involve the use of a vegetarian diet.

The importation of Buddhism from India further influenced the development of a sophisticated vegetarian cuisine, since one of the five abstentions of orthodox Buddhism is an injunction against taking life. Fine vegetarian cuisine developed first in the Buddhist monasteries. According to Hsiang Ju Lin and Tsuifeng Lin in their book *Chinese Gastronomy* (Hastings House, NY, 1969), "Buddhists are vegetarians, consequently a small pocket of gastronomy has developed, fascinating in its attempt to create the ordinary flavors and appearance of fish and meat by using vegetarian ingredients. The Buddhists, whether monks or ordinary people, mingled freely with the non-vegetarians, and because the manners of Chinese society are all-embracing and diffuse, felt obliged to provide food which looked and almost tasted like meat. This was a sign of hospitality." Wealthy ladies would make pilgrimages to the city temples, having ordered a vegetarian lunch in advance. This was apparently one of the few occasions on which wealthy women could go out by themselves.

The authors continue: "The school of cooking which originated in the temple kitchens expanded and was taken up by the Yangchow cooks, specializing in delicate pastries and noodles. The challenge of simulating textures and appearance was irresistible. They were, in fact, able to reproduce even the intricate diamond pattern of duck skin, by lightly scoring smooth bean curd and filling in the cuts with a soy sauce mixture. Vegetarianism, which had originated for ethical reasons, finally became the gastronome's business, and fell into the fine hands of the pastry cook."

Even today, when most Chinese Buddhists are not orthodox enough to be vegetarians, they flock to Buddhist vegetarian restaurants during times of penance, or special days such as New Year's or the first and fifteenth days of each lunar month. Others will frequent vegetarian restaurants when they are prescribed a vegetarian diet by their Chinese medical practitioner or simply because they enjoy eating something different.

Chinese vegetarian cuisine is basically vegan, since dairy products are almost totally unused in Chinese cooking and an orthodox Buddhist will not eat eggs or fish. Western nutritionists should take note of the fact that Chinese vegetarians have thrived over the centuries on a nutritionally balanced diet of vegetables, fruits, nuts, mushrooms and various fungi, beans and bean products, and grains and cereal products.

Vegetarian travelers to China and Hong Kong often come home with stories of having great difficulty adhering to their diets until they were introduced to or stumbled upon vegetarian restaurants and Buddhist monasteries which serve meals to the public. Then one hears tales of sumptuous ten-course vegetarian banquets featuring "Buddha's meats" and vegetable dishes with poetic names such as "Two Immortals in the Apricot Garden."

I believe that Chinese vegetarian cooking has a major contribution to make to ever-evolving Western vegetarian cuisine, primarily in the use of fresh, high-quality produce and ingredients, interesting flavor combinations, and cooking techniques which heighten the flavor and nutrition of each dish.

YIN AND YANG FOODS, CHINESE MEDICINE, AND VEGETARIANISM

Chinese medicine depends largely on the interpretation of the balance between yin and yang in the body (yin being cold, dark, wet, sweet, and expansive, and yang being bright, hot, and dry). If a Chinese practitioner feels that you are too yin, you will be prescribed more yang foods to balance your system and vice versa.

Foods are broadly divided into the two categories, but the nature of the food can be intensified and even to some extent changed, by the way it is cooked. The methods of cooking are classified from "coolest" to "hottest," with boiling regarded as cool, stir-frying medium, and deep-frying hot. The length of cooking time is also considered, with quick-cooking being more cooling than long-cooking, regardless of the method.

YIN FOODS

Duck and pork are classified as yin, along with tofu and other soy products, bean sprouts, all bland or boiled foods, the cabbage family, carrots, celery, cucumbers, some fish and fruits (like pears), American ginseng, most greens, honey, melon, milk, potatoes, seaweed, water, watercress, winter squash, and most white foods, including white turnips.

Whiskey and beer are considered cooling. A traditional cooling beverage is sugar cane juice.

YANG FOODS

Beef, broiled meats, catfish, chicken and chicken soup, eggs, fatty meats, shellfish, pigs knuckles, and pork liver are considered yang. *All* fried foods, of whatever origin, are also considered yang.

Eggplant, garlic, ginger, Korean ginseng, glutinous rice, green peppers, hot and spicy foods, leeks and onions, mushrooms, peanuts, persimmons, sesame oil, tangerines, vinegar and wine, brandy, sour foods, and red foods (beans, peppers, tomatoes, etc.) are all vegetarian foods which are considered yang.

The time of the year and the climate also have a bearing on what is eaten—for instance, one would eat more yang foods (warming) in the winter and more yin foods (cooling) in the summer.

Sometimes people will tell me that they used to be vegetarian, but they started to eat meat because they were told they needed to eat more yang foods. However, this is an oversimplification of the nature of yin and yang. Some animal foods are considered yin. Chinese practitioners will also tell you that eating too many sweets (yin) can set up an imbalance which will then need yang foods to rectify, so some vegetarians who seem to need more yang may actually be consuming too many sweet foods.

WHAT ABOUT ANIMAL FOODS AS MEDICINE?

The Chinese, as in most cultures, long ago discovered leaves, seeds, tree bark, and roots that have medicinal properties. Many of these have been proven to be efficacious. However, Chinese folk practitioners sometimes prescribe the internal organs of animals, including those of endangered species. Dr. Gerald Choa, former director of the Hong Kong government's Medical and Health Department, has described this as "sympathetic magic." In an address to the Royal Asiatic Society in October 1966, he commented: "The Chinese also practice organotherapy—and it is here, particularly, that we run into ideas of sympathetic magic. When people have a weakness or supposed weakness in a certain organ, or when they want to improve its functioning or power, they eat the corresponding organ of an animal."

There are activists in Asian communities working to educate people about the plight of endangered animals, such as bears, tigers, rhinoceri, and elephants. Chinese medicine has many facets and can be extraordinarily helpful, but it is not necessary to cling to unproven folk remedies of any culture, especially if they are harmful to these magnificent animals. There are dietary and herbal prescriptions, acupuncture, acupressure, massage, and various types of exercises within Chinese medicine which can be used to treat any ailment that might have once been treated with "sympathetic magic."

Therefore, you need not abandon your vegetarian principles in order to follow Chinese medical practices. Chinese Buddhist monks and nuns, after all, are strict vegetarians.

FOOD SYMBOLISM

The colors and shapes of fruits and vegetables have special significance for the Chinese. Green vegetables recall the color of jade and are associated with youth and healthfulness. Red foods denote good fortune. Gold, the color of money and of the sun, is prized above all. Round fruits are said to resemble the moon and thus bring good fortune.

Pineapples are said to be signs of prosperity, and bananas bring luck if eaten first thing in the morning. Fruits with seeds are symbols of fertility. Tangerines or mandarin oranges, being both round and "gold," are particular tokens of wealth and good fortune.

Chapter II

THE REGIONAL COOKING OF CHINA

"If there is anything [the Chinese] are serious about, it is neither religion nor learning, but food."
Lin Yutang, *My Country and My People*

China is a vast country with a wide range of climates and terrain, and so encompasses many schools of cooking within its cuisine. The climate, geography, and native ingredients of these regions influence their cooking style. Some food ideas have moved beyond their original boundaries to become absorbed in a "national" cuisine; others have retained their regional character.

The cooking of China is divided into four main culinary "schools": the North (Mandarin, Peking, or Beijing-style), encompassing Shandong, Hebei, Shanxi, and others; the East (Shanghai-style), encompassing Shanghai, Zheijiang, Jiangsu, and Fujian; the South (Cantonese-style), including Guangxi and Guangdong; and the West (Sichuan-style), including Sichuan, Hunan, Guizhou, and Yunnan.

NORTHERN CUISINE (MANDARIN, PEKING, OR BEIJING-STYLE)

The northern "Eternal City" of Beijing, formerly Peking (laid out by Kublai Khan in the 13th century), has long been a focus for artistic, intellectual, political, and culinary activity. From early times, culinary art in Beijing became highly sophisticated, elegant, and imaginative in order to honor visitors to the official court. After China opened its doors to foreigners in 1844, this sophistication reached even greater heights. This "school" is also probably the most eclectic in China, as it incorporates Imperial Palace delicacies and Mongolian and Moslem dishes along with northern provincial dishes.

Because of the fertile terrain and extreme temperatures in this region, wheat, barley, millet, corn, and soybeans are staple crops. For this reason, wheat flour-based breads, pancakes, noodles, and dumplings, rather than rice, dominate the table. Cabbage family vegetables abound, and fruits such as apples, pears, grapes, and persimmons are common. This area has the heaviest dependence on meat dishes, due to Mongolian and Moslem influences.

Northern cuisine is characterized by sweet-and-sour sauces, wine-based cooking, hoisin sauce, garlic, sesame oil, green onions, yeast doughs, and generous use of soy sauce. Vinegar is a commonly used seasoning. The area is also known for its fermented bean pastes.

EASTERN CUISINE (SHANGHAI-STYLE)

The great city of Shanghai, the largest city in China and a major industrial and trade center, resides at the mouth of the Yangtse River. The fertile river valley of the Yangtse accounts for the nickname "Heaven on Earth" which is sometimes given to this region. The climate is basically subtropical, with warm, wet summers and cool winters, allowing for a year-round growing season. Major crops are wheat, barley, rice, corn, sweet potatoes, and soybeans. Numerous vegetable and fruit varieties flourish here. It was in this region that Chinese vegetarian cuisine developed into a highly sophisticated art form. The city of Suchou is noted for its superb pastries, and Yangchou for its noodles and egg rolls.

Shaoxing wine, black vinegar, a variety of pickles, and what is reputedly the best soy sauce in China all come from this region. It is famous for its talented chefs and highly complex cooking techniques. However, the area is also famous for homey braised (red-cooked) dishes.

SOUTHERN CUISINE (CANTONESE-STYLE)

This is the style of Chinese cooking most familiar to North Americans, for the simple reason that it was from this area that waves of Chinese immigrants came to North America in the 19th century. The food served in North American Cantonese restaurants was cheap and tasty, but not necessarily authentic Cantonese—the cooks made what they thought would appeal to their customers.

But real Cantonese food is far from dull. It has great variety and depth due to the diversity of local food and also to the fact that Kuangchou (Canton) was a prosperous trading port where wealthy Chinese merchants and foreigners resided. The moist, tropical climate affords a long growing season for rice, vegetables, and fruits. For this reason, the Cantonese appreciate fresh ingredients with subtle seasoning. The food is light and generally mild.

Cantonese food has also been influenced by the Mandarin style and by foreigners from

Portugal, Holland, and other countries who brought new ingredients, such as peanuts, corn, tomatoes, and white potatoes.

Though the Cantonese use a wide variety of cooking techniques, they are famous for stir-fried dishes and for their dim sum dishes. Black bean sauce and oyster sauce are favorite seasonings. (Vegetarians can use "oyster" sauce made with mushrooms—see p. 116.) They excel at barbecuing and roasting.

WESTERN CUISINE (SICHUAN-STYLE)

The delicate flavors of Cantonese cooking seem the exact opposite of the spicy robustness of western-style cooking, characterized by that of Sichuan and Hunan, two regional cuisines now very popular in North America. The semi-tropical climate here is favorable for growing chiles and other spices. The close proximity to Burma, Pakistan, and India has influenced its use of highly seasoned condiments.

Sweet, sour, and salty flavors are favored here in the "Land of Abundance," as it is sometimes called. It is one of the major "rice bowls" of China and is one region that has rarely experienced famine. Rice is eaten at every meal. Bean curd (tofu) is very popular here, usually permeated with hot, spicy flavors.

Red chile peppers, black mushrooms, wood ears, Sichuan peppercorns, garlic, onions, chili oil, dried tangerine peel, and ginger are common ingredients. Often flavorings are combined to create a complicated blend of hot, sour, sweet, and salty in one bite. Stir-frying and steaming are the most common cooking techniques; it is a cuisine noted for its generous use of oil. Sometimes more than one cooking technique will be employed within a dish.

CHINA

Peking

Szechuan

Shanghai

Hunan

Canton

Hong Kong

Chapter III

A GUIDE TO INGREDIENTS

"Chinese cooking has been called the 'marriage of flavors.' This is very apt, for the individual ingredients should preserve their identity while complementing each other."

Hsiang Ju Lin and Tsiufeng Lin
Chinese Gastronomy

Chinese home cooking does not require a hundred strange ingredients. Certain seasonings are essential, but most are now commonly found in larger supermarkets. Chinese cooks who have emigrated to the far corners of the world work their culinary magic with the produce at hand and make it their own. You can do the same.

If you live in an isolated area, check the mail-order sources on p. 185. Otherwise, stock up on the essential ingredients when you are in a large city. Most of them keep for a long time and are very inexpensive. Then you can use whatever fresh produce you have on hand.

Here are some descriptions, explanations, and directions for ingredients which are not commonly known, might be confusing, and are used throughout this book.

ESSENTIAL INGREDIENTS

Black beans, salted or fermented (Tou Shih)

The use of these salted or fermented black soybeans predates soy sauce in China. They are still used by poor rural Chinese when they cannot afford soy sauce, because they are cheap and easy to make at home. The beans give foods a pleasing, wine-like flavor and are particularly delicious combined with broccoli, asparagus, and "mock meats." Once used all over China, they are now primarily used in Cantonese cooking. Some chili pastes have a bit of fermented black bean added.

The beans come in plastic bags, jars, or cardboard cartons, and last indefinitely. Sometimes they are flavored with dried ginger or orange peel, which is fine, but avoid those flavored with star anise or five-spice powder. The flavor is strong and not suitable to most dishes. After you open the package, transfer the beans to covered jars. They do not need refrigeration.

To use the beans, do not bother rinsing them, as many recipes suggest. I find this diminishes the flavor. If you use the salted variety, go easy on other salty ingredients in your dish. The beans should be chopped with a knife or cleaver or crushed with the back of a fork before using. This is often done along with any grated ginger, chopped or crushed garlic, and/or wine that is also being used. Usually only a tablespoon or two is added to a dish.

I prefer the beans to the bottled black bean sauces; the beans are cheaper and cleaner tasting. There is really no substitute for the fermented beans.

Brown bean sauce or paste (Yuan Shai Shih); also yellow bean sauce or paste, bean paste, soybean condiment

Originally known as jiang or chiang, this is the oldest soybean sauce in Chinese cooking. (Miso is a Japanese derivative.) Light miso, slightly watered-down, may be used as a substitute if you absolutely can't get the Chinese variety. Brown bean paste is simply fermented soybeans and can be whole or ground. The ground variety (mo yuen shih) is sometimes very salty, so do some taste tests.

Modern "duck sauces" often call for hoisin sauce mixed with sugar and sesame oil, but the authentic version uses plain bean sauce. It is used often in Sichuan and Hunan cooking and is frequently added to noodle dishes.

Chili garlic paste or sauce (La Chiao Chiang, Tou Pan Chiang)

Although chilis are a "new world" product, they were quickly adapted into the cuisines of Sichuan and Hunan. Look for "chili paste with garlic," "chili paste with soybean," or "Sichuan (Szechuan) chili sauce" in jars or cans. You can use the Southeast Asian varieties (look out for shrimp), but they aren't as flavorful as the Chinese, which often have some fermented black beans or brown bean paste added. If you are absolutely desperate, use cayenne pepper or bottled hot sauce, but go easy and don't expect the same results.

Cornstarch and other thickeners

The Chinese prefer cornstarch as a thickener because it thickens to a clear sheen with no taste. It is also used for batters, because it gives a crunchy crust. Cornstarch should be used with a light hand—gloppy sauces are not what you are looking for. It should be mixed with two or three times as much *cold* water and stirred into the sauce just at the end of cooking.

I use cornstarch because it is cheap, readily available, and gives good results. It is not an item I depend upon for nutrition, so it doesn't bother me that it is refined. In fact, all starch thickeners are highly refined. However, if you are allergic to or prefer not to use cornstarch, here are two common Chinese alternatives that can be used exactly as cornstarch.

Wheat starch is the starch left over from washing wheat flour dough to make gluten (which is the protein). It is found in most Asian grocery stores and some supermarkets, either in the flour section, allergy section, or Asian section. Health food stores may carry it as well.

Water chestnut flour (Ma T'i Fen) is made from ground dried water chestnuts. It gives a clear sheen to sauces and a crunchy texture to fried foods, but it's expensive and harder to dissolve than cornstarch. It is found in eight-ounce boxes in Asian grocery stores and perhaps the Asian section of some large supermarkets.

I have omitted arrowroot and kuzu powder, two rather expensive thickening powders which are commonly used in natural foods cooking. They are both highly refined and have no special nutritional advantages. They both require a longer, lower-temperature simmering time to thicken. This will not work in rapid-fire Chinese stir-fries—the vegetables would be overcooked.

Hot bean sauce, Sichuan hot bean paste

This is brown bean paste (Yuan Shai Shih) with chili, and sometimes garlic, sesame oil, and sugar added. You can simply use bean paste and add your own seasonings.

Mushrooms, dried Chinese black (Hsian chun), *dried shiitakes, black forest mushrooms, black winter mushrooms, brown oak mushrooms, fragrant mushrooms*

When you visit an Asian market, you will see bags of all sizes and varying prices containing dried mushrooms. They may range in size from one to three inches in diameter, with brown or black caps that are smooth and thin, or thick with white fissures. (Thicker is better.) Although the Japanese and Koreans eat these mushrooms both fresh and dried, the Chinese prefer them dried.

You will find the widest variety of sizes, types, and prices in Chinese herbalist shops, since dried mushrooms have long been used in Chinese medicine for heart disease and blood pressure problems. Some varieties may cost over $30 a pound, but there are inexpensive varieties available in most large supermarkets. They keep for a long time. (You may want to store them in the freezer to keep bugs at bay.)

All are delicious, but the more expensive varieties are exceptionally meaty and flavorful, so treat yourself once in a while. Save the soaking broth for stock, by the way.

See p. 42 for directions on how to prepare the mushrooms for cooking. See p. 42 for directions on how to prepare the mushrooms for cooking.

Noodles (see Chapter X)

Rice (see introduction to Chapter IX, p. 91)

Sesame oil, roasted

This amber-colored oil is an absolute must for Chinese cooking, especially vegetarian cooking. Because it is more expensive than cooking oil, it is usually drizzled over a dish at the end, but I often reject convention and use it for stir-frying when I want to cut down drastically on the amount of oil used but still have full flavor. (Japanese chefs often deep-fry with half sesame oil and half cooking oil for rich flavor, so I don't consider it grossly heretical to stir-fry with a bit of it.) It is also used in salads and dipping sauces.

Do not substitute the pale, unroasted health food store variety. Only the roasted Asian variety has full, rich flavor. You can tell the difference by the color. Read labels carefully—some bottles reveal in the small print that they contain only some sesame oil. You want pure sesame oil. Prices vary widely, so shop around in large supermarkets and Asian grocery stores. Try to buy it in glass bottles, which helps keep it from becoming rancid so quickly. It doesn't matter whether you buy the Chinese or Japanese variety. Two recommended brands are the Kadoya brand (Japanese) "pure sesame oil" and the Chinese Kinlan and Dynasty brands.

I use roasted sesame oil in my Western cooking too. It lends a flavor reminiscent of smokey bacon fat.

Soy sauce (Chiang Yu) (see entry under Soyfoods, pp. 26-27)

Sugar, unbleached

I use unbleached sugar, not because it is more nutritious than ordinary sugar, but because cane sugar is usually bleached with ash made from beef bones. Beet sugar is not bleached this way. I specify "light unbleached" in some recipes—this would be the turbinado type, a pale beige, fairly coarse-grained sugar. "Dark unbleached" is more like brown sugar (ordinary brown sugar is just bleached sugar coated with molasses). Granulated sugar cane juice (there are organic brands) can be used in this instance, if you prefer.

Tofu (see entry under Soyfoods, pp. 27-29)

Vegetable oil

Many cooks don't realize that lard was, and still is in some areas, used for stir-frying and other uses in China. Now, cooking oil is produced so cheaply that it is usually used instead. Canola oil, peanut oil, corn oil, and safflower oil are all acceptable in Chinese cooking, but canola and peanut oil are the first choices. They contain more monunsaturated fats, which are more healthful, and they have a higher smoking point. (See Chapter XIII, about oils for deep-frying and for more information about oils and health.)

Refined, commercial oils have little flavor, which may be what you want in certain dishes. If you are cutting down on the amount of oil you use, you may want every teaspoon to count in terms of flavor. Cold- or expeller-pressed peanut and corn oils are more flavorful, but be careful—I have had some that were so unpleasant tasting that they must have been rancid. Expeller-pressed oils *must* be kept away from light, heat, and air. Buy from a store with a fast turnover and keep the oil in a tightly sealed glass bottle in a cool, dark place.

Many Chinese cooks have a preference for peanut oil (as I do), especially for frying, because it has a pleasant flavor, it burns only at very high temperatures (about 500°F), and does not take on odors and flavors from foods

as readily as other oils. (Another plus—it is almost as high in monounsaturates as olive oil.) The commercial supermarket brands are virtually flavorless, which is fine for deep-frying, but for tasty stir-frying, I recommend cold- or expeller-pressed peanut oil. It's more expensive but you can buy expeller-pressed Asian brands in 20-ounce bottles right up to 1-gallon cans for reasonable prices in Asian grocery stores. A good cold-pressed Asian peanut oil should have the fragrance of freshly-roasted peanuts, just as good extra-virgin olive oil is redolent with olive aroma and flavor. Buy small bottles of different brands at first to taste test them. Lion and Globe brand from Hong Kong is excellent and readily available.

> *Allergy Note:* I am aware that peanut allergies are serious and possibly life threatening. If you have such an allergy, of course, you will need to substitute another oil when I suggest peanut oil.

You may want to buy only organic oils. This is especially true for canola, which may be genetically modified if it is not organically grown. You will have to buy organic oils in natural food stores, and they will be more expensive.

Unless I specify sesame oil in my recipes, you can use whichever oil you prefer.

Vinegar

Vinegar is an age-old seasoning and medicinal used throughout Asia. Vinegars are made from rice, millet, barley, and fruits. Rice vinegar, either Chinese or Japanese, is inexpensive and easy to find. Avoid the seasoned varieties, which contain salt and sugar. You can usually substitute cider vinegar or white wine vinegar with excellent results.

Chinese black vinegar is made from wheat, malt, glutinous rice, millet, and sorghum, and has a rich, sweet, smokey quality. It is not as easy to find as white rice vinegar, however, and is sometimes diluted. I recommend Gold Plum's "Chinking Vinegar," Tientsin Vinegar, and Narcissus Brand "Yongchun Loagu."

Fortunately, balsamic vinegar makes a fine substitute. The really fine balsamic vinegars are prohibitively expensive (about \$100 for 3 ounces), but you can find acceptable "industri-ale" versions in supermarkets. Some are very harsh tasting, so some testing is necessary. You should not choke when the vinegar hits the back of your throat! Safeway bottles an inexpensive, acceptable variety.

Wine

Wine is used quite frequently in Chinese cooking, and, in my opinion, many dishes are lacking that certain something without it. It may be just a splash in a stir-fry, or as much as half a cup in a braised dish. (There are some Chinese dishes referred to as "drunken" which contain one or two bottles!) But it definitely adds depth of flavor, especially in vegetarian dishes.

China's most famous rice wine (Shaoxing wine, Shao Hsing, Hua Daio) has been made for over 2,000 years in Shaoxing in Zhejiang province. Made from glutinous rice, it is aged for about 10 years in earthenware jars stored in underground cellars. The only good substitute is dry sherry, which is very similar in color, bouquet, and alcohol content. (Do not use white wine or sake.) I have called for dry sher-ry in my recipes, simply because it is so much easier to find. If you can get rice wine (blue-labeled 624 ml bottle and red-labeled 750 ml bottle, both Pagoda brand), then by all means use it. Do not buy the yellow-labeled bottle, which is sweetened.

If you prefer to use nonalcoholic wines, you will have to experiment with the sweeter vari-eties. I honestly don't know if there is any vari-ety that comes close to a good dry sherry, but Ariel is a good brand to investigate first.

Vegetables, fresh

Because so many vegetables (Asian and Western) are used in Chinese cooking today, I am only commenting on unusual varieties or those which I think need additional informa-tion on selecting, purchasing, storing, sprout-ing, preparing, etc. I am assuming that every-one knows about garlic, snow peas, asparagus, and broccoli, for instance.

Bean sprouts (see mung beans, dried, p. 21, and soybean sprouts, p. 25)

You can sprout just about any legume for stir-frying, using the general directions given for these beans, but you might want to consult a book specifically devoted to sprouting or talk to a sprout enthusiast for more details.

Bok choy (see entry Greens, Chinese, p. 18)

Cabbage, napa (celery cabbage, Chinese cab-bage) (see entry Greens, Chinese, p. 18)

Chinese broccoli (Chinese kale, Gai Lan) (see entry Greens, Chinese, p. 18)

Chinese mustard greens or cabbage (Gai choy) (see entry Greens, Chinese, p. 18)

Eggplant (Chinese, Asian, or Japanese)

Asian eggplants are small and thin and require no salting and draining, as do the large Western types. They are sweet, tender, and seedless, but they spoil quickly, so use them up within a couple of days of purchase. Large eggplants can be used instead, but if they are not young and fresh, they will need to be sliced, salted, left to drain for 30 minutes, and then rinsed before cooking.

Ginger, fresh

It would be very hard to cook Chinese (or any Asian) dishes without fresh ginger. Valued as much for its medicinal properties as its culinary ones, ginger has been cultivated in Asia for longer than recorded history. It is a wonderful cure for nausea, aids digestion, combats cold symptoms, and is said to stimulate the appetite—for sex as well as food! It has a clean, spicy flavor which goes exceptionally well with garlic.

Knobby "roots" (they are actually rhizomes or underground stems) of fresh ginger are easily found in any supermarket—the challenge is keeping them from rotting before you use them all! My solution used to be to peel them, cut them into chunks, and store them in the refrigerator in a jar of dry sherry. This works just fine, and the ginger-flavored wine can be used in Chinese dishes, but I have discovered an easier way, thanks to Chinese cooking expert Barbara Tropp. Simply store your ginger, unpeeled, in a sturdy paper bag inside of a tightly sealed plastic one. If the paper bag gets soggy and tears, just replace it with a new one. The ginger keeps for months this way! Don't freeze your ginger—it will lose flavor.

Buy the hardest, heaviest rhizomes you can find, with smooth, unwrinkled skins. Check where the knobs have broken—if there are a lot of fibers, the rhizome is older. If you are grating the ginger, this doesn't matter because the fiber will stay behind. But if you are cutting the ginger into slices or slivers, fiber will be objectionable.

The Chinese often use very finely cut or slivered ginger. I prefer to grate it, because many people don't like to bite into pieces of ginger, however small. I use a tiny little metal box grater with a plastic top—it's about 2 inches high and very inexpensive. I find that this is the most efficient tool for grating both ginger and citrus peels. I don't peel ginger before grating it, but sliced or slivered ginger should be peeled.

Greens, Chinese

Since these entries can be used interchangeably in many cases, I have grouped them together. The Chinese use many kinds of greens, including watercress, turnip tops, radish tops, and many varieties not available to most of us. I have suggested substitutions using common North American greens where appropriate.

Bok choy (Chinese white cabbage, pak choi), flowering bok choy, and baby bok choy

Although Chinese farmers grow as many as 20 varieties of bok choy, we are lucky to see three kinds—the large chard-like variety with a bulbous bottom of white stalks and dark green leaves; the baby bok choy which is simply a miniature, immature version of that; and the flowering kind which looks very similar, but has thinner stalks and has yellow flowers growing out of the center. It is one of the most popular and readily available types of Chinese greens, but if you can't find it, Swiss chard or tender kale could be substituted.

Cabbage, napa (celery cabbage, Chinese cabbage)

This is probably the second most widely available Chinese vegetable in North America. It is more common in northern China, whereas bok choy is more common in the south. Napa cabbage is widely used in Japan, as well as Korea (where it is used to make the famous hot pickle, kimchi). It looks a bit like bok choy, but it is pale green to nearly white and the heads are larger and more dense.

You can use savoy cabbage as a substitute—it actually has more flavor, in my opinion. You could use regular green cabbage, but it's much tougher than either napa or savoy.

Chinese broccoli (Chinese kale, gai lan)

This is one of my absolute favorite Chinese vegetables, and it is becoming more widely available. It's also very easy to grow. If you've never tried it, you are in for a treat! It's dark to dull green in color and looks like broccoli that didn't head properly—with smaller, smooth stems, large leaves, and small clusters of white flowers. It's very tasty—slightly more bitter than broccoli, but not as bitter as the Italian broccoli rabe (rapini). It is one of the most nutritious vegetables available.

It can be prepared as you would broccoli, but in Chinese restaurants, it is usually blanched (whole) and then stir-fried with a very simple seasoning of oil and salt, and perhaps a bit of soy sauce or vegetarian "oyster" sauce.

You could substitute regular broccoli, but it won't have the same intensity of flavor, and if you used rapini, that would be much more bitter. A better substitute might be kale or collard greens.

Chinese mustard greens or cabbage (gai choy)

This exceptionally nutritious green deserves to be more popular. It is like bok choy with a hot bite to it. There are many varieties, most grown for preserving. The greens are wonderful in soups and stir-fries too. You could substitute turnip greens or radish tops.

Shanghai bok choy

This is another of my favorite Chinese greens. The leaves and stems are flatter than bok choy and spoon-shaped; the color is light green but darker than napa cabbage or Chinese cabbage. It can be anywhere from 6 to 12 inches high and is cooked like bok choy. You could substitute Swiss chard, tender kale, collard greens, or savoy cabbage.

Yow choy or Yow choy sum

This is a very common vegetable in Hong Kong, and I see it more and more in my area. It has narrow stems and oval leaves of a medium green color with a delicious mustard-like tang. It's wonderful in stir-fries.

You could substitute kale, collard greens, or turnip greens.

Shanghai bok choy (see entry Greens, Chinese, p. 18)

Soybean sprouts (see entry under Soyfoods, p. 25)

Water chestnut flour (see p. 14)

Water chestnuts, fresh

Although most North Americans are quite familiar with canned water chestnuts, most have not had the pleasure of tasting the fresh variety—more's the pity! The fresh ones are crisp and reminiscent of fresh coconut meat. They are not chestnuts at all, but the underwater stem tips (corms) of a type of water grass.

Buy only those that are rock hard and not discolored. The corms must be scrubbed and then the skin pared off with a small, sharp knife. They can be placed in cold water briefly before using.

If you can only find the canned variety, use them only in dishes where you want some crunch, not flavor, and rinse them well. Blanching them in boiling water for 15 seconds may take away some of the canned taste.

Vegetarian broth, powders and cubes (p. 109)

Vegetarian stir-fry "oyster" sauce (see p. 116)

OTHER INGREDIENTS

DRIED, CANNED, AND PRESERVED FOODS

Agar-agar (kanten, Chinese gelatin)

Asians are fond of molded jellies. Some are made from fruits and nut milks, others are made with sweetened beans and even corn. They are gelled with a seaweed-derived gelatin called agar-agar (kanten in Japanese) rather than the gelatin that is derived from animal hooves and skins commonly used in Western cooking. For this reason, agar has been adopted by Western vegetarians. It is available in natural food stores, in bar, flake, and powder form. A further advantage over animal gelatin is that it will set at room temperature.

The bars of kanten are more difficult and time consuming to use, so I recommend flake or powder form. To gel 2 cups of liquid, you need 1 teaspoon of agar powder or 2 tablespoons of agar flakes, soaked in the liquid for several minutes and then simmered or microwaved until it dissolves. It does not need to be strained. You need to use 6 times more flakes than powder.

Certain ingredients interfere with the gelling of agar, so you may have to experiment to see if you need more than the recommended amount of agar to achieve the degree of firmness you want. Acid foods like lemon juice, vinegar, and fruit juices often pose problems, and as do foods containing oxalic acid, such as chocolate, spinach, and rhubarb. Try using half again as much agar, especially with citrus juices, tomato, and pineapple.

Gluten powder, pure (vital wheat gluten—do-pep)

Gluten is the protein in wheat. It is an essential ingredient for making seitan and "mock meats." Because it is often used in bread machine recipes, it is widely available in natural food stores. Be careful when purchasing gluten flour—read the label carefully. It should contain pure wheat gluten only. Sometimes gluten flour is 80% gluten powder mixed with 20% white flour.

Gluten powder is mixed with cold liquids and sometimes seasonings. It can be boiled, braised, or fried (see Chapter VI).

"Golden needles" (dried tiger lily buds)

Despite their name, these are actually the dried unopened flowers of yellow and orange day lilies. (I guess "tiger lily" sounds better!)

The name "golden needles" refers to their color and shape. They should be golden and flexible, not dry and brown. Store them in a tightly-covered jar, away from light. They need to be soaked in warm water for about 20 minutes before using. Cut off the hard tips and shred them. They are commonly used in Buddhist vegetarian dishes, often in concert with tree ear fungus.

Lotus leaves, dried (see p. 97)

"Mock meats" (see Chapter VI)

Mung beans, dried

Mung beans are second only to soybeans in Asia. They are used to make noodles called pea starch or cellophane noodles, but their main use in China is for sprouting. The cream-colored, crispy sprouts that are available in every supermarket and Asian grocery store in North America today are mung bean sprouts.

If you shop often, you'll probably want to buy them already sprouted. Use them within a day or two—they don't keep well. Forget the canned sprouts—they are soggy and tasteless!

If you don't live near a store, you can sprout them yourself. Use any sprouting arrangement you like. I use 2-quart jars with plastic sprouting lids which can be purchased in natural food stores. About ¼ cup of beans will yield around 7 cups of sprouts (approximately 1 pound).

Soak the beans overnight, then drain them. Keep them in a dark warm place at about 70°F. Rinse them *at least* twice a day (preferably 3 or 4 times a day).

In about 3 or 4 days, you will have sprouts 2 to 3 inches long. Cover them with cold water in a large bowl, and swish them around. Any unsprouted beans will sink to the bottom. (You may get a broken tooth, if they are not removed from the batch!) A lot, but not all, of the green skins will float to the surface and can be skimmed off. You may want to do this with several changes of water. Drain them well and store in a sturdy paper bag inside of a plastic bag in the refrigerator for a few days.

Mung bean sprouts can be used raw in salads. The Chinese prefer to blanch them in boiling water for 5 seconds, rinse in cold water, and drain them well. They need only a few seconds of stir-frying, so add them at the last minute.

When I don't have mung bean sprouts for a recipe, I substitute shredded cabbage—green, savoy, or napa.

Nutritional yeast flakes

Nutritional yeast is *not* the same thing as brewer's yeast or baking yeast. Nutritional yeast flakes have a cheesey taste when used alone, but they can also add an egg yolk flavor to tofu egg substitutes and have a chickeny taste when used with soy sauce (see Breast of Tofu "Chicken," p. 45). Red Star Vegetarian Support Formula is the most widely available brand in natural food stores.

Nutritional yeast is not a live yeast and is guaranteed to be candida albicans free. It is a concentrated source of protein, B vitamins, and minerals, contains no fat and few calories, and is an important seasoning in vegan cooking.

Pickled or preserved Chinese vegetables (plum vegetables, Sichuan preserved vegetables, Tientsin preserved vegetables, preserved turnip, red-in-snow, sour mustard greens, dried salted white turnips, preserved cucumbers, tea cucumbers)

Chinese preserved vegetables are one of those things, like jook or congee, that people rarely taste in a Chinese restaurant. They are salt-cured, an ancient way of preserving vegetables for winter. Each region has its own specialty, which accounts for the proliferation of names and varieties.

Some are sold in decorative crocks, some in jars, and some in cans. "Preserved vegetable" or "red-in-snow" means pickled mustard or turnip greens. You can also buy a fermented variety of "red-in-snow." "Preserved turnip" is actually pickled daikon radish. Sichuan preserved vegetable or Sichuan preserved mustard stem, or Sichuan preserved radish are very popular. They are rubbery green lumps that are cured with salt and red chili. They can be added to Hot and Sour Soup (p. 112), stir-fries, dipping sauces, and dumpling stuffings.

Chopped Chinese pickles are used as a condiment or salty seasoning in congee, for instance. You may want to rinse them to cut down on the saltiness or chili heat. They should be used with restraint.

Good sauerkraut or Japanese salted mustard greens can be used in place of Chinese preserved vegetables. Add some chili paste if you are substituting for Sichuan preserved vegetables.

Sea Vegetables (Seaweed)

Dulse flakes

Dulse is a very nutritious reddish-purple sea vegetable which lends a mild "seafood" flavor to batters for deep-fried foods (Chapter XIII). The flakes, which are much less expensive than the whole dried pieces, are available in natural food stores.

Kombu (konbu, kelp)

Kombu is used in Japanese soup stocks as a flavor enhancer and digestive aid. Many people add it to beans. It comes in hard, gray-green strips about six inches long. In Chinese markets it comes in 8-ounce packages labeled simply "Dried Sea Weed." I use it in the broth for my Seitan "Seafood" (p. 45).

Nori (Laver, purple seaweed)

This is the familiar wrapping for sushi and can be found in many supermarkets, natural food stores, gourmet stores, and most Asian grocery stores. It ranges from dark green to purple and is very nutritious. It is also possible to buy nori flakes. You'll find the largest selection in Japanese markets.

The Chinese use it shredded in soups. It lends a "seafood" flavor when chopped and added to batter for deep-fried foods (Chapter XIII) or to broths. For "mock fish" you can experiment with wrapping it in softened yuba, steaming it, then frying it as you would Buddha's Chicken (pp. 55-56). You could also add a mushroom filling to the roll, such as the "Seafood" Mushroom Filling (p. 72). Another "mock fish" idea would be to wrap it around slices of tofu and fry it.

Soy protein products, dried textured (see pp. 50-51)

Tree ear or black fungus, dried (Mu-er, wood ear, cloud ear)

This fungus has been heralded in China for many centuries for its cholesterol-combatting properties, which are now being reported by the Western medical press.

The fungus has little flavor, but a pleasant crunchy texture. It is commonly included in mu shu mixtures, Hot and Sour Soup (p. 112), and in many Buddhist vegetarian dishes. The mushrooms need to be soaked in boiling water for about 30 minutes. They quadruple when reconstituted!

Water chestnuts, canned (See water chestnuts under Fresh Vegetables p. 20)

HERBS AND SEASONINGS, CONDIMENTS, AND PASTES

Chili oil (hot pepper oil, hot oil, Sa-te oil, sesame chili oil)

A few drops of this oil can be added to dipping sauces and salad dressings for a fiery bite. However, I dislike buying commercial varieties, because they are often rancid and made from inferior oils.

It's easy to make your own chili oil, and that's what I recommend. (It makes a great gift for adventurous cooks, by the way.) Coarsely chop a cup of small, dried red chili peppers. Heat them slowly in a nonaluminum pan with ¾ cup of peanut or canola oil until the peppers begin to foam, watching carefully for any burned flecks. At the first sign of blackening, turn off the heat. Cover and let sit for 4 to 6 hours. Strain the oil well into a glass jar, cover tightly, and store away from heat and light.

If you like, you can add ¼ cup of roasted sesame oil to the chili oil.

Citrus peel

You can buy dried orange or tangerine peel in Chinese markets. It's a very popular flavoring in Chinese cooking. I prefer using the fresh peel from organic fruit. When we peel organic tangerines, I save the peels and freeze them for future use. Sometimes I dry a few of them on a sunny window sill. Tangerine peels have almost none of the bitter white layer that orange peels have, so they can just be chopped. Orange peels should be grated. I use a 2-inch metal box grater. You can also use a citrus zester.

Five-spice powder

This spice mixture usually has more than five spices in it, but the number five once had symbolic power, ensuring healthfulness. It commonly contains star anise, fennel or anise, cinnamon, cloves, licorice root, Sichuan peppercorn, and sometimes ginger. It is inexpensive and can be purchased in any Asian market and at many supermarkets. It usually comes in a plastic bag, so you'll have to transfer it to glass jars. In my opinion, it is often overused in Chinese-style cooking. It is very strong, completely taking over the flavor of whatever it's used in—so go easy with it.

Hoisin sauce (Hai Hsien Chiang)

This sweet, spicy sauce with a star anise flavor can be very cloying and should be used with discretion, not as a condiment on its own. It can be thick or runny, depending on the brand and is best used as an ingredient in barbecue sauces.

Sichuan peppercorns, roasted

Sichuan pepper was once a popular condiment all over China—even wines were flavored with it. When black pepper was introduced, it fell from favor, although it is still widely used.

The dried reddish-brown berries are not related to our black peppercorns. They have a clean, spicy fragrance which goes well with roasted and fried foods. The peppercorns are sold in Asian markets and must be roasted before using.

To roast, place the peppercorns in a dry, heavy skillet and toast them over medium heat for about 5 minutes. They'll smoke, but don't burn them. Grind in a spice grinder or electric coffee mill that is not used for coffee. Store in a covered jar.

To make "seasoned salt," you can roast 2 parts Sichuan peppercorns with 3 parts coarse salt before grinding.

Star anise

These are beautiful, little, eight-pointed pods from an evergreen that grows in southwestern China and northern Vietnam. Star anise is not related to aniseed, which is a member of the parsley family. The Chinese use star anise, often along with cinnamon, in many meat and poultry dishes, especially "red-cooked" dishes (foods braised in dark soy sauce). Star anise is one of the essential spices in five-spice powder. Although it has a lovely aroma and flavor, I use it cautiously, as it tends to overwhelm other flavors, especially with more delicate vegetarian foods.

SOYFOODS

Soyfoods rate their own special section because they are so important to Chinese cooking—vegetarian and nonvegetarian alike. Soybeans are one of the "Five Sacred Grains" and are used daily by Chinese and other Asians of all economic classes. Soybeans will yield 33% more protein from an acre of land than any other crop. This is 20 times as much usable protein as can be raised on an acre of land devoted to grazing cattle or raising cattle feed! In an area with chronic overpopulation and food shortages, there is little wonder that soy has been so important over the centuries.

Soy protein is very high quality. Soybeans also contain fiber, iron, calcium, antioxidants such as isoflavones, and other important nutrients. Over the centuries, the Chinese have found an amazing number of inventive and delicious ways to use the soybean—for making milk, tofu "meat of the fields," flavorings, and a myriad of "mock meats."

Green soybeans (edamame, sweet beans)

These are soybeans picked at the green stage. They are sweet, nutty-tasting, and delicious. The beans are boiled or steamed in the pod, salted, and eaten as a snack in both Japan and China. They are positively addictive! To eat them, put the whole pod in your mouth, hold onto the end, and pull the pod out between your teeth. This pops the beans into your mouth. Discard the pod.

You can buy frozen green soybeans in the pod in Asian grocery stores and natural food stores under the Japanese term "edamame." They are also sold shelled and frozen or in cans in North American supermarkets and natural food stores under the name sweet beans. They can be eaten as a hot vegetable like peas or corn, used in soups, salads, stir-fries, and casseroles, or used instead of lima beans or cooked beans in dips and spreads. You might like to try growing green soybeans in your garden. The Chinese eat them in salad-like dishes with a light soy sauce dressing.

Miso (Japanese fermented soybean paste)

Miso is a Japanese derivative of the ancient Chinese condiment, brown bean paste or sauce (p. 14). It has been adopted into Western vegetarian cooking, and so is readily available in natural food stores. It comes in many varieties. The light, or white, variety, can be used in place of Chinese bean paste. The red, or dark, varieties can be used in place of Chinese red fermented bean curd. I also use light miso in place of dried shrimp as a flavoring when converting some Chinese recipes to vegan dishes.

Soybeans, whole dry (Ta-tou in Chinese, meaning "great beans")

These soybeans are harvested when fully mature. Most varieties are yellow or beige. There are also delicious brown and black varieties, which are used for making salted or fermented black beans (p. 14). Whole soybeans are an excellent source of fiber, isoflavones, and protein, and have the most calcium of any dry beans.

Whole dry soybeans are not usually eaten just as a bean, except fried as a snack food, but they are used to make a myriad of important soyfoods which make Chinese vegetarian cuisine so versatile. They are often sprouted for use as a fresh vegetable.

When buying whole dried soybeans, look for beans that are mostly whole, with not many split beans. They should be clean, with no dirt, stones, or foreign matter. They will keep for about a year if stored in dry, cool conditions in a sealed dry container.

Soybean sprouts

These sprouts are nutritious and easy to grow at home from organic, dried whole soybeans. The sprouts should not be eaten raw, but they only need brief stir-frying or steaming to make them edible. They should still be crunchy. The Chinese use soy sprouts as a base for vegetarian broth and in stir-fries. Soy sprouts are grown in the same way as mung beans (see p. 21), but they may take five to seven days to mature. They *must* be rinsed three or four times a day while sprouting. They are more prone to spoiling during the sprouting process than other beans, so use organic beans from a store with a good turnover—old beans will not sprout well.

When the fully grown sprouts are placed in indirect sunlight for a few hours, they will turn green, which I find more appetizing. Before using, submerge them in cold water and agitate; most of the hulls will then float to the top. Drain well and refrigerate in a sturdy paper bag inside of a plastic bag for several days.

Soy sprouts can be used instead of green soybeans in some recipes. You may be able to find them in Asian (particularly Korean) grocery stores.

Soymilk (soy beverage or soy drink—dou-jiang)

The Chinese, along with other Asians, often drink hot sweetened or savory soymilk as a breakfast beverage. It is available in many supermarkets, as well as in natural food stores and Asian markets. It can be used to replace cow's milk in baking and other recipes, as well as on cereal, in hot beverages, etc. Several modern processing techniques make it possible to produce a soymilk with a greater taste appeal to Westerners than the traditional Asian-style soymilks, which are often beany tasting, thin, and quite sweet.

The fat content of modern soymilks will be 1 to 3 percent. Soymilk is lactose- and cholesterol-free, and now often comes fortified with calcium, vitamin D, and other nutrients.

Note: Do not use soymilk in place of infant formula. If you cannot breastfeed, use a specially formulated soy-based infant formula.

"Soynuts" or roasted soybeans

Available in natural food stores, these are soaked whole or split dried soybeans which are lightly cooked and then roasted in the oven until crunchy like nuts, for which they can be used as a substitute. They have lots of protein, fiber, isoflavones, and calcium and are lower in fat than nuts, so they make an excellent snack food. They are usually sold salted and can be flavored with various spices and herbs.

The Chinese generally deep-fry soybeans as a snack food, but the roasted ones are less greasy. To make your own, soak the beans overnight in enough water to cover generously. Drain and rinse them and place in a pot of fresh water to cover. Bring it to a boil, lower the heat, simmer for 10 minutes, and drain.

Preheat the oven to 350°F. Spread the beans in a single layer on lightly oiled cookie sheets. Roast them for about 45 minutes, or until they are golden and crispy, stirring several times while roasting. Cool thoroughly and store in an airtight container.

You can coat the soybeans with a tiny bit of roasted sesame oil or flavorful peanut oil, if you like. Use a pump-sprayer, if you have one. Then salt them, or add spices such as garlic granules, five-spice powder (not much), cayenne pepper, or chili flakes.

Soy protein products, dried textured (see pp. 50-51)

Soy sauce, shoyu and tamari

These fermented soy products lend a rich, meaty flavor to many vegetarian recipes as well as Asian recipes. Though ubiquitous, soy sauce is used with restraint in Chinese cooking. It is considered bad form to pour soy sauce on your food at the table. This is an insult to the cook. Soy sauce is not poured on plain rice either. The rice is flavored with the sauce or sauces from the dishes offered.

Shoyu is the Japanese word for soy sauce; tamari is actually the dark liquid by-product of the miso-making process. It is delicious and expensive. (Most of what is labeled "tamari" is actually just a naturally brewed soy sauce.)

The Japanese learned the art of making soy sauce from the Chinese about one thousand years ago. Real Chinese soy sauce (jiang-you) is a traditional product made by natural or temperature-controlled fermentation and comes in light and dark (or "black") varieties.

Light soy sauce (sheng-chou) is sometimes referred to as thin or regular soy sauce. Many Chinese cooks consider the brand Pearl River Bridge "Golden Label Superior Soy" the premium brand light soy sauce for most cooking. Pearl River Bridge also makes "Superior Soy," which is not quite as prized but still good. Both are very inexpensive. Do not confuse either with Pearl River Bridge "Soy, Superior" in a bottle with a red label, which is a dark soy sauce. Koon Chun Sauce Factory's "Thin Soy Sauce" is also acceptable. Another acceptable inexpensive brand that is available in my area is Rooster Brand Superior Light Soy Sauce. They make a mushroom soy sauce, as well.

Do *not* use cheap imitation soy sauces with phony Chinese names that contain hydrolyzed vegetable protein and caramel coloring. The label should state that it contains only soybeans, salt, water, and sometimes wheat. Most supermarkets carry at least one brand of naturally brewed, inexpensive light Chinese soy sauce and sometimes Chinese dark and/or mushroom varieties. If not, use a Japanese brand of shoyu. Chef Barbara Tropp, an expert in Chinese cuisine, considers the Japanese-American brand Kikkoman "a middle ground between the sweeter Japanese-made soy sauces and the saltier Chinese soy sauces." Many other Chinese-American chefs depend on Kikkoman when brands from China are not available.

Kikkoman and some other Japanese brands make a reduced-salt version sometimes labeled "Lite," which is about 15% less salty than regular Japanese soy sauce and must be kept refrigerated. One brand of Chinese reduced-sodium soy sauce is Gold Orchid Light Soy.

Dark soy sauce (sometimes called thick, rich, or black soy sauce—lao ch'ou) is fermented for a longer time than light soy sauce and has a hint of molasses or caramel. It is used in heartier, long-cooking dishes. Mushroom soy sauce is considered in the dark category and is widely available in supermarkets. The Pearl River Bridge Mushroom Soy is an excellent brand. Their red-label "Soy, Superior Sauce" is a dark soy sauce as well. Koon Chun Sauce Factory makes a decent "Black Soy Sauce." I use Rooster Brand Mushroom Soy Sauce.

If you prefer organic foods, there are organic "tamari" and soy sauces available in natural food stores.

Tofu (bean curd, bean cake, or soybean curd—doufu)

Tofu is widely available these days in many varieties. It originated in China over two thousand years ago and is still one of the most widely used foods in Asia today. The average Taiwanese eats 64 pounds of tofu a year! Every province of China makes its own varieties of tofu with their own names and pronunciations. In this book I will use the Japanese word "tofu," which is universally accepted in North America and is close to the Mandarin word for soybean curd, "doufu" (pronounced tdoe-foo). The Cantonese word is "dowfu" (pronounced "dow-foo"). What we refer to as extra-firm tofu comes in small cakes of pressed tofu in Chinese shops, called "doufu kan" or "dowfu gar."

Tofu can best be described as a soft cheese made from soymilk that is curdled with mineral salts and then drained and pressed into different textures. It is used widely in Asian cooking and vegetarian cooking. This isoflavone-rich soyfood is extremely versatile, takes on flavors easily, and can be used to substitute for dairy products, meat, poultry, seafood, and eggs.

If you can purchase freshly made tofu (made the same day), you will be surprised at its fresh, clean taste and you will appreciate how Asians can eat plain tofu with just a little light soy sauce and perhaps some green onion as a condiment.

Most supermarkets and natural food stores will carry several different types of tofu—you may find *soft tofu* (used mainly for drinks and desserts), *regular* or *low-fat medium-firm* (the Japanese style), *firm* (the Chinese style), or *extra-firm* (also called pressed), which is excellent for marinating, stir-frying, and making kebabs. Firm or Chinese-style tofu is always preferable to medium-firm or Japanese-style in Chinese cooking. The medium-firm will not stand up to the rough and tumble of Chinese stir-frying. "Dessert tofu" is a soft tofu that is sweetened and flavored and often served cubed with fruit in Asia. It can be used in puddings, shakes, and frozen desserts.

You may find some varieties of tofu in bulk in large tubs of water or in vacuum-packed plastic tubs or sealed packages. If you use bulk tofu, try to buy it from a store that gets it fresh each day. If you live in a city with a sizable Asian population, the best place to find it is a tofu shop, Asian grocery store, or a large supermarket that caters to an Asian population. Vacuum-packed tofu that is opened should be covered with fresh water daily and kept in a sealed container in the refrigerator. There are organic brands of tofu available.

If you freeze tofu (anything from medium-firm to extra-firm) for 48 hours or more and then thaw it out, it takes on a very chewy texture after you squeeze the water out of it. In Asian cooking, the thawed frozen tofu (called tung-doufu or ping-doufu) is generally cubed and added to stews, where it soaks up the flavor of the cooking liquid.

In Asian markets, tofu shops, and some large supermarkets you can find savory tofu (wu-hsiang kan), which is pressed tofu marinated in a mixture of soy sauce, oil, and seasonings. It is used in place of smoked ham as an hors d'oeuvre. Unfortunately, it is often quite thin and hard, with star anise overwhelming the flavor. You can substitute some of the new varieties of baked and marinated tofu that you find in natural food stores, or try marinating your own extra-firm tofu (see Breast of Tofu "Chicken" p. 43). Soy-sauce pressed tofu (chiang-yu doufu-kan) is similar, but is not spiced. You will also find some Japanese and Chinese varieties of fried tofu (age in Japanese, yu-doufu or cha-dofu in Chinese). These are cubes or triangles of golden deep-fried tofu which are excellent for use in barbecues, stews, soups, and sweet-and-sour sauces. Asian grocery stores and some large supermarkets carry them. Thick Chinese fried tofu triangles are the most common variety. Another popular variety is doufu-kuo, hollow fried tofu cubes, which can be stuffed. Although these are fried, boiling water is poured over them and most of the oil is squeezed out before they are used. These varieties are concentrated sources of protein and isoflavones.

Sautéed tofu (kuo-lao doufu) is thinly sliced tofu, pan fried until it becomes a rich golden brown. You will probably have to visit a Chinese tofu shop to purchase this variety.

In Chinese markets you will find jars of Chinese fermented tofu, called doufu-ru. It is sold in its brining liquid, which contains alcohol and salt. This comes in a white variety (pai doufu-ru), a hot spicy version (la doufu-ru, la-chiao furu, or la furu), and a red version (hung doufu-ru, nanru, or nanyu) to which red fermented rice is added for a deep, rich red color and distinctive flavor. There are other less common varieties, such aswu-hsiang furu, flavored with five-spice; mayu-la doufu-ru, a red pepper variety with sesame oil; and tsao-doufu, aged in rice wine and its lees. In China, doufu-ru is used as a condiment and to add richness to sauces and marinades. The brining liquid (doufu-ru chih) is also used as an ingredient. The white variety has a flavor similar to that of blue cheese. Doufu-ru keeps for a long time refrigerated, even after opening. It takes some time for Western palates to get used to it, but it is worth getting a few jars for the recipes in which it is an essential ingredient. If you absolutely can't find it, experiment with using Japanese miso as a substitute. It's not the same, but it does have a fermented quality that is pleasantly similar.

There are many modern varieties of tofu available in natural food stores; smoked tofu, baked tofu, and marinated tofu can replace Chinese pressed savory tofu, meats, poultry, and even smoked fish or smoked cheese. The milder-tasting varieties can be used in stir-fries and stews; the stronger-tasting varieties are best used as Chinese appetizers.

For an excellent overview of tofu, including a chapter on "Tofu and Yuba (bean curd skin) in China, Taiwan, and Korea," read *The Book of Tofu: Food for Mankind* by William Shurtleff and Akiko Aoyagi, Autumn Press, 1975.

Western style soy meat substitutes

These are now available in literally hundreds of brands and forms in natural food stores and supermarkets around the world. They usually contain tofu or tempeh, textured soy protein, and soy concentrates and/or isolates, and may also contain some seitan (wheat gluten). The types that resemble ham or Canadian bacon (back bacon) and poultry cutlets or nuggets would be most useful for Chinese cooking. Most are very low in fat and can be either frozen or refrigerated. They usually require only heating, not long cooking. Some brands may contain egg products, but most are vegan—read the labels. Many brands are very delicious and are available in supermarkets where they are purchased not only by vegetarians but also by shoppers who want to lower fat and cholesterol in their diets.

Yuba (bean curd skin—tou-p'i, doufu-p'i, or doufu-i)

I'm going to refer to this product by its Japanese name (yuba); it is shorter and less confusing than the various English translations from the Chinese names. Considered a delicacy in Japan, yuba is more common in China and Taiwan where each city will have a number of shops or market stalls selling only bean curd skin and products made from it. It is made by simmering soymilk and lifting off the "skin" that forms on the top, just like that which forms on dairy milk. This "skin" can be used fresh, or it can be dried in sheets or rolled-up sticks. The sticks are used in soups, stews, and stir-fries, and can also be barbecued. The sheets can be cut up like noodles, or used in soups, stews, and stir-fries as well. They can be rolled around fillings and baked, steamed, or fried for delicious appetizers or used as a crispy "skin" around vegetarian poultry substitutes.

Yuba is a very concentrated soyfood. The dried version, available in Asian markets and some large supermarkets, must be soaked in warm water before using.

Fresh sheets are also available in large cities in Chinese tofu shops and must be frozen for future use. They often come in 16-inch-wide round or semi-circular sheets. These are sometimes labeled "fresh spring roll skins or wrappers," but are not to be confused with the wrappers made from flour. The package will tell you that the ingredients are only soybeans and water. Some varieties are very thin, some are as thick as canvas. The sheets are folded into many forms and sizes to make rolls and stuffed pouches, or they are molded and steamed.

The Chinese have used amazing ingenuity to create mock meats using yuba. In Chinese yuba shops, you will find replicas of chickens, ducks, fish, hams, rolled meats, sausage links, etc., all made primarily from yuba. These dishes, with names such as Buddha's "Chicken" or Buddha's "Duck" (see pp. 55-56), are served on cold plates at fine restaurants or family banquets.

Often, these mock meats are made from a similar product called pai-yeh (sometimes translated as "one hundred leaves" or "one hundred pages"). Should you find it, feel free to substitute it for yuba. Pai-yeh is made by pressing firm soybean curds under very heavy weights for several hours until the sheet of bean curd looks like a 6 to 12-inch square of canvas with a cloth-like pattern imprinted on both sides. The sheets are flexible and very attractive. They are, unfortunately, harder to find outside of urban centers with large Chinese populations, so I have not called for this product in these recipes.

A thicker form of yuba is called er-ju bean curd sheets. They are brown and come in stacks of 5- x 1½-inch sheets tied together with string or wrapped in paper. They can be soaked and then cooked with soy sauce and seasonings to make vegetarian "ham" or "bacon."

SPECIAL INGREDIENTS

A word about MSG (Wei-Ching): Monosodium glutamate (also known as Accent, taste essence, aji-no-moto, and vetsin) is not a synthetic additive, but a natural salt that occurs in many foods—the monosodium salt of glutamic acid, an amino acid. In 1908, the Japanese discovered how to extract it from wheat, soy, shrimp, and seaweed proteins. Now it's made from sugar beet molasses or glucose solutions fermented with special bacteria. It is used to enhance flavor and often to make up for a lack of flavor.

It doesn't seem to bother most people when eaten in natural trace amounts, but the concentrated form, used with a heavy hand in many Chinese and Japanese restaurants, can cause allergic reactions in some (headache, flushing, numbness, chest pains, and difficulty breathing). It is used particularly in soups and can cause a quick reaction after ingesting soup on an empty stomach, which is often the case, since soup is usually the first course.

Although it does not seem to cause harm to anyone who's not sensitive to it, it's not necessary to use it, so I don't!

Chapter IV

CHINESE COOKING EQUIPMENT, TECHNIQUES, AND THE MODERN KITCHEN

"The Chinese chef is engaged in visual harmony—in the size and shape of the food, the fragrances, and in contrasting tastes and textures. Above all, he sets out to attain a balance among all of these elements."

Ken Hom

The most basic, sparsely equipped North American kitchen is likely to be light years ahead of the average Asian kitchen in terms of convenience. Chinese cooking has developed using very few pieces of essential equipment and little fuel. You probably have everything you need in your kitchen already, but I recommend that you purchase a good wok (more about that later).

Your stove is an important piece of equipment. You need a burner that is hot enough to stir-fry efficiently. Most people prefer gas burners for stir-frying, and many of the new designs have a special burner which burns very hot and is ideal for this purpose. I have a fairly recent electric range which has one burner that gets *very* hot, so I have never had a problem stir-frying, but older electric stoves may not be up to scratch. While you can turn the flame on a gas burner up or down for instant temperature changes, on an electric range this will have to be accomplished by moving the wok off and on the burner at the right moment.

An exhaust fan above your stove is a great advantage while cooking Chinese dishes, which often use extreme heat and generate some smoke. However, I don't have one. I just open the windows when necessary!

Although you don't absolutely need it, a wok is such a great piece of equipment that I urge you to buy one. You'll use it for stir-frying (and not just Asian foods), deep-frying, braising, and steaming. They are inexpensive, and good ones last for many years. I have three woks—two are 14 inches and one is 12 inches. One of my woks predates the birth of my youngest daughter, who is almost 30. I have them hanging near the stove, where they are convenient to use at a moment's notice and don't take up precious cupboard space.

Chinese food just tastes better when made in a wok, and there's even a term for that mysterious quality, that "wok-charred" taste. The Chinese call it "wok hey"—the sign of a well-seasoned wok.

A wok has a concave form which makes it easy to toss and turn foods during stir-frying. Its shape makes it possible to use very little oil when deep-frying or stir-frying. There are no corners for food to get stuck in. Above all, the shape of a wok convects heat up the sides with maximum efficiency, making it a great fuel conserver.

Woks come in all sizes, from 8 inches (great for a single person) to 4 feet across (the restaurant version). The 14-inch size is the most versatile for the home kitchen. It's easy to stir-fry a small amount in a large wok, but not so easy to cook a large amount in a small wok! The wok may have two metal handles, one long wooden handle, or a long wooden handle on one side and a smaller wooden handle on the other.

Traditional woks have round bottoms, which are placed in a hole in a Chinese wood or charcoal stove, or over a brazier. If the power ever goes out and you have a wood stove with a removable round plate above the firebox, you can place your wok in the hole and stir-fry your dinner! (I once cooked a five-course Chinese meal for company this way, one dish at a time.)

Most woks come with a round ring which is placed over the burner for the wok to sit in—this steadies the wok. Flat-bottomed woks have been designed specifically for electric burners, increasing the heat contact between the burner and the wok. For safety reasons, you should always use a flat-bottomed wok with an electric burner, or a ring with the round-bottomed wok on either a gas or electric burner when deep-frying, steaming, or braising.

The most inexpensive, efficient, and long-lasting wok is made from heavy-gauge carbon steel. Carbon steel conducts heat better than aluminum, stainless steel, or copper. Forget electric woks for stir-frying. The temperature usually does not get hot enough and drops when you add the food. Electric woks are handy for deep-frying and steaming.

A carbon steel wok has to be seasoned. To do this, thoroughly wash it inside and out with soapy hot water, using an abrasive scouring pad to remove the oily protective coating. Wipe it dry and heat the wok on the stove over medium-high heat for several minutes. Put oven mitts on both hands. With a folded paper towel, rub on some refined cooking oil to thoroughly coat the entire inside surface of the wok. (Unrefined oil has too many residues for this job.) Add ½ teaspoon of fine salt, and rub the entire surface. Soon the wok will begin to darken and smoke. (You should have an exhaust fan over your stove for this, or open some windows!) Do this several times, using fresh paper towels and more oil and salt, until the paper towel finally comes away clean. Rotate the wok carefully so that all the lower sides of the wok come into contact with the heat. This may take 15 to 20 minutes. Let the wok cool, then wash it in warm water with a nonabrasive pad, wipe dry, and dry over high heat for a few minutes.

There will be a dark brown area over the center of your new wok. Over time, with proper use and cleaning, that dark area will grow. The whole wok will become shiny and dark, developing a natural nonstick patina to keep food from sticking and the wok from rusting.

To clean and store your wok after use, wash it right away, while it is still hot, with soapy warm water. Use a non-abrasive scrub pad (like Scotch-Brite) or salt to get any stuck food off. Rinse well, wipe dry, and then stove-dry over high heat for a minute or two. ***This is essential.*** Even though your wok may look dry, unseen moisture in its pores may cause rusting. ***Never*** let a wet wok drain dry. Some people recommend oiling the wok before storage, but I think this just attracts dust, so I never do. If you use your wok often and keep it well seasoned, oiling is unnecessary. After the wok cools, hang it up in a convenient place. This way you will use it more often, and that is what will keep it well seasoned. You don't need to scrub the black patina off the outside, so your wok won't look pretty after continued use, but it will become one of your most valued cooking implements.

Note: Repeatedly using a wok for steaming or braising foods for long periods in acid ingredients can remove the seasoning from a wok. If you steam in a wok and then fry in it the next time, that will renew the seasoning. Just make sure to dry it properly after steaming. If you steam often, use other pots or have a wok that is used only for steaming.

Woks come with a variety of handy accoutrements. It should have a domed lid and a flat stainless steel stir-frying spatula (a "wok spatula") that is designed to fit the curvature of the wok and not scratch the wok's surface. It is stronger than an ordinary spatula and more efficient for scraping food as you turn it.

You may also get a wire draining rack that fits over one side of the wok to place fried food on when you remove it from the hot oil. Or you could purchase a round, brass, basket-like wire deep-fry skimmer on a bamboo handle and a ladle.

If the wok does not come with these or you got it at a second-hand store, you can purchase them cheaply in Asian grocery stores, or you can use implements that you already have. (I do recommend the lid and the wok spatula.)

If you do not have a wok, you can use a heavy 12- to 14-inch skillet, a "chicken fryer," sauté pan with deep sides, or a paella pan. They can be made from spun steel, anodized aluminum (like Calphalon), stainless steel over heavy-gauge aluminum, or cast-iron. Ideally, it should have gently sloping sides. You can even use a Dutch oven or a wide-bottomed stock pot, about ten or more inches in diameter and no more than six inches deep.

For steaming equipment, p. 35.

Read about pots for braising and stewing and Chinese clay pots on pp. 149-150. Read about pots for cooking rice on p. 93.

The food processor is a marvelous invention, and I couldn't live without mine, but when preparing foods for frying and stir-frying, use a knife or a cleaver—it doesn't cause the food to exude so much juice. You can use the food processor for mincing, fine chopping, and grating as well as puréeing and mixing. It's ideal for kneading noodle and bread doughs, and mincing large quantities of onions, garlic, and ginger. Firm vegetables may be neatly sliced in the food processor, because they don't exude much juice, but they might not look as pretty as hand-cut slices.

A good knife and/or a Chinese cleaver is another absolutely essential piece of equipment. You will be doing a lot of slicing, dicing, chopping, and mincing.

A vegetarian cook needs only a lightweight Chinese vegetable cleaver with an 8-inch blade. A vegetarian cook does *not* need heavyweight butchering, poultry, or bone-chopping cleavers, for obvious reasons. The lightweight cleaver is much easier to handle than the heavy or medium-weight ones. The vegetable cleaver has a light wooden handle and a rectangular, "two-toned" blade (a black band across the top of the blade), which is slightly curved on the bottom for making "rocking" cuts. Metal handles are said to be more evenly balanced, but are heavier to handle. The vegetable cleaver is ideal for cutting, chopping, slicing, crushing, mincing, and scooping up food to place in the wok. If you are patient, you can even use the handle as a mortar to grind spices in a small, heavy bowl. It looks clumsy, but once you get the hang of it, you'll find it efficient, speedy, and easy to use. (See pp. 36-37 for cutting techniques.) It needs to be razor sharp, and the best way to insure this is to learn how to sharpen it regularly on a whetstone.

A carbon steel knife, though not as pretty, is a better choice than stainless steel, because it can be sharpened. However, like the carbon steel wok, it needs to be stored *absolutely dry*. The first time you use it, scrub off the protective coating with warm, soapy water and a non-abrasive pad. Rinse it and wipe it absolutely dry. Coat it with a thin film of mineral oil. Clean it immediately after use, and wipe it dry, dry, dry. (Some people recommend oiling before storage, but I think it just gets mucky, so I never do.) If you don't have a Chinese cleaver, you can use a large, sharp French chef's knife.

Of course, you will need a good wooden cutting board or two on which to use your cleaver. It should be at least one inch thick.

You might like to try using long cooking chopsticks if you're handy with them. They are inexpensive and often very pretty.

A mini-chopper, mini-processor, or hand mixer with a chopping attachment is handy to have for chopping garlic, mixing fermented black beans with other ingredients, making pastes and sauces, chopping nuts, etc. If you are handy with a cleaver, then you can easily chop nuts, garlic, etc. with it. You can also use an old-fashioned manual nut chopper; it works well for small amounts.

I am partial to using a tiny metal box grater, about two inches high, with a plastic top for grating small quantities of unpeeled ginger and citrus rinds. It works quickly and efficiently, it's easy to clean, and takes up little room.

You can use your microwave oven for dissolving agar mixtures, making sauces, quick-soaking dried mushrooms, and partially steaming hard vegetables.

CHINESE COOKING TECHNIQUES

Over the centuries, Chinese chefs have devised over 50 different cooking processes with subtle variations in technique and heating temperature. However, for the purposes of a home cook, only a few techniques need be discussed. First, read the information on equipment which preceded this section.

You'll find all you need to know about cooking rice in Chapter IX. Detailed directions for stir-frying are given at the beginning of Chapter XI. The techniques of braising and stewing, including "red-cooking" and cooking with Chinese clay pots and "sandpots," are discussed in Chapter XII.

Although the recipes in my previous books have been very low in fat, I decided that a Chinese cookbook would not be complete without a section of fried foods. In general I have used less oil in these recipes than would most traditional Chinese cooks. In some cases, a low-fat alternative version (oven-frying or grilling) produces good results. In other cases, only deep-frying produces the light, crunchy results that are expected. These foods are eaten in small amounts as part of a larger meal and, if cooked properly, should not be greasy. I have found that they can be an occasional part of an otherwise low-fat diet. Helpful instructions for deep-frying, twice-frying, shallow-frying, pan-frying, and the low-fat alternatives—oven-frying, broiling, and grilling—are found at the beginning of Chapter XIII.

That leaves the techniques of steaming and the various cutting techniques, which are essential to Chinese cooking.

STEAMING

Since traditional Chinese homes don't have ovens, many foods that we might bake or roast are steamed over simmering water. This includes breads and cakes, which turn out delightfully fluffy and light from the steamer. Although vegetarians do not have to be concerned about techniques for steaming fish, poultry, meat, and savory egg custards, which are very popular in China—dumplings, breads, cakes, puddings, vegetables, and even soups are all steamed foods which vegetarians enjoy. Since no oil is used in this method, it generally produces low-fat, digestible food and tends to accentuate the natural flavors of foods.

Steaming is simply cooking food on a rack, basket, or plate above simmering water in a cooking pot. The wok is the all-purpose pot of China. There are various ways to steam food in a wok.

1. Foods may be placed in a clay pot or on a plate on a round wooden or metal trivet or cake rack that fits across the bottom of a wok.

2. You can use a collapsible metal steaming basket or a conventional metal steaming rack.

3. A plate or pot of food can be balanced on two chopsticks placed across the inside of the wok or 4 chopsticks stacked "tic-tac-toe" style.

4. You can use traditional Chinese round bamboo steaming baskets which you can stack and which are attractive enough to serve the food in. There is a special latticed bamboo lid which fits on the top basket and lets just the right amount of steam escape. There are also aluminum versions of these stackable baskets; they aren't as aesthetically pleasing but they are more durable and easier to clean since they don't mildew or absorb cooking odors the way the bamboo baskets do. The bamboo baskets need to be carefully cleaned and dried.

Use the domed wok lid for all methods except the steaming baskets.

If you don't have a wok, you can devise a steamer from pots or use a special steaming pot with a basket. You can improvise a steamer using a large pot with a tight lid. An electric wok or frying pan with a domed lid also makes a good steamer. The lid should be one to two inches above the food so that the steam can circulate around the food. To hold the food above the water, you can use cans with the ends removed or scrunched up aluminum foil. The food should be supported at least two inches above the simmering water.

These are important things to remember when steaming:

✓ Juicy foods should be placed on a heatproof plate or in a glazed ceramic Chinese bowl before being placed in the steamer so that their juices don't escape.

✓ Check the water level regularly, and add boiling water if it gets low.

✓ If you are steaming small pieces of food, place them on top of a couple of layers of cheesecloth, or place them on leaves of lettuce or napa cabbage.

✓ Place breads and dumplings on squares of foil, waxed paper, cooking parchment, oiled brown paper, or layers of cheesecloth so that they don't stick to the steamer surface.

✓ Avoid burns by opening the steamer carefully with oven mitts and tilting the cover away from your face.

CUTTING THE CHINESE WAY

Note: If you usually use a food processor, for slicing, dicing, or chopping, see my comments on p. 33.

To use the cleaver, hold it in your "chopstick hand," as the Chinese say (your writing hand), move your hand all the way up the handle so that your thumb is on one side of the blade and your index finger on the other. Curl your index finger slightly, and grasp the blade firmly between the thumb and index finger. This gives you more control than simply wrapping your hand around the handle.

Use your free hand to hold the food in place, curling your fingertips under (see illustration). Rest the flat side of the blade alongside the first knuckles of your free hand as you slice or chop. This keeps the fingers out of the way. Your knuckles guide the blade. Never uncurl the fingers of your free hand, and never raise the blade higher than the first knuckle. Use a firm downward and slightly forward motion.

Proper hand position
for cutting

Dicing

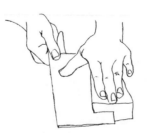

Parallel cutting

Diagonal-cutting or slant-cutting: This technique is used for long, thin vegetables, such as asparagus or string beans. It creates larger pieces that actually cook faster than smaller pieces because more of the interior of the vegetable is exposed to the heat.

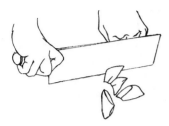

Roll-cutting: This is an attractive preparation method for long vegetables, such as carrots or zucchini. It also exposes more surface area of the vegetable so that it cooks faster.

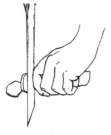

Thin slicing

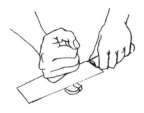

Crushing: The flat of the blade can be used to smash or crush garlic and ginger, making them easier to peel and chop.

Chapter V

HOW TO PLAN, ORCHESTRATE, AND SERVE A CHINESE MEAL

"Planning a Chinese meal can be likened to a general's planning a battle. You must have a calculated written plan, starting with the dishes you would like to serve down to the measuring of the tea leaves in the pot."
Karen Lee, *Chinese Cooking Secrets* , Doubleday & Co., Inc., Garden City, N.Y., 1983

While most of us are not as organized as Karen Lee would have us be, planning ahead does help ensure the success of a Chinese meal, whether it be a casual family dinner or a feast for company. Don't be too ambitious—even the most experienced Chinese grandmother who has cooked for a large family for years will hire a restaurant for a lavish banquet on some special occasion.

To avoid disasters or exhaustion on your part, become familiar with Chinese cooking before you attempt a dinner party. Read through this book and others, and glean all the tips you can. Try out one recipe at a time on your family until you have a repertoire of dishes that you like and can do well. *Never* try a new recipe that you have never made before on company!

SUPER-FAST CHINESE MEALS AND ONE-DISH MEALS

Before I get into the subject of planning dinner parties and full-scale meals, I must remind you that if you are in a hurry, you'll find many speedy one-dish meal possibilities in this book. The one-dish meal is a great way to become acquainted with Chinese cooking and try out dishes before serving them to company. Many Chinese dishes include both vegetables and protein and need only be served on rice or noodles to make a full meal. Noodle dishes and soups often contain everything you need for a balanced meal.

A stir-fry (see Chapter XI) with rice, noodles, or Mandarin Pancakes (pp. 87-88) is a good candidate for experimentation. Choose one with few ingredients. Put the rice on to cook or the water for the noodles to boil first. Use white rice, or quick-cooking brown rice, if you prefer.

Cooking rice or noodles (including the time it takes for the water to boil) takes about 20 minutes. By the time you have cut the ingredients, mixed the cooking sauce, and set the table, the rice or noodles are cooked, and you can make your stir-fry. The actual time you spend at the stove is usually about five minutes! If you use reheated leftover rice or noodles (they reheat nicely in a microwave) or eat your stir-fry rolled up in a Mandarin pancake, tortilla, or a pita pocket, you can have dinner even sooner!

Other quick one-dish meals can be found in Chapter IX, and Chapter X. You can have a great noodle and vegetable soup with tofu on the table in ten minutes if you have all the ingredients on hand and know your way around the kitchen.

PLANNING A CHINESE MENU

Some experts tell you to plan a meal that includes a soup, three dishes featuring three different kinds of protein (for a vegetarian, this might be a tofu dish, a textured soy protein or yuba dish, and a seitan dish), a dish featuring only vegetables (the protein dishes will probably also contain some vegetables), and rice (or in Northern China, wheat pancakes, noodles, or steamed bread).

Others will tell you to serve a soup and then one stir-fried dish, one braised or stewed dish, one steamed dish, one deep-fried dish, and one roasted dish.

It is customary in restaurants to order one dish for each diner, not counting the soup and rice. So, if there are four diners, you order four different dishes, if there are six diners, you order six different dishes, and so on. This can get a little complicated for the home cook, so you can pare down the number of dishes and make a larger quantity of each.

Note: The recipes in this book have serving sizes indicated. This is generally the serving size if the dish is to be served as the only main dish, along with a starch. If the dish is to be part of a larger Chinese-style meal, double the amount of servings.

Variety and balance are much prized within a Chinese meal (the yin and yang again). You want contrasts of sweet and sour, spicy and subtle, soft and crisp, richly colored and pale, hot and cool, chewy and silky, and so on. You cannot achieve all of this with one dish, or even two, so at least for company, try to make three dishes or more.

Although the Chinese love sweets, they are rarely served after meals. Rather, they are enjoyed with tea. Fruit and tea may be served after the meal. If you want to serve a light dessert after your meal, see Chapter XIV for recipes and suggestions.

When planning a Chinese meal, ask yourself:

Can I realistically pull this off? Do I have the equipment I need? What can I do ahead of time? Can I fit everything on my stove? Can I cook everything at the same time and eat with my guests, or will I be at the stove the whole time?

A Chinese cook can prepare a six-dish meal in half an hour in a tiny kitchen with no oven. This takes practice, of course, but it is achievable in our modern kitchens. The Chinese cook will stir-fry or deep-fry some of the dishes in turn, transferring the finished dish to a heated serving plate with a cover while the next dish is completed. Stir-frying and deep-frying, when all of the ingredients are prepared ahead of time, takes only minutes.

However, if the thought of all this last-minute cooking makes you nervous and will keep you from your guests, you must chose your dishes with care and prepare as many things ahead of time as you can. Have all the vegetables chopped and all the cooking sauces mixed. See about stir-frying (Chapter XI) and about deep-frying (Chapter XIII) for tips on organizing foods before cooking by these rapid-fire methods. Instead of planning two or three stir-fried dishes, plan only one stir-fry, one braised or stewed dish (that can be made ahead), a soup (that can be made ahead), a steamed or baked dish (such as filled buns, which can be made ahead and reheated), a cold dish (such as Vegetable-Noodle Salad with Sesame, p. 103, or an appetizer plate, that can be made well ahead of time), and perhaps a deep-fried dish (use the twice-fried technique on p. 170, so that you need only finish the pre-fried food in hot oil at the last minute).

Here is a little story that may be instructive to some of you—it certainly was to me! I got a little too ambitious with one meal I planned for company. I had carefully planned two braised dishes and a soup that could be made ahead. I had one dish out on the porch (it was in the winter), keeping cool, and I placed the other in the microwave oven, all ready to reheat. However, I was in such a flap serving the soup and steaming dumplings, and doing two stir-fries, and I can't even remember what else, that I totally forgot about the two braised dishes, which I discovered in their resting places the next morning! This is where I should have used that "battle plan," or list, that Karen Lee wrote about!

HOW TO SERVE A CHINESE MEAL

In family-style meals, the dishes are usually served all at the same time. Banquet-style means serving one course at a time. You don't have to prepare a banquet to serve this way! Although it means you will be in the kitchen more (unless you have another cook or two to help you), serving one course at a time may be less stressful than trying to have everything ready at the same time.

It's still important to prepare as many things ahead of time as possible. Have each dish prepared in advance to the point of last-minute cooking or reheating. (And remember that list—your "battle plan"!)

Serving a meal banquet style allows your guests to savor each dish on its own. Rice, noodles, or Chinese breads are served throughout. For real food afficionados, this also allows time to discuss the qualities of each dish, how it was made, and the wonderful skills of the cook!

What to Drink with a Chinese Meal

Tea is traditional with Chinese meals in restaurants, although this is not actually a common practice in China. If you prefer tea, you can use a Chinese green tea, jasmine tea, or a myriad of other varieties. Buy small packets of Chinese teas at an Asian grocery store and try them out—make your own blends. However, do not brew Chinese tea as strong as orange pekoe.

At family meals, tea is not generally served until after the meal. The beverage may be soft drinks or beer, or soup may be sipped like a beverage between courses. At banquets, warm rice wine or heavy spirits are often served throughout the meal.

Western grape wines can be served with Chinese meals. A slightly sweet, fruity white wine, such as Riesling, Chenin Blanc, Gewurtztraminer, or Sylvaner, or a rosé, goes well with most Chinese dishes. Sparkling wines, slightly sweetened sparkling sodas or mineral waters, and sparkling ciders are other good choices. If the food is very spicy, beer may be the best thirst-quencher of all.

A glaring omission from most Chinese vegetarian cookbooks is a chapter on how to make Chinese Buddhist-style vegetarian "mock meats." Yet, visit any Chinese Buddhist restaurant and a large portion of the menu is based on these foods! What gives? My theory is that most Chinese vegetarian cookbooks (thus far) have been written by omnivores who can have meat whenever they choose, so they see no need to give recipes for "mock meat" and "mock seafood" dishes, concentrating instead on the delicious vegetable-based dishes of the cuisine. This is great, as far as it goes, but these recipes often contain real oyster sauce, desserts with animal-based gelatin, and chicken broth, as well. These books overlook the hearty stews and other "mock meat" dishes that vegetarians crave, especially in the winter. I wanted this book to fill a need for real vegetarian recipes devised by a vegetarian.

Chinese "mock meats" can be bought prepared from any Buddhist restaurant, if you have one nearby. The products vary from restaurant to restaurant, but they are all delicious. They can be made from seitan (wheat gluten), tofu (bean curd), yuba (bean curd skin), mushrooms, textured soy protein, and a variety of vegetables from land and sea. Tofu, for instance, will often replace chicken; textured soy protein will replace pork or chicken; seitan chunks are made to replace pork, beef, and seafood; bean curd skin is seasoned and fashioned into delicious "crispy delights" for sweet-and-sour, or "roast duck" or "roast chicken"; batter-fried mushrooms may be used in place of meat or fish. Sometimes batter-fried walnuts are used, but I find these too rich.

Asian grocery stores will carry cans of "mock meats"—everything from braised seitan, braised "dried bean curd," mock "abalone" (plain or curried), mock "roast duck," and curried seitan chunks ("Curried Buddhist Chicken") to "scallops" canned by Worthington Foods or other Seventh Day Adventist brands. If you have a store near you that carries these products, buy some and try them out. You might not like them all, but you will probably love some of them, and they are very convenient for quick meals. Companion and Longevity brands are good.

You can use some of the new western-style soy and seitan-based "mock meats" in Chinese cooking too. Most natural food stores sell

Chapter VI

HOMEMADE "MOCK MEATS"

"To a Chinese cook, imitating certain meat dishes with non-meat ingredients is not simply a matter of replacing the meat. It is instead an effort to show off the great culinary art of China, to make the impossible possible."

Stella Lau Fessler, *Chinese Meatless Cooking*

Preparing Dried Chinese Black Mushrooms For Cooking

Dried Chinese black mushrooms (see p. 15) are used in many recipes. To prepare them, cover the dried mushrooms with hot water, cover the bowl, and let them soak for 20 to 30 minutes, or until they are soft. Drain the mushrooms, saving the soaking water to use in broth or as a broth—it's very tasty. Cut off the stems and discard them. Now the mushrooms are ready to use.

If you are in a hurry, you can microwave the mushrooms in a covered bowl for about 10 minutes. Leave plenty of room for the water to boil up. The time depends on how many mushrooms you are rehydrating at once—if you are doing a large amount, it's probably just as fast to soak them the ordinary way.

already prepared seitan cutlets, sometimes chicken-style as well as beef-style. Frozen "mock chicken" cutlets and nuggets can be used in stir-fries, and the vegetarian deli "ham" and "Canadian back bacon" are excellent seasonings in many Chinese dishes. Some of the firm "burgers" can be sliced and used in stir-fries, and the various types of marinated, baked, smoked, and otherwise flavored tofu and tempeh products make good "mock meats" too.

I like making my own, for the most part. They are cheap, easy to make, and delicious. They can be made ahead and frozen for quick meals. The seitan products are made from pure vital wheat gluten powder, so there is no arduous kneading and rinsing involved, and you can add seasonings right into the dough.

I hope you have fun preparing your own "mock meats." The recipes give you options for using homemade or commercial versions.

In a Hurry Vegetarian "Chicken"

If you don't have any Breast of Tofu "Chicken" (p. 43) marinating in your refrigerator, or reconstituted textured soy protein chunks, "brests," or cutlets (pp. 50-51) ready in the freezer, but you want to make a vegetarian "chicken" stir-fry, all you need is 12 ounces of firm or extra-firm tofu. This is equal to about 2 large chicken breasts.

If you are following a non-vegetarian Chinese recipe that calls for chicken breast slivers or cubes that marinate in a seasoning mixture while you ready the other stir-fry ingredients, simply substitute the firm or extra-firm tofu for the chicken breasts. Otherwise, toss the tofu slivers or cubes in 1 or 2 tablespoons of vegetarian stir-fry "oyster" sauce (p. 116) before stir-frying or deep-frying. This gives the tofu some depth of flavor and the rather sticky sauce clings well to the tofu.

If you have no vegetarian stir-fry sauce, use a mixture of 2 tablespoons light soy sauce, 1 tablespoon dry sherry, 1 teaspoon light unbleached sugar, 1 teaspoon roasted sesame oil, and 1 teaspoon cornstarch.

BREAST OF TOFU "CHICKEN"

Yield: 32 slices

1½ to 2 pounds extra-firm or pressed tofu

Marinade:

1½ cups water

¼ cup light soy sauce

3 tablespoons nutritional yeast flakes

½ teaspoon onion powder

½ teaspoon garlic granules

Prepare the marinade by mixing all of the ingredients together in a 5 cup rigid plastic container with a tight lid. Slice the tofu about ¼ inch thick or into ½-inch cubes, and place in the marinade so that it is fairly tightly-packed and covered with liquid. Cover and refrigerate for up to 2 weeks, shaking daily.

To use in a stir-fry instead of chicken, cut into bite-sized slivers and marinate in whatever ingredients would be used to season chicken (usually soy sauce and sherry, sometimes with a bit of sugar and maybe some cornstarch). Stir-fry as directed for chicken.

To make crispy slices, coat the slices with Seasoned Flour (p. 49). Heat a heavy-bottomed, 10- to 12-inch cast-iron skillet over high heat. When very hot, add about 1 tablespoon of oil. Expeller-pressed Asian peanut oil is good. When the oil is hot, turn the heat down to medium and add 8 to 10 coated slices. You may have to play with the heat on your stove. On mine, medium is perfect for browning the slices without danger of burning, but your stove may be cooler or hotter. They brown more slowly when cooked this way than they do when a lot of oil is used.

Cook, watching carefully, until golden brown and crispy on the bottom. Turn the slices over and cook the other side until golden and crispy. Drain thoroughly on paper and repeat the process if you want to cook more slices.

Per 2 slices: Calories 45, Protein 4 g, Fat 1 g, Carbohydrates 2 g

I always have some extra-firm tofu slices marinating. They will keep refrigerated for up to 2 weeks—ready for a quick, delicious meal. Coated with Seasoned Flour (p. 49) and fried in a minimal amount of oil, a crispy "skin" results that makes this an excellent replacement for chicken in fried dishes, such as Lemon "Chicken" (pp. 177-178). They can be deep-fried if you prefer the more traditional Chinese cooking method. The cold fried slices can also be used on Chinese appetizer plates in place of chicken.

Used "as is," the marinated slices can be used in any stir-fry that calls for chicken. I prefer the texture of Breast of Tofu "Chicken" to that of seitan in vegetarian "chicken" dishes. Instead of slices, you can marinate chunks, for using on skewers or in stews.

Note: Nutritional yeast flakes are not a traditional Chinese item, but, combined with soy sauce, they provide a remarkably "chickeny" taste that I feel any Buddhist vegetarian cook would approve of.

Traditional Chinese gluten recipes use an unflavored dough that is either boiled or deep-fried, and then cooked in a flavored broth or sauce. I have added a baked or oven-fried version, which can be used like deep-fried gluten, but without the fat.

Following this basic recipe are a number of ways to use the cooked gluten. The Braised Chinese Seitan and variations can be used in dishes that call for pork or textured soy protein chunks. I have devised a Chinese-Style "Beefy" Seitan, as well. These seem to suit Chinese recipes better than the seitan "pork" and "beef" that I make for other styles of cooking.

Mock Abalone is my version of the canned Chinese variety. It is good in hotpots, soups, and stir-fries. I have also devised my own Seitan "Seafood."

You can use the Deep-Fried or Baked Seitan in stir-fries, hot-pots, and stews, or bake or grill with barbecue sauce or sweet-and-sour sauces to make a dish like "ribs."

This recipe makes a large amount because it freezes well.

RAW GLUTEN DOUGH

Yield: 96 pieces

2½ cups pure gluten powder (vital wheat gluten)
2 cups cold water

To make the raw gluten, mix together the gluten flour and the water. Mix until it forms a smooth, firm dough. Knead briefly. Cut the dough into 96 fairly equal pieces. Keep your hands wet while you handle the dough.

Per 4 pieces : Calories 57, Protein 12 g, Fat 0 g, Carbohydrates 2 g

BAKED SEITAN BALLS

Form the pieces into little balls as if you were making little dinner buns. Pull two sides of the dough down, and pinch it tightly on the bottom, so that the top is smoothly rounded. Place the balls 2½ inches apart on lightly-oiled cookie sheets. Bake at 350°F for 10 minutes. Turn them over and bake for 5 to 10 minutes longer, or until puffy and golden.

BOILED SEITAN CHUNKS

Drop the gluten chunks (in about 4 batches) into a large pot of boiling water, and boil for 5 minutes. Scoop out with a slotted spoon, and drain in a colander.

DEEP-FRIED SEITAN CHUNKS

Heat about 2 cups of oil in a wok or medium pot to 325°F. Add a few pieces of gluten at a time. They puff up quite dramatically and stick together easily, so don't crowd the pot. Keep turning and separating them until they are puffed up and golden all over. Remove with a slotted spoon, and drain on paper. (They will deflate.)

You can freeze any of these forms of seitan in plastic bags or rigid freezer containers for future use. Or go ahead and flavor them as directed in one of the following recipes.

Seitan "Seafood"

Yield: 1½ pounds cooked seitan (8 to 10 servings)

1 recipe Raw Gluten Dough (p. 44)

Cooking Broth:

4 cups water
6-inch piece kombu seaweed
1½ tablespoons salt
4 dried Chinese black mushrooms
2 tablespoons lemon juice
1 tablespoon sugar
1 teaspoon dried garlic

For "scallops": Shape the raw gluten dough into a long roll about 1 inch in diameter. Cut into little rounds like very thin scallops. Mix the cooking broth ingredients, and bring to a boil. Drop in the gluten rounds, and simmer for 30 minutes. Refrigerate overnight in the cooking broth.

For "fish": Flatten the raw gluten into very thin "fillet" shapes. If your pieces are too big, just cut them. Mix the cooking broth and bring to a low boil. Add the gluten "fillets" and return to a low boil, rather than a simmer, and cook for 30 minutes. This makes a softer seitan. Refrigerate overnight in the cooking broth.

For "clams": Tear the raw gluten into tiny bits. Bring the cooking broth to a boil, and drop in the gluten pieces. Boil for 3 minutes and refrigerate overnight in the cooking broth.

For "shrimp": Cut the raw gluten into little wedge shapes about 1½ inches long and ½ inch thick. Mix the the cooking broth, and bring to a simmer. Drop in the gluten and simmer for 30 minutes. Refrigerate overnight in the cooking broth.

Note: Remember that seitan expands quite a bit, so whatever shape you cut, make the pieces at least half as small as you want them to be.

Per serving: Calories 164, Protein 32 g, Fat 1 g, Carbohydrates 7 g

Seitan "Seafood" can be used in stir-fries, or batter-fried (pp. 171-173) and served with a dipping sauce. Adding some nori or dulse seaweed flakes to the batter gives it a more seafood taste.

Ground Seitan

Use seitan made by any method, in any shape. Cut into chunks and run them through a regular meat-grinder or a food processor. You can then freeze this in any convenient measurement.

By weight, ½ pound seitan is equal to about a pound of meat.

Mock "Abalone"

Yield: 48 pieces

This is one product that is readily available in cans if you have an Asian grocery store nearby, but it's not hard to make. The finished pieces can be frozen. They can be sliced and used in stir-fries, soups, and hot-pots.

48 pieces Deep-Fried or Baked Seitan (p. 44)
10 medium dried Chinese black mushrooms, soaked in hot water for 20 to 30 minutes until soft and stems discarded (save soaking water)
2 tablespoons light soy sauce
1 tablespoon dry sherry
1 teaspoon grated fresh ginger
1 teaspoon unbleached sugar

Place the gluten in a pot with the mushroom soaking water, drained mushrooms, and remaining ingredients. Cover and simmer for 20 to 30 minutes, or until the liquid has almost evaporated. Remove the mushrooms and use them in other dishes, or freeze for future use. Pack the "abalone" in a rigid plastic container or a pint jar, and refrigerate or freeze.

Per 2 pieces: Calories 64, Protein 12 g, Fat 0 g, Carbohydrates 3 g

Braised Chinese Seitan

Yield: 24 pieces

You can buy this in cans, but it's much less expensive and very easy to make yourself. You can double or quadruple the recipe if you like. You can use it as a pork substitute.

24 pieces Boiled, Baked, or Deep-Fried Seitan (p. 44)
Cooking Liquid:
½ cup water
2 tablespoons light soy sauce
2 tablespoons dry sherry
1 tablespoon light unbleached sugar
1 tablespoon maple syrup
½ tablespoon brown bean sauce
½ tablespoon roasted sesame oil

If the chunks seem too big, cut them in half. Combine the seitan chunks and the cooking liquid ingredients in a large, heavy or non-stick skillet. Cook over medium-high heat—10 minutes for the baked gluten, 20 minutes for the boiled or deep-fried gluten. Stir frequently until most of the liquid is absorbed. If the liquid evaporates too quickly, turn the heat down a little and/or add a little water from time to time, but cook for the full length of time specified. Store in a covered container with the leftover sauce in the refrigerator or freezer.

Per piece: Calories 66, Protein 12 g, Fat 0 g, Carbohydrates 3 g

RED-BRAISED SEITAN

Yield: 24 pieces

1 tablespoon roasted sesame oil
24 pieces Boiled, Baked, or Deep-Fried Seitan (pp. 44-45)
20 small or 10 large dried Chinese black mushrooms, soaked in
   hot water for 20 to 30 minutes until soft and stems discarded
   (save soaking water)
2 tablespoons dry sherry
2 tablespoons dark or mushroom soy sauce
1 tablespoon unbleached sugar
¼ teaspoon salt
Optional: **1 small onion, sliced**
2 slices fresh ginger
2 cloves garlic, smashed

In a heavy pot or saucepan, heat the oil over medium-high heat. Add the mushrooms and stir-fry for a few minutes. Add the mushroom soaking water, seitan, and the rest of the ingredients. Cover and simmer for 30 minutes. If the liquid hasn't cooked down to almost nothing by the end of this time, remove the cover and raise the heat to cook it down until it is almost all absorbed, watching carefully. Store the gluten and mushrooms separately.

Per piece: Calories 71, Protein 12 g, Fat 1 g, Carbohydrates 3 g

Variation
Curried Braised
Chinese Seitan

Add ½ tablespoon curry powder or paste to the cooking sauce. Omit the sugar.

You can also add some minced garlic and/or ¼ to ½ teaspoon chili garlic paste, if you like.

This recipe can use boiled, fried, or baked seitan. It is cooked with a large amount of dried Chinese black mushrooms to make a seitan with a rich, subtle flavor. The mushrooms can be used as a dish on their own, or added to other dishes which call for rehydrated dried mushrooms. Both the mushrooms and gluten can be frozen for future use. This can be used as a pork substitute.

Be sure to check out the delicious recipe for Vegetarian "Barbecued Pork" on pp. 58-59.

Chinese-Style "Beefy" Seitan

Yield: 48 pieces

While this is not a traditional recipe, it is (almost) a traditional method of cooking. I vary it by using some of the flavored cooking broth as the liquid in the gluten, so that it has more flavor. Cut the cooked pieces into slivers for stir-fries, or use them in barbecues, stews, or kebabs.

Broth:

1 cup cold water

2 tablespoons dark or mushroom soy sauce

2 tablespoons ketchup

**2 teaspoons Marmite, yeast extract, or dark miso mixed with
    ½ cup hot water until dissolved**

¼ teaspoon garlic granules

¼ teaspoon onion powder

Optional: **2 teaspoons Kitchen Bouquet or other gravy browner**

1¼ cups pure gluten powder (vital wheat gluten)

Additional Ingredients:

1 tablespoon light soy sauce

1 tablespoon dry sherry

1 tablespoon roasted sesame oil

Mix the broth ingredients together. In a small bowl, mix the gluten powder with 1 cup of the broth. Stir until a dough forms. Roll the dough into a "log" and cut it into 48 more or less equal-size slices or chunks.

Mix the remaining broth with ½ cup water and the additional soy sauce and sherry in a medium saucepan. Bring to a boil. Drop in 12 pieces of gluten. Boil for 4 minutes, then remove them with a slotted spoon to a sieve or colander placed over a bowl. Add ½ cup more water to the pot, and let it come to a boil again, then drop in 12 more pieces, and boil for 4 minutes. Repeat this 2 more times until all the gluten is cooked, adding more water, plus any broth that has dripped into the bowl back to the pot. You may have to add more than ½ cup of water the last time. Just make sure the gluten pieces are more or less covered with liquid while they cook.

When all the gluten is cooked, heat the sesame oil in a large, heavy skillet, and add the gluten pieces along with the remaining broth. Cover and cook over medium-low heat for about 20 minutes, or until all the broth is absorbed and the gluten is firm. You may have to add a splash of water from time to time. Stir frequently as it cooks.

Place the gluten in a covered container, and refrigerate or freeze.

Per piece: Calories 19, Protein 3 g, Fat 0 g, Carbohydrates 1 g

Seasoned Flour

2 cups whole wheat (or other wholegrain) flour
¼ cup nutritional yeast flakes
1 teaspoon salt
Optional: **1 teaspoon onion powder**
Optional: **Freshly ground black pepper to taste**

Mix all the ingredients together, and store in a tightly covered container in the refrigerator.

Variations

Other seasonings that you can try are garlic granules, five-spice powder, and/or finely ground dried red chili flakes. Start with ½ teaspoon and add more after tasting.

To quickly rehydrate the granules

Mix an almost equal amount of very hot or boiling liquid with them, cover, and let soak for 5 minutes or so. Water is fine for soaking if the granules are to be added to a spicy mixture, but you can also use a flavorful broth or just add 1 or 2 tablespoons light soy sauce to the hot water. The general rule is ⅞ cup liquid to each cup of textured vegetable protein granules. This yields about 1⅓ cups.

To reconstitute the dry chunks, "Brests," and cutlets

Cook 1½ cups dry chunks in 3 cups water with 3 tablespoons soy sauce, 3 tablespoons ketchup or tomato paste, and 1 tablespoon nutritional yeast flakes for 15 to 30 minutes, depending upon how tender you like them. "Brests" or cutlets need to cook for 30 to 40 minutes, generally in a vegetarian chicken-like broth. Cool and store in the cooking broth. (I usually make 4 or more times this amount and freeze it in 2-cup portions.) Drain the chunks

ABOUT TEXTURED SOY PROTEIN

Textured soy protein (or TVP® or textured vegetable protein, as it is sometimes called) is a low-fat, inexpensive dry product, used as a meat substitute. It is *not* the same thing as hydrolyzed plant protein or soy isolate, and contains no MSG or other additives. It is made from soy flour that is cooked under pressure and then extruded to make different sizes and shapes.

Textured soy protein has the advantage of being chewier and lower in fat than tofu. It can take the place of frozen tofu in many recipes. Even if you object to the use of meat alternates on a regular basis, it makes a great transitional food for people who are accustomed to eating meat and, despite the best of motives and intentions, miss those familiar flavors and textures. I have had great success in serving textured soy protein dishes to nonvegetarians. Textured soy protein chunks and cutlets have such a meaty texture that when I have cooked them in a flavorful mixture, some anxious vegetarians have asked me if I'm sure their food includes no meat!

Although textured soy protein is not a traditional Chinese food, I find it being used more and more in Buddhist Chinese vegetarian restaurants. There are some Chinese companies that make Chinese-style textured soy protein products specifically for the Chinese restaurant market. Your favorite restaurant might sell you some of the products they use, but they are not generally available to the public. I suggest that you use unflavored textured soy protein products from your natural food store or natural foods mail-order source (see pp. 185) and flavor them yourself.

Textured soy protein will keep for a long time, has no cholesterol, almost no fat or sodium, and is an excellent source of protein and fiber. An organic variety is available. It is easily rehydrated for use in soups, stews, casseroles, and sauces. In fact, if your mixture is very "brothy," you can just add the textured soy protein in its dry state, and it will absorb the flavorful broth.

The most readily available types are the granules and the chunks. In Chinese cooking, the granules can be used for patties, "sausage," "meatballs," and "meat" stuffings for dumplings and stuffed breads. The chunks make wonderful stews, stir-fries, deep-fried "nuggets," and are an excellent substitute for small sweet-and-sour spareribs. I reconstitute large amounts of them and keep them frozen in 2-cup containers, in their cooking broth, in the freezer. Then I can quickly thaw them out and make an elegant, but quick and easy, dish for dinner at the last minute.

Reconstituted textured vegetable protein granules, ground seitan, and crumbled frozen tofu can be used pretty much interchangeably in many recipes. When I'm substituting for meat in a recipe, I figure that 1 pound of meat is equal to about 2 cups of reconstituted textured vegetable protein granules or chunks, crumbled frozen tofu, or ground seitan.

The chunks, cutlets, and "brests" take a little longer to reconstitute, but have an amazingly meat-like texture and a pleasant, mild flavor. The chunks are available in most health-food stores and some supermarkets, but you may have to order cutlets or "brests" by mail-order (see p. 185), or ask your local Chinese vegetarian restaurant if they will sell you some.

The Chinese vegetarian restaurant that we frequent in Victoria, B.C., the Lotus Pond, sells their customers small textured soy protein cutlets. They prepare them somewhat differently than I have been accustomed to, but they are equally delicious. The Lotus Pond method of reconstituting textured soy protein chunks or cutlets is to cover them with plenty of boiling water and let them soak for at least 2 hours, or even overnight. (You may need a plate with a bottom that goes below the level of the top of the bowl to keep the cutlets under the water.) When they are expanded and softened, drain them and squeeze out most of the water. Flavor them by adding 2 tablespoons light soy sauce, 1 tablespoon dry sherry, 1 teaspoon unbleached sugar, and 1 teaspoon roasted sesame oil for every 1 ounce of dry soy protein. I put the cutlets in a covered container with the mixture and shake them. They readily soak up the flavoring. Next, flour the cutlets or chunks lightly and deep-fry, shallow-fry, or oven-fry them until crisp and golden and ready to use in your recipe. (See Chapter XIII on frying.)

before using them, and pat them dry before coating with flour, frying, or marinating.

Besides stews, the chunks can be used in stir-fries, barbecues, kebabs. They can be deep-fried or shallow-fried, pan-fried with less oil, or oven-fried (see Chapter XIII). Cutlets and "brests" can also be fried or oven-fried this way.

Note: If you make seitan, you can also reconstitute textured vegetable protein chunks in leftover seitan cooking broth of any flavor.

Vegetarian Chinese "Sausage"

Yield: 14 to 20 links (about 1 pound)

Chinese sausage is sweeter than North American sausage, with a more fermented taste. Try to use the red fermented tofu (doufu-ru) in this recipe for the most authentic flavor. It is used in rice dishes, casseroles, and stuffings.

Note: I recommend making these ahead of time and cooling them before use; this firms them up. The sausages can be frozen or refrigerated.

1 cup dry textured soy protein granules
¾ cup boiling water
1 tablespoon dark or mushroom soy sauce
1 tablespoon dry sherry
1 tablespoon unbleached sugar
3 ounces medium-firm tofu mashed with 2 cubes red doufu-ru (see pp. 28-29), or 4 ounces medium-firm tofu mashed with 1 tablespoon red Japanese miso
1 tablespoon roasted sesame oil
1 teaspoon liquid smoke
½ teaspoon salt
½ teaspoon five-spice powder
¼ teaspoon freshly ground black pepper or dried red chili pepper flakes
Optional: 1 tablespoon minced cilantro
Optional: 2 green onions, minced
Optional: ½ teaspoon ground roasted Sichuan peppercorn
½ cup pure gluten powder (vital wheat gluten)

In a medium bowl, soak the soy protein in the boiling water, soy sauce, sherry, and sugar for about 10 minutes, or until the soy protein has soaked up all the liquid. Add the mashed tofu and doufu-ru, sesame oil, seasonings, and any optional ingredients. Set aside to cool. You can speed the cooling by spreading the mixture on a plate and putting it in the freezer for a few minutes. (Cooling keeps the gluten from clumping into strings as you mix it.)

When cool, add the gluten powder and mix well with your hands. Shape into 14 to 20 small sausage "links."

Steam them on a plate or a steaming basket, covered, over simmering water for 20 minutes. Or *microsteam* them in a plastic microwave steamer in a covered bowl over 1 cup water for about 5 minutes. Microsteam half the recipe at a time. This makes a moist product which firms up nicely when cooled. They can then be browned in a nonstick or heavy skillet in a little roasted sesame oil until crisp and golden on all sides. Add them to recipes that call for Chinese sausage.

Per 2 links: Calories 93, Protein 12 g, Fat 2 g, Carbohydrates 5 g

Ground "Pork"

For Ground "Pork" to use in egg rolls, dumpling fillings, etc., use the recipe for steamed "Pork Balls" on pp. 60-61, either raw or cooked, according to the particular recipe's directions in this book, or whether you are substituting it for raw or cooked ground pork in a recipe.

VEGETARIAN GROUND "CHICKEN"

Yield: 8 patties or 24 to 26 balls (1 pound)

¾ cup dry textured soy protein granules
¾ cup boiling water or mushroom soaking water
2 tablespoons light soy sauce

½ cup mashed tofu (4 ounces)
1 tablespoon nutritional yeast
1 teaspoon onion powder
½ teaspoon garlic granules

½ cup pure gluten powder (vital wheat gluten)

After it is cooked, this recipe can be crumbled and used in egg rolls, dumplings, etc.

In a bowl, soak the textured soy protein granules in the boiling water and soy sauce. When liquid is absorbed, add the tofu, nutritional yeast, onion powder, and garlic. Set aside to cool.

Mix well and form into 8 patties or 24 to 26 balls. If the recipe calls for cooked minced chicken, steam according to any of the methods in the recipe for Vegetarian Chinese "Sausage" on p. 52 . If the recipe calls for raw ground chicken, don't steam it. Recipes in this book will direct you whether to use the mixture cooked or uncooked.

Per patty: Calories 76, Protein 13 g, Fat 1 g, Carbohydrates 4 g

CHINESE MUSHROOM-RICE "SAUSAGE"

Yield: 16 patties

One sometimes comes across Chinese recipes for a "sausage" made with rice. This is my version, using lots of mushrooms in place of meat. It's moist and delicious and makes an excellent dim sum dish. It can also be crumbled over simple rice, noodle, or scrambled tofu dishes.

Variation
Chinese Vegetarian "Pork" Patties

Omit the liquid smoke, five-spice powder, and fermented tofu. Use only 1 tablespoon sugar. Use light soy sauce. Add 4 teaspoons grated fresh ginger. You can use the chili flakes, or use some freshly-grated white or black pepper instead. Use expeller-pressed Asian peanut oil instead of the sesame oil, if you wish, or half and half.

1 medium onion, finely minced (in a food processor, if possible)
6 cloves garlic, crushed
1 pound fresh mushrooms (button, crimini, shiitake, portobello, or a mixture), finely chopped (in a food processor, if possible)
½ cup minced green onions
3 tablespoons dry sherry
2 tablespoons dark unbleached sugar
4 cubes red fermented tofu (doufu-ru, pp. 28-29), mashed, or
   2 tablespoons Japanese red miso
½ tablespoon dark soy sauce or mushroom soy sauce
1 teaspoon salt
1 teaspoon liquid smoke
½ to 1 teaspoon five-spice powder
½ teaspoon dried red chili flakes
2 cups cooked short grain rice (cooked in vegetarian broth)
¾ cup soft fresh breadcrumbs
2 tablespoons roasted sesame oil

In a large non-stick skillet, dry-fry (see p. 122) the onion and garlic over high heat, stirring constantly. Add drops of water as needed to keep the mixture from sticking and browning. When the onions are soft, add the mushrooms, green onions, and sherry. Stir over high heat until the liquid the mushrooms exude is pretty much absorbed, about 5 minutes.

Scrape the mixture into a bowl, and add the remaining ingredients, except the oil. Mix everything together very well. The mixture can be refrigerated for a couple of days at this point, if you wish. Form the mixture into 16 patties.

Cover a wide steamer basket with plastic wrap, and poke a few holes in the wrap. Place the patties on the plastic wrap. (You may have to do 2 batches.) Cover and steam them over boiling water for 7 minutes. (See pp. 35-36 about steaming.)

The patties need to be chilled before browning. If you are in a hurry, you can speed this up by placing them in the freezer until they are cold.

In a large heavy skillet over medium heat, brown the patties on both sides in two batches, using 1 tablespoon sesame oil per batch.

Per patty: Calories 65, Protein 1 g, Fat 2 g, Carbohydrates 10 g

Buddha's "Chicken"

Yield: 4 servings

**3 large round sheets fresh yuba (bean curd skin) about
16 inches in diameter, cut in half, or 3 large rectangular sheets
dried yuba**
⅓ cup vegetarian broth
1½ tablespoons light soy sauce
2 teaspoons light unbleached sugar
½ tablespoon roasted sesame oil
Oil for deep-frying

This is a traditional yuba (bean curd skin) recipe used by Chinese Buddhist vegetarians. It makes a delicious hot or cold appetizer. Leftovers can be chopped and used in stuffings or rice or noodle dishes.

If you use fresh yuba, which needs no soaking, this dish is very quick to prepare. It's very easy to make whether you use fresh or dried.

If using the dried yuba, handle the sheets carefully and soak in warm water for 5 to 10 minutes. Pat them dry and cut in half.

Mix the broth, soy sauce, sugar, and sesame oil in a small saucepan, and heat until the sugar is dissolved. Pour into a bowl and allow to cool slightly.

Spread a 12- x 6-inch piece of fine cheesecloth or thin white cotton sheeting over a cookie sheet. Place a half-sheet of the fresh or reconstituted dried yuba on the sheet.

Brush the yuba with the soy sauce mixture. Cover with another piece of yuba and brush. Repeat until all of the yuba and sauce is used up. If there is some sauce left, pour it over the yuba and brush evenly towards the outside edges.

Variation
Buddha's Roast "Duck"

Follow the same procedure as for Buddha's "Chicken," but for the sauce, use Chinese mushroom soaking water instead of broth, 2 tablespoons light soy sauce, 2 teaspoons roasted sesame oil, only ¾ teaspoon light unbleached sugar, and add 2 teaspoons dry sherry.

Instead of rolling the brushed sheets of bean curd skin, fold the short side in, once, and then once again, so that it is folded in thirds, and flatten lightly. Steam and fry as directed.

Variation
Mock Peking Duck

Serve thinly sliced Buddha's Roast "Duck" with Manadarin Pancakes (pp. 87-88), Duck Sauce (p. 119), and finely-shredded green onions. Guests place a bit of "duck" along with about 1 teaspoon of the sauce and a few shreds of green onion in a Mandarin pancake, roll up, and eat with their hands.

Roll the stack of sheets into a compact cylinder, and wrap it in the cloth. Tie the ends with white string. Steam the roll, covered, over boiling water for 10 minutes.

Remove the cloth carefully and cut the roll into 4 sections, diagonally. Heat the oil to 350°F in a wok, skillet, or deep-fryer. Drop in the rolls, standing back to avoid splattering, and deep-fry until golden-brown. This will take only a few seconds. Drain the rolls on paper.

To serve, slice diagonally into ½-inch rounds, and serve hot or cold.

Per serving: Calories 155, Protein 13 g, Fat 8g, Carbohydrates 7 g

Dim sum translates literally as "dot heart" or "point on the heart." In culinary terms, that means "heart's delight." And, indeed, these little dishes and dainties delight even the most jaded heart or palate.

The Chinese have been enjoying dim sum in tea houses since the 10th century. Dim sum are small dishes, savories and sweets that are often steamed, deep-fried, or pan-fried—all typical fuel-saving Chinese cooking techniques.

In my pre-vegetarian days, we used to visit dim sum restaurants in Vancouver, boisterous with families enjoying a meal together, the air redolent with intoxicating odors. The waiters would wheel up carts of foods in little steamer baskets and plates and bowls. We would point to what we wanted (sometimes not having any idea what it was!), and they would leave the containers on the table. A little while later, they would come by with some more treats. After we had finished stuffing ourselves, the dishes and baskets would be counted up and we would be presented with our (very reasonable) bill.

Some restaurants and tea houses serve dim sum all day every day, others just at specific times and days. Tea is always served throughout the meal.

It is difficult, if not impossible, to enjoy this ritual as a vegetarian, unless you live near a Chinese Buddhist vegetarian restaurant that serves dim sum, so I have learned to make some of my favorites. Many of these dishes can be made ahead, so you might like to make up several and have a dim sum meal with friends, surprising them with the wonderful variety of flavors.

Although I have a separate chapter for dumplings and breads (Chapter VIII), they are usually considered dim sum as well.

These recipes make wonderful western-style appetizers for parties too.

Chapter VII

SAVORY SNACKS AND APPETIZERS

DIM SUM

"To eat well requires a sense of fitness (taste) and an adventurous spirit. Like good explorers, we must know when we have found something, then return to it, charting the approaches, so that it will be known to others."

Hsiang Ju Lin and
Tsiufeng Lin,
Chinese Gastronomy

This is China's answer to the Mediterranean grilled pepper. It's delicious, quick, and very easy. If you don't have an exhaust fan over your stove, keep some windows open!

Chinese Appetizer Plate

Make or buy a selection of Chinese vegetarian "mock meats" (see Chapter VI), such as "roast duck," "chicken," "ham," etc. You can include some western vegan deli items, such as slices of vegetarian "turkey," "ham," or "Canadian back bacon," and slices of commercial baked or savory tofu. Slice these "mock meats" thinly, or cut into small pieces and arrange artistically on a platter. You could arrange them in concentric circles, placing contrasting colors together. Decorate the platter with radish roses, green onion "fans," etc.

PAN-ROASTED SICHUAN PEPPERS

Yield: 4 servings

2 large green peppers, seeded and quartered

Cooking Sauce:

4 green onions, chopped

2 tablespoons dry sherry

1 tablespoon fermented black beans, mashed with a fork

1 tablespoon oil

1 teaspoon light soy sauce

1 teaspoon rice, cider, or white wine vinegar

¼ teaspoon salt

Heat a large wok or heavy skillet over high heat. When it's very hot, add the peppers and cook over high heat, turning them often with a spatula, until they are slightly charred on the outside and starting to get a little soft on the inside. (They will soften further when cooled.)

Add the cooking sauce and toss the mixture for a couple of minutes. Place on a serving platter, and let come to room temperature before serving.

Per serving: Calories 55, Protein 1 g, Fat 3 g, Carbohydrates 3 g

VEGETARIAN "BARBECUED PORK"

CHAR SIU

Yield: 4 to 6 servings

Char Siu Sauce:

⅓ cup light unbleached sugar

¼ cup light soy sauce

¼ cup dry sherry

¼ cup red fermented bean curd (doufu-ru) and brine, or
2 tablespoons red Japanese miso

3 tablespoons water

12 cloves garlic, peeled and crushed

1 tablespoon roasted sesame oil

2 teaspoons five-spice powder

2 teaspoons grated fresh ginger

Gluten Chunks or Balls (makes 48)

1¼ cups pure gluten powder (vital wheat gluten)

1 cup cold water

To make the char siu sauce, mix all the sauce ingredients in a food processor, blender, or with a hand blender.

To make the gluten dough, mix the gluten powder and water in a medium bowl until a dough forms. Knead briefly. Roll the dough into a thick rope. Cut the dough into 48 slices, more or less evenly sized. Boil, bake, or deep-fry the gluten slices (see Chapter XIII).

To make the Char Siu with boiled seitan slices, mix them in a medium bowl with half of the sauce mixture. Heat a lightly oiled 10- to 12-inch heavy skillet over high heat. When very hot, add the gluten chunks with sauce and keep turning them over the high heat until they are glazed and golden and even slightly charred. Turn the heat down to low, cover, and cook for 10 minutes.

Pour in the rest of the sauce, and mix well. (At this point, the gluten can be refrigerated or frozen for future use. Refrigerated pieces can be heated up by going on to the next step. Frozen ones will have to be thawed first.) Place the gluten and sauce on a lightly oiled or nonstick shallow baking pan or cookie sheet. Broil the gluten 3 to 4 inches from the heat until they are slightly charred, about 3 minutes on each side; watch them closely.

To make the Char Siu with baked or fried seitan chunks or deep-fried tofu cubes, mix *all* of the sauce with the gluten or fried tofu in a large skillet. Bring to a boil, lower the heat, and simmer gently until the chunks have absorbed some of the sauce, but not all. (At this point, they can be refrigerated or frozen for future use. You can heat up refrigerated pieces by going on to the next step. Frozen ones will have to be thawed out first.) Spread them out on a lightly greased or nonstick cookie sheet or shallow baking pan, and char them slightly under the broiler (as directed above) before serving.

Per serving: Calories 244, Protein 31 g, Fat 3 g, Carbohydrates 19 g

This delectable recipe for Vegetarian Barbecued "Pork" may look long and complicated, but it isn't really. The space is taken up giving you several different choices of protein and ways to cook it.

If you prefer not to make this dish with the gluten chunks or balls (which would be the ingredient of choice in Chinese vegetarian cuisine), use the sauce on 48 one-inch cubes of commercial Chinese or Japanese deep-fried tofu, cooking them according to the directions for using baked or deep-fried seitan.

Whichever protein you use, you can make these several hours or days ahead of time. Serve them at room temperature or reheat them briefly under the broiler. The dish can also be frozen.

They are addictive as an appetizer, and they are delicious cold too! Use them as an ingredient in any dish that calls for Chinese barbecued pork, including Steamed Savory Filled Buns (pp. 78-80).

Chinese "Pork" Balls

Yield: 24 to 26 balls (equal to 1 pound meat)

Meatballs are served as dim sum, used in soups and casseroles, or served in a sauce. They can be used steamed or fried crisp on the outside.

Note: I recommend making these ahead of time and cooling them before use—this firms them up. The balls can be frozen or refrigerated.

If using the balls in a soup, brothy casserole, or a sauce, add them at the last possible moment so that they do not absorb too much moisture and fall apart.

Variation
Vegetarian Ground "Pork"

This mixture can be used as a basic "ground pork" for egg rolls, dumpling fillings, etc. Simply omit all of the optional seasonings and minced vegetables, and steam the mixture as directed in the recipe, but form it into 4 large patties.

1 cup dry textured soy protein granules
¾ cup boiling water
3 tablespoons light soy sauce
½ cup mashed medium-firm tofu (4 ounces)
3 tablespoons minced drained Chinese preserved vegetables
1 tablespoon minced green onion or fresh cilantro
1 teaspoon roasted sesame oil
½ teaspoon white pepper
¼ teaspoon salt
Optional: **3 tablespoons chopped water chestnuts (preferably fresh)**
Optional: **1 tablespoon grated fresh ginger and/or crushed garlic**
½ cup pure gluten powder (vital wheat gluten)

In the bowl of your food processor, combine the textured soy protein, boiling water, and soy sauce, and let soak for about 10 minutes until the soy protein has absorbed all the liquid. Add the rest of the ingredients, and process for several minutes until the soy protein is not so coarse. Set aside to cool. You can speed up the cooling process by spreading the mixture on a plate and putting it in the freezer for a few minutes. Cooling keeps the gluten from clumping into strings when it is added.

When cool, add the gluten powder and process briefly until the mixture forms a loose ball. With wet hands, shape the mixture into 24 to 26 small "meatballs," about 1 heaping tablespoon per ball. The mixture will be soft but will hold its shape. Roll the balls between the palms of your wet hands to make them smooth.

Important Note: The balls must be steamed first even if they are to be served deep-fried.

Steam them on an oiled plate or in an oiled steaming basket with little holes, covered, over simmering water for 20 minutes. You can also **microsteam** them by placing them in an oiled plastic microwave steamer in a covered bowl over 1 cup water and cooking for about 5 minutes. Microsteam only half the recipe at a time. This makes a moist product which firms up nicely when cooled.

They can then be reheated by steaming or microsteaming, or they can be browned in a nonstick or heavy skillet, using a little roasted sesame oil, until crisp and golden on all sides. You can also roll them in cornstarch and deep-fry until golden brown. (See Chapter XIII for deep-frying directions.)

Each ball: Calories 17, Protein 2 g, Fat 0 g, Carbohydrates 1 g

Pearl Balls

Yield: 24 to 26 balls

½ cup uncooked white, glutinous, "sweet" or sticky rice, for coating
1 cup dry textured soy protein granules
⅔ cup boiling water
3 tablespoons light soy sauce
1 tablespoon dry sherry
½ cup mashed medium-firm tofu (4 ounces)
6 large dried Chinese black mushrooms, soaked in hot water for 20 to 30 minutes until soft, stems discarded, and chopped
½ cup very finely grated raw carrot
1 tablespoon minced green onion
1 tablespoon grated fresh ginger
1 teaspoon roasted sesame oil
¼ teaspoon salt
½ teaspoon white pepper
½ cup pure gluten powder (vital wheat gluten)

Before you start making the "meatball" mixture, rinse the sweet rice in cold running water until the water runs clear. Drain the rice and place it in enough cold water to cover. Let it soak for 1 hour. Drain the rice and spread it evenly on a cookie sheet.

In the bowl of your food processor, soak the textured soy protein, in the boiling water, soy sauce, and sherry for about 10 minutes, or until the soy protein has soaked up all the liquid. Add the tofu, mushrooms, carrot, green onion, ginger, sesame oil, salt, and white

Variations for "Pork" Balls

Instead of the preserved vegetables, you can use:

- minced drained sauerkraut
- minced fresh mushrooms
- dried Chinese black mushrooms soaked in hot water for 20 to 30 minutes until soft and stems discarded

Pearl balls, a famous dim sum dish, originated in Hunan province, one of China's primary rice-growing regions. The name comes from the pearly coating of steamed glutinous rice. (Brown glutinous rice will not work in this recipe due to the long cooking time.) They are generally served as fingerfood with light soy sauce as the only accompaniment. Use a more strongly flavored dip or sauce, if you wish.

Note: If you absolutely can't find glutinous rice, then use plain Japanese-style short grain (or pearl) white rice (not flavored sushi rice).

pepper. Process for several minutes, or until the soy protein is not so coarse. Set aside to cool. Cooling this mixture keeps the gluten from clumping into strings. You can speed up the cooling by spreading the mixture on a plate and putting it in the freezer for a few minutes.

When cool, add the gluten powder and process briefly until the mixture forms a loose ball. With wet hands, shape the mixture into 24 to 26 small "meatballs," about 1 heaping tablespoon per ball. The mixture will be soft, but will hold its shape. Roll the balls between the palms of your wet hands to make them smooth. Roll each ball in the soaked rice completely coating each ball.

Line 2 steam baskets or trays with iceburg lettuce leaves, cooking parchment, cheesecloth that has been moistened with water, or waxed paper that has been punched with holes. Arrange the balls on the trays ½ inch apart. Stack the steamer trays over plenty of boiling water in a large wok or cooking pot, and cover. If you have no stacking trays, you will have to steam them in batches. Steam over high heat for 25 minutes, replenishing the water as necessary from a kettle of boiling water. Let them cool for a few minutes, then serve immediately.

They can be frozen or refrigerated for a few days. You can steam them (as above) for a few minutes just to reheat them.

Per ball: Calories 24, Protein 2 g, Fat 0 g, Carbohydrates 3 g

CRISPY GARLIC "CHICKEN" BALLS

Yield: about 25 balls

These make great cocktail snacks. Serve with Plum Sauce (p. 117) or commercial plum sauce or any other dipping sauce. They could also be used in a sweet-and-sour recipe or be added to noodle casseroles and soups.

1 recipe Vegetarian Ground "Chicken" (p. 53), steamed, cooled
4 teaspoons cornstarch dissolved in 4 teaspoons dry sherry
6 to 8 cloves garlic, crushed
1 tablespoon grated fresh ginger
1 tablespoon light soy sauce
¼ teaspoon white pepper
Cornstarch for coating balls
Oil for deep-frying

Mix the Ground "Chicken," dissolved cornstarch, garlic, ginger, soy sauce, and white pepper in a medium bowl, mixing well with your hands to make a cohesive mixture. Form the mixture into about 25 walnut-sized balls, squeezing and pressing the mixture together well and rolling between the palms of your hands. Roll the balls in cornstarch to coat.

Heat the oil in a wok or heavy pot over high heat to about 360°F. Fry in several batches until the balls are crispy and golden brown. Do not crowd the balls while frying. (See Chapter XIII about deep-frying.) Drain on paper towels and serve hot.

Per ball: Calories 27, Protein 4 g, Fat 0 g, Carbohydrates 2 g

SHANGHAI SPRING ROLLS

Yield: 24 to 25 rolls

Seasoning Mixture:

1 tablespoon light soy sauce
1 tablespoon dry sherry
Pinch of salt
½ teaspoon unbleached sugar
1 tablespoon roasted sesame oil
1 tablespoon cornstarch dissolved in 2 tablespoons cold water

Filling:

1½ cups textured soy protein reconstituted with 1⅓ cups boiling water
3 tablespoons light soy sauce

1 tablespoon oil
½ cup minced onions or green onions
6 large fresh mushrooms or dried Chinese black mushrooms, soaked in hot water for 20 to 30 minutes until soft, stems discarded

Shanghai Spring Rolls are deservedly popular delicious, crispy appetizers. However, they are often a greasy travesty of the delicacy they should be. They are often called "egg rolls," but egg rolls are made with a thicker, noodle dough wrapper which contains egg and are a specialty of the Canton region. Spring rolls are traditionally fried but not in a batter. They should not drip oil if they are properly cooked.

Authentic Chinese filling is mostly made of vegetables, with just a little meat or seafood added, so it's not difficult to make a vegetarian version. If you prefer an all-vegetable version, simply leave out the protein and the 3 tablespoons soy sauce in the filling recipe. Use twice as much mushrooms, carrots, and bean sprouts and/ or cabbage. You may need a little more salt in this simple filling, or you might like to add a tablespoon of brown or yellow bean sauce or vegetarian stir-fry "oyster" sauce (p. 116).

I am giving you the traditional frying method, plus an option for oven-frying them which is not traditional but still excellent. Spring roll skins or wrappers might also be called "Shanghai spring roll skins." They are often available in the produce section of supermarkets. "Egg roll" skins or wrappers are a bit thicker, usually contain egg, and don't make as delicate a product.

Shanghai spring roll wrappers are either round and resemble 7-inch doilies, or 8- x 8-inch squares. They dry out very easily, so they should be double bagged in plastic before placing them in the refrigerator or freezer. They freeze well.

If you are allergic to wheat, you can make spring rolls with Vietnamese dried rice paper wrappers (banh trang). Buy 8-inch round ones. Dip them in cold water and spread out on a clean, damp towel. Only work with two at a time. In seconds the wrappers will soften. Fill and wrap them as instructed in the recipe. They can be oven-fried or deep-fried. If oven-fried, bake them as directed, but for 10 minutes, then turn and cook for 10 to 15 minutes more, or until golden.

1 cup grated carrots
½ cup celery, thinly sliced
3 cloves garlic, minced
1 tablespoon grated fresh ginger

2 cups fresh bean sprouts

1 (10- to 12-ounce) package (Shanghai) spring roll wrappers or skins (flour and water only)
2 cups oil for frying
Sweet-and-Sour Dipping Sauce (p. 119) or Plum Sauce (p. 117)

Sealing Paste:
2 tablespoons flour
2 tablespoons water

Combine the seasoning mixture ingredients, and set aside.

Heat a heavy skillet or wok over high heat. When it's hot, add the 1 tablespoon oil. When the oil is hot, add the onions and stir-fry until they begin to soften. Add the mushrooms, carrots, celery, garlic, and ginger, and stir-fry for about 2 more minutes, just enough to wilt them. Add the bean sprouts.

Quickly pour in the seasoning mixture, and stir until it thickens. (You don't want this mixture to be runny or it will cause holes in the rolled spring rolls.) Remove from the heat and spread it on a platter to cool in the refrigerator. You can cool it in the freezer for about 15 minutes, if you're in a hurry. *Important*—Do not fill the rolls until the filling is thoroughly cooled.

Filling the rolls: Fill the rolls right before they are to be cooked. Mix the sealing paste ingredients until smooth. Place about 3 tablespoons of the filling on the end of a spring roll wrapper nearest you (see illustrations). Fold in the two ends, then roll it up away from you. Use the sealing paste to seal the edge.

Frying the rolls: Heat the oil in a wok or heavy skillet to about 360°F. The oil should be at least 1½ inches deep. (See Chapter XIII about deep-frying and shallow-frying.) Fry as many rolls at a time as can fit in the pan in one layer. Fry for 3 to 4 minutes, adjusting the heat as necessary if they brown too quickly or too slowly.

When they are golden brown, remove them with a slotted spoon to drain on paper towels.

Oven-frying the rolls: The rolls don't get quite as crispy this way, but they are delicious and light when served immediately. (They soften as they cool.) Preheat the oven to 400°F. Place the filled rolls on oiled dark cookie sheets. (Dark sheets brown foods better.) Brush the rolls lightly with oil, and bake until golden, about 7 minutes. Turn them over and bake for 7 to 8 minutes more, or until crispy and golden on the top and bottom.

Serve the rolls immediately, hot and crispy, with sweet and sour sauce or plum sauce. (You can also offer light soy sauce, hot mustard, and vinegar.) Or let them cool, then refrigerate or freeze in plastic bags. Refrigerated rolls can be reheated on cookie sheets in a 350°F oven for 15 minutes or until hot all the way through. Reheat frozen rolls for 25 minutes.

Steaming the rolls: For a delicate, low-fat snack, the filled spring rolls can be steamed for 8 minutes, using the same method as Beijing-Style Steamed Dumplings (p. 71). They can be served with Spicy Peanut Sauce (p. 120).

Per roll: Calories 51, Protein 3 g, Fat 1 g, Carbohydrates 5 g

Variations for Shanghai Spring Rolls

In place of the soy protein, you can use 2 cups frozen tofu, thawed, squeezed, and crumbled, or 2 cups crumbled extra-firm tofu.

In place of the soy protein or tofu with 3 tablespoons soy sauce, use any of the following:

* 2 cups ground seitan of any kind

* 2 cups crumbled commercial marinated tofu

* 2 cups any savory or baked tofu, or 1 recipe Vegetarian Ground "Pork" (p. 70), steamed

Instead of bean sprouts you can use a mixture of finely shredded greens, or napa or savoy cabbage added with the mushrooms.

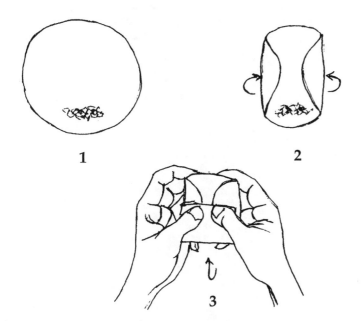

1

2

3

Spicy Braised Yuba

Yield: 6 servings as an appetizer

This is a vegetarian version of a well-loved Chinese dim sum dish made from—dare I say it?—tripe. My mother suggested that yuba sticks (bean curd skin), soaked and cut into pieces make a good substitute for tripe in the Mexican soup menudo and in some old-fashioned Italian dishes, so I tried it with this dish. It's delicious!

1 (6- to 8-ounce) package dried yuba sticks (bean curd skin)

Sauce:

1 tablespoon oil

2 green onions, chopped

3 large cloves garlic, chopped

1 tablespoon fermented black beans, chopped

1 to 3 teaspoons grated fresh ginger

2 tablespoons light soy sauce

2 tablespoons dry sherry

1 to 1½ teaspoons chili garlic paste

½ tablespoon roasted sesame oil

Soak the yuba in a large bowl or pot of warm water for about 1 hour. Drain it and cut into 1-inch pieces, discarding any parts that didn't soften.

Heat a large wok or heavy skillet over high heat. When it's hot, add the oil. When the oil is hot, add the green onions, garlic, black beans, and ginger. Stir-fry briefly, then add the yuba and all of the seasonings, except the sesame oil. Cook over high heat, stirring from time to time, until most of the liquid is absorbed. Drizzle in the sesame oil, and stir. Serve hot or at room temperature.

Per serving: Calories 203, Protein 14 g, Fat 12 g, Carbohydrates 6 g

The basic staple in the Chinese diet has always been grain—rice in the south and wheat in the north (although millet was frequently used in earlier times). Because of the lack of fuel, since about the fifth century B.C. wheat has been ground into flour and made into foods that require much less cooking time than whole wheat kernels do—such as dough stuffed with savory fillings, noodles, and steamed or pan-fried breads. During the Tang dynasty (618-906 A.D.), China's "Golden Age," wheat gradually surpassed millet as the desired taste for delicate wheat breads, cakes, and dumplings grew. There was an explosion of sophistication in cooking, agriculture, and general economic prosperity during the Sung dynasty (960-1279 A.D.). Restaurants became popular—from lavish multi-level establishments for the rich to humble noodle shops. Some shops specialized in steamed buns or deep-fried pastries. Marco Polo was amazed at the level of sophistication to be found in Chinese cities.

While foods made from wheat originated in the north, the more delicate ones, such as dumplings, made their way into the more highly spiced southern cuisine. Wheat delicacies were used as sacrificial offerings to the dead and to the gods, a practice codified during the Zhou dynasty (1100 B.C.), which ruled from the north.

During the Ming dynasty (starting 1370 B.C.), when the Chinese regained power from the nomadic Mongols, agriculture and cuisine regained their former importance. By the Ch'ing dynasty in the early 1700s, there was a tremendous population explosion, due partly to the introduction of new foods from the West (potatoes, sweet potatoes, carrots, peanuts, and corn) and partly to the intensified cultivation of rice in the south. Through the times of extreme poverty, war, and revolution, ninety percent of the food supply came from grains, the very poor existing primarily on millet, hand-milled wheat, and cornmeal, and eating rice and wheat noodles whenever they could.

Today, the average Chinese eats better than during those hard times, but grains remain a staple and fodder for the inventiveness and creativity of the Chinese cook.

Delicate dumplings are a favorite snack food in the south (dim sum, see Chapter VII), but sturdier versions are eaten as a main dish in the north. Dumplings are almost always eaten during holidays.

Chapter VIII

DUMPLINGS AND BREADS

"Although Buddhist monks are vegetarians, like all Chinese they see no virtue in insipid meals."

Emily Hahn, *The Cooking of China*, Time-Life Books, N.Y., 1968

The whole family may gather together to fill hundreds of dumplings at a time (much the way Ukrainian families make perogies or Mexican families make tamales by the dozen for Christmas and New Year).

It seems that each region has its own version of one dumpling or another—too many for me to even mention here. I had a hard time choosing which recipes to include because I love them all! But I decided to leave out the dumplings made with transparent wrappers of tapioca starch (they are very delicate to handle), and the tiny open steamed dumplings that are somewhat picky to make. Still, the recipes here will offer you many hours of cooking and eating pleasure, especially for a vegetarian who loves Chinese dumplings and does not live near a vegetarian Buddhist restaurant. (Most dumplings contain meat or seafood!)

The delicate steamed dumplings and "potstickers" can be used for dim sum (see Chapter VII), along with stuffed breads (bao). These little savory buns are a favorite in Chinese bakeries and dim sum parlors, but it is often hard to find vegetarian versions. Fortunately, they are easy to make at home. You have the option of making an easy homemade dough (it takes seconds to mix in a food processor) or using a commercial frozen bread dough.

Dumpling and spring roll wrappers may contain egg, so if you use the commercial variety, check the labels. The most common wrappers in supermarkets are the square egg-dough wonton skins and larger egg roll wrappers, however, you may be able to find the delicate flour-and-water Shanghai wonton wrappers. I use the more easily obtainable round gyoza wrappers (gyoza is Japanese for potsticker), which are made from flour and water, instead of square wonton skins. I also use them for steamed and boiled dumplings, or I make my own. This is somewhat time consuming, but very inexpensive and not difficult. You can make a flour and water dough or a vegan version of an egg dough which is made with soy flour (pp. 100-102).

Please read the section on steaming foods in Chapter XII.

POTSTICKERS OR SAVORY STEAM-FRIED DUMPLINGS

BEIJING-STYLE GUO TIE

Yield: 80 dumplings

Spicy Dipping Sauce (p. 116) or one of the following mixtures:

- 3 tablespoons light soy sauce with 1 tablespoon Chinese black vinegar or balsamic vinegar
- 3 tablespoons light soy sauce with 1 tablespoon chili oil
- 2 tablespoons light soy sauce with 1 tablespoon roasted sesame oil, 1 tablespoon Chinese black vinegar or balsamic vinegar, and 1 teaspoon crushed garlic
- 4 tablespoons roasted sesame oil with crushed garlic to taste

Filling:

2⅔ cups dry textured soy protein granules, reconstituted with 2 cups plus 2 tablespoons boiling water for 5 minutes

2 large carrots, grated, or 2 cups fresh bean sprouts, or 1 cup of each

1 cup minced green onions

4 large cloves garlic, minced or crushed

4 teaspoons grated fresh ginger

¼ cup light soy sauce

1 teaspoon salt

Homemade Dumpling Wrappers (or see sidebar on p. 70):

3½ cups unbleached white flour

1⅓ cups hot water

(*Note:* If you are steaming the dumplings instead of stem-frying them, add 2 tablespoons oil to the dough.)

For Steam-Frying:

3½ tablespoons oil mixed with 1 tablespoon roasted sesame oil

Make the various components of the recipes in the order given.

Make the dipping sauce and set aside.

To make the filling, mix all of the ingredients together well, preferably in a food processor.

Guo tie are called potstickers because of the unique cooking method used to make them. The juicy dumplings fry and steam at the same time, leaving them delicately soft on top and crispy on the bottom. They are so popular in Japan that they have been assimilated into Japanese cuisine, under the name "gyoza." I've seldom met anyone who could stop eating them unless the plate was taken away! For this reason, I'm giving you a large recipe. If you can't use it all at once, they freeze well. You might as well make a large batch while you are putting out the effort.

The dumplings can be made in the morning, covered with plastic wrap, and refrigerated until cooking time. Or they can be frozen. Then you can cook a few whenever you want.

This is my vegetarian version of the traditional pork-and-vegetable stuffed potstickers, using either textured soy protein, ground seitan, or frozen tofu. You can also use the steamed "Seafood"-Mushroom dumpling filling on p. 72.

Two time- and effort-savers

Use the commercial, round, egg-free dumpling wrappers (sometimes called "gyoza wrappers"). They are often available frozen or in the produce section of large super-markets where egg roll and wonton wrappers are found. A 1-pound package may contain from 50 to 75, depending on their thickness, so buy 2 packages for this recipe. Extras can be frozen. If frozen, thaw them out before filling.

You can also use a little gadget called a potsticker press for filling and sealing dumplings. It's a little hinged, white plastic gadget that's available in Asian and gourmet stores for under $10. It pleats and seals the dough with just a little pressure on the handles. With it, even a novice cook can make perfect potstickers and dumplings.

Variations

Instead of the textured soy protein, use about 3⅔ cups of one of the following:

- frozen tofu, thawed, crumbled, and squeezed
- ground unflavored seitan

Filling Variation

- Green Tofu Filling for steamed buns (pp. 82-83)

To make the wrapper dough, place the flour in a medium bowl or food processor. Add the hot water and knead by hand on a floured board for 5 minutes or in a food processor for 30 seconds until it forms a ball on the blade. Place the dough in a bowl covered with plastic or a wet tea towel.

To make the wrappers for steam-fried dumplings, roll the dough into a long "rope," and cut it into 80 equal-sized pieces. Keep them covered while you work. Flatten each piece into a thick round with your fingertips, then on a lightly floured board, roll each round out into a circle about 3½ inches in diameter. (The circles don't have to be exactly round.)

The best way to make a circle that is of equal thickness all around is to start rolling in the center of the round and roll straight away from you. Turn the round a quarter-turn, and roll like this again. Keep doing this until the wrapper is the size you want. You can place it over the open potsticker press to check the size, or cut out a paper circle the right size and use that for comparison. After a while, you'll get a fast rhythm going.

To fill the dumplings by hand, place a scant tablespoon of filling in the center of each circle. Fold one side of the wrapper over the filling, and press the edges together, making 5 tucks (see illustration).

To use a potsticker press, center a wrapper on the opened press, moisten the wrapper edge with water, and add a scant tablespoon of filling in the center. Close the press, using pressure to seal the wrapper. Pop the dumpling out and repeat.

Arrange the dumplings on floured cookie sheets, and cover with clean tea towels as you work.

To freeze the uncooked dumplings, place them on floured cookie sheets in the freezer until frozen solid. Loosen the frozen

dumplings by banging the pan on the table. Place them in plastic bags or rigid freezer containers, and fasten airtight before returning to the freezer. Freeze up to a month. Cook them about a minute longer than unfrozen ones.

To steam-fry the dumplings, you will need to decide how many skillets and what size to use. A 10-inch skillet will hold about 15 dumplings, a 12-inch skillet about 18, and a 14-inch skillet about 30 dumplings, but with a skillet this large you will probably have to move the outer ones to the middle and vice versa for even browning. If you are cooking all of the dumplings at once, you will need several skillets, or you'll have to cook them in batches. Use heavy skillets, such as cast-iron.

Heat the skillet(s) over high heat until very hot. Add 1 tablespoon of the mixed oil to a 10-inch skillet, 1½ tablespoons to a 12-inch skillet, or 2 tablespoons to a 14-inch skillet. Swirl the oil around and lower the heat to medium-high. Remove the pan(s) from the heat while you place the dumplings in the pan(s), not quite touching, pleated side up. Return the pan(s) to the heat. When the bottoms of the dumplings begin to brown, about 1 minute, add about ⅓ cup of hot water to a 10-inch skillet, about ½ cup to a 12-inch pan, or ⅔ cup to a 14-inch pan. Cover and cook until the water evaporates—about 5 minutes. Cook 2 to 3 minutes more until a dark-brown crust forms on the bottom, the dumpling dough is translucent on top, and they start to puff up. Remove from the pan and serve them brown-side-up with a little bowl of dipping sauce for each diner.

Clean each skillet out thoroughly before cooking another batch of dumplings in it.

Per 4 dumplings: Calories 140, Protein 8 g, Fat 3 g, Carbohydrates 20 g

Variation
Beijing-Style Steamed Dumplings (Cheng Jiao)

Add the optional oil to the wrapper dough, if making your own. Use the pot-sticker filling (p. 69), the boiled dumpling filling (pp. 73-74), or the "Seafood"-Mushroom Filling (p. 72).

If you use bamboo steamers, line them with a couple of layers of cheesecloth, or place a little square of foil under each dumpling and place them ½ inch apart. You can stack two steamers at a time. Steam over high heat for 8 minutes, and serve immediately. Or you can arrange the dumplings on an oiled plate, and steam in a wok or other pot over medium-high heat for 8 minutes.

Steamed dumplings are usually served with a simple dipping sauce of rice vinegar. Instead of rice vinegar you can use cider or white wine vinegar with shredded fresh ginger added.

pleated pinch

"Seafood"-Mushroom Filling

Yield: enough filling for 80 dumplings

This filling is delectable and so delicious that a dipping sauce is really unnecessary.

1 tablespoon roasted sesame oil
1 recipe Vegetarian Ground "Pork," steamed as directed (p. 70)
8 large dried Chinese black mushrooms, soaked in hot water for
   20 to 30 minutes until soft, stems discarded, and chopped
½ cup chopped white mushrooms oyster mushrooms
½ cup chopped green onions
2 tablespoons dulse flakes
2 tablespoons dry sherry
2 tablespoons grated fresh ginger
2 tablespoons light soy sauce
1 tablespoon vegetarian stir-fry "oyster" sauce (p. 116)
1 teaspoon unbleached sugar
Pinch of white pepper
Optional: ¼ cup minced water chestnuts (preferably fresh)
2 tablespoons cornstarch dissolved in ¼ cup cold water

Heat a large, heavy wok or skillet over high heat. When it's very hot, add the sesame oil. When the oil is hot, add the mushrooms and green onions. Stir-fry for about 2 minutes, then crumble in the Ground "Pork." Stir-fry briefly, then add all of the remaining ingredients, and stir just until the mixture is thickened. Cool thoroughly before filling the dumplings. Cooling can be speeded up by spreading it on a cookie sheet or plate and placing it in the freezer for about 15 minutes.

Per 4 dumplings: Calories 38, Protein 3 g, Fat 1 g, Carbohydrates 3 g

Northern-Style Boiled Dumplings

Jiao Zi

Yield: 80 dumplings

Soy-Vinegar Dipping Sauce (p. 120), or Black Bean Dipping Sauce (p. 118)

Filling:

3 tablespoons roasted sesame oil

1 medium onion, minced

3¼ cups finely chopped or processor-pulsed Chinese greens (pp. 18-19) and/or Savoy cabbage, Swiss chard, or kale

18 ounces firm or extra-firm tofu, crumbled, *or* 3 cups reconstituted textured soy protein granules, *or* 3 cups ground plain boiled unflavored seitan (p. 44)

9 medium dried Chinese black mushrooms, soaked in hot water for 20 to 30 minutes until soft, stems discarded

4½ tablespoons vegetarian stir-fry "oyster" sauce (p. 116)

3 tablespoons light soy sauce

1½ tablespoons dry sherry

1½ tablespoons grated fresh ginger

3 cloves garlic, crushed or minced

Dumpling Wrappers:

Use 80 round commercial egg-free "gyoza," or 1 recipe Steam-Fried Dumpling Wrappers (pp. 69-70)

Or to make your own wrappers:

4 cups unbleached flour

1½ cups cold water

Make the various components of the recipe in the order given.

Mix the dipping sauce in a bowl, and set aside.

Jiao zi are the "ravioli" or "perogie" of Northern China. They are almost always eaten on holidays and, unlike steamed dumplings which are usually eaten as a snack, they can be a whole meal in themselves. I'm giving a large recipe for dumplings because I guarantee that your guests will have to be told to stop eating them if any other dishes are to follow! If by some chance you don't want to cook them all, they freeze well, so you might as well make a big batch while you are going to the effort.

The dumplings can be made in the morning, covered with plastic wrap, and refrigerated until time to cook them. Or they can be frozen and a few cooked whenever you want them.

The wrapper dough is a very simple one, using cold water instead of hot. The wrappers are slightly thicker than potsticker wrappers, since they must withstand the rigors of boiling water.

Variation fillings

- Filling for potstickers (p. 69)
- "Seafood"-Mushroom Filling (p. 69)
- Green Tofu Filling for steamed buns, (p.)

To make the Filling heat a large wok or heavy skillet over high heat. When hot, add the sesame oil. When the oil is hot, add the onion and chopped greens. Stir-fry until the greens are wilted and all the liquid is absorbed. *Do not scorch*. Mix all of the filling ingredients together well, preferably in a food processor. (If you don't have a processor, make sure that the tofu is well-mashed.) Spread the filling on a platter or cookie sheet and let it cool thoroughly in the refrigerator before filling the wrappers (or speed it up by cooling it in the freezer for 15 minutes).

For instructions on how to make the wrapper dough, fill the dumplings by hand, or to use a potsticker press, and to freeze the uncooked dumplings, see the Potsticker recipe on pp. 69-71.

To boil the dumplings, bring 3 quarts. of water to a boil in a large pot. Add 2 teaspoons of salt. Cook the dumplings in three batches of 27, 27, and 26. Add the first batch of dumplings. Bring it back to a boil.

Add 1 cup cold water. Bring it back to a boil again. Add 1 more cup cold water. When it comes back to a boil again, the dumplings should be done. Take one out and test it. Frozen dumplings take about a minute more to cook than fresh ones. Dumplings made with store bought wrappers, which are thinner than homemade, take slightly less time. Remove them with a slotted spoon to a colander. Drain briefly and place on a plate immediately. Repeat with the remaining dumplings. Serve hot with the dipping sauce, or serve in a soup (see p. 109).

Per 4 dumplings: Calories 137, Protein 5 g, Fat 3 g, Carbohydrates 20 g

Wontons

Yield: about 75 wontons

Filling:

½ cup textured soy protein granules

⅓ cup boiling water

½ cup medium-firm tofu, mashed

4 dried Chinese black mushrooms, soaked in hot water for 20 to 30 minutes until soft, stems discarded

2 tablespoons finely minced green onion

2 tablespoons finely minced water chestnut (preferably fresh)

1 tablespoon light soy sauce

1 tablespoon dry sherry

½ tablespoon roasted sesame oil

1 to 3 teaspoons finely grated fresh ginger

¼ teaspoon salt

Optional: ½ tablespoon vegetarian stir-fry "oyster" sauce (p. 116)

*Optional:*1 tablespoon dulse or nori flakes (for a "seafood" flavor)

Wrappers:

Use 75 round commercial egg-free "gyoza" (1 to 1½ packages, depending on thickness)

Sealing Paste:

2 tablespoons water

2 tablespoons flour

To make the filling, pour the boiling water over the textured soy protein granules in a medium bowl. Stir and let them soak for 5 minutes, mash in the tofu, and then the other filling ingredients. Make sure that the vegetables are very finely chopped so that they don't cause holes in the dough. Mix very well.

Have a little dish with the sealing paste handy to dip your finger into for sealing the dumplings.

Wontons are tiny, delicate filled dumplings from the south of China. They are extremely popular in North American Chinese restaurants—for a good reason! They are usually served boiled in soup, but the boiled dumplings can also be served as a dim sum with a dipping sauce of light soy sauce with a little roasted sesame oil. They are also served fried for a crispy snack.

Variation

Although most wonton wrappers are made with an egg dough, Shanghai wonton wrappers are made with only flour and water.

You can also use round, commercial potsticker flour and water wrappers, instead of the usually square wonton wrapper.

Homemade Wrappers

Use the Wonton Wrapper Dough (pp. 100-102).

If you make your own Wonton Wrapper Dough, read the special notes in the noodle recipe which refer specifically to rolling and handling dough for wontons.

Note: You can make the filling several hours or days ahead of time and keep refrigerated.

Freezing Filled Wontons

Freeze the uncooked wontons on sheets of waxed paper sprinkled with cornstarch between the layers in rigid plastic containers.

Keep the wrappers covered while you work. Place ½ teaspoon (no more!) of the filling on the bottom middle edge or corner of the wrapper. Fold the wrapper away from you toward the middle until it is almost rolled in half. Place a dab of sealing paste on each end of the rolled-up section. Fold the ends of the rolled-up section toward each other. Press firmly to seal. (See illustrations below.)

Do not over-fill the dough, and make sure that no filling gets into the seal on the edges, or it may break open when cooking.

Place the filled wontons aside (not touching) on cookie sheets covered with waxed paper that has been sprinkled with cornstarch. Set the filled wontons with the "pouch" (filled side) up—this keeps them from getting soggy on the bottom and tearing. Cover them with dry, clean tea towels while you work. You can refrigerate the wontons for up to 3 hours before you cook them. Place the cookie sheets inside large plastic bags and close with twist-ties. Or freeze them (see sidebar).

Cook the wontons in a large pot of boiling water in 2 or 3 batches, dropping them one at a time into the rapidly boiling water. Cook them for 1 minute once the water has come back to a gentle boil. Don't let the water boil so hard that the dumplings come apart. Watch over them and stir gently with a slotted spoon to make sure none have stuck to the bottom. When cooked, quickly lift them out with a slotted spoon. Serve immediately.

Per each: Calories 24, Protein 1 g, Fat 0 g, Carbohydrates 5 g

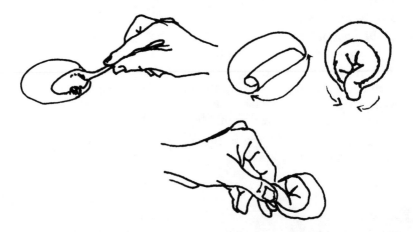

WONTONS IN SOUP

Yield: 8 servings

12 cups water with 10 vegetarian bouillon cubes, or 12 cups Homemade Vegetarian Broth (p. 108)
About 4 cups chopped or sliced Chinese greens (see pp. 18-19) or Swiss chard, kale, and/or collard greens
2 tablespoons light soy sauce
2 large green onions, chopped
Roasted sesame oil

1 recipe wontons

Have the broth ready before you put the wontons on to boil. Also have a large pot of boiling water ready.

Bring the broth to a boil with all the other ingredients, except the green onions and sesame oil, and then remove from the heat. Boil the wontons in the water for 1 minute, then scoop them out with a slotted spoon and place in the soup. Serve as soon as they are all cooked. Sprinkle each bowl with the green onions. Pass roasted sesame oil for each diner to sprinkle on as desired.

Per serving: Calories 305, Protein 21 g, Fat 0 g, Carbohydrates 52 g

Storing Wrapper Dough

To store the steamed dumpling dough wrappers, dust them with cornstarch and stack them between 3-inch squares of waxed paper. Wrap the stack in foil, then place it in a plastic bag or rigid container. They will keep in the refrigerator for up to 3 days, or in the freezer for up to 2 months.

Note: Uncooked refrigerated wontons need 1½ minutes to cook; raw frozen wontons need 2 to 2½ minutes.

Crispy fried wontons are a favorite in Chinese restaurants. You can fry them in two ways—pan-frying with oil and water like potstickers (p. 69) or deep-frying (Chapter 167-173). Serve them with Sweet-and-Sour Dipping Sauce (p. 119) or vinegar with chili paste added to taste.

The Chinese like fried wontons with a strongly-flavored filling and no dipping sauce. You can use the Curried "Chicken" steamed bun filling (p. 81) in the wontons.

Make sure all of the filling ingredients are very finely minced or mashed, and thoroughly cooled before filling the wontons.

The Chinese also make sweet versions of deep-fried wontons, often in a long, rolled "firecracker" shape, with sweet red bean, nut, or date fillings. I have not included any sweet fillings, but you can easily devise one from pitted dates cooked to a paste with orange juice, flavored with a little orange rind, peanut butter (or other nut butter), and flaked coconut.

Fried Wontons

Follow the directions for making Wontons on pp. 75-76.

For potsticker-type fried wontons, heat a large cast-iron or other heavy frying pan over medium heat. Add 2 to 3 tablespoons oil. When the oil is hot, add as many fresh or frozen wontons as you can without crowding too closely. Cook the wontons until they become golden on the bottom, then add ⅓ to ½ cup water. Cover the pan and cook until the water evaporates. Take the cover off and continue cooking until the wontons become puffy and are crusty-brown on the bottom. Turn them over on a plate to serve.

To deep-fry wontons, heat 2 or more inches of oil in a large wok or a heavy frying pan to 350°F. Fry a few wontons at a time in the hot oil until they are crispy, golden, and light, about 2 minutes. Don't crowd them. (See Chapter XIII about deep-frying.) Drain them on paper towels, and keep them hot in a 200°F oven with the door open a bit. If you need to cook them ahead of time and reheat them, place them in a 450°F oven for about 3 minutes, or read about twice-frying on p. 170.

Steamed Savory Filled Buns

Bao Xian

Yield: 16 buns

1 pound loaf of dairy-free, commercial, frozen white bread dough

Or homemade dough:

1 teaspoon unbleached sugar

2 teaspoons regular dry active yeast

1 cup plus 2 tablespoons warm water (use 1 cup warm soymilk and 2 tablespoons warm water if the buns are to be baked)

2½ cups unbleached flour

1 tablespoon oil

1 teaspoon salt

To make the homemade dough, mix the sugar and yeast with the water (or soymilk and water, if the buns are to be baked) in a 2-cup bowl or measuring cup. Let it stand for about 5 minutes, or until it becomes frothy.

To make the dough without a food processor, combine the flour, oil, and salt together with your fingers or a fork to mix it well. Stir in the dissolved yeast, and knead the dough on a lightly floured or oiled surface for about 10 minutes.

To make the dough in a food processor, mix the flour, oil, and salt by pulsing it in the processor bowl with the metal blade until mixed. With the motor running, pour in the dissolved yeast through the top. When the dough has formed a ball on the blade, process for 30 seconds more, and turn off the machine.

Place the dough in an oiled bowl with room to expand. Turn it over so the top is oiled, cover the bowl with a plastic bag, and let the dough rise in a warm place until doubled in size, about 1 hour.

If you are using frozen bread dough, take it out of the package, brush it with oil, and cover it with plastic wrap. Let it stand at room temperature for about 2 hours, or thaw it in the microwave, according to package directions.

Punch the dough down and divide it into 16 equal pieces. Roll each piece into a ball, and keep the balls covered with a damp towel or a plastic bag as you work. Roll each ball out on a lightly floured surface with a rolling pin to make a circle about 4½ inches across. (It doesn't have to be perfectly round.) Make sure there are no thin spots or holes in the dough.

To fill the buns, use one of the fillings following this recipe. Make sure that the filling has cooled. Divide it into 16 equal portions of about 2 tablespoons each. Place one portion of the filling in the center of each circle of dough. Pull the edges of the dough over the filling into the center, pleating the edges in and pinching them together tightly in the middle to seal in the filling. Give the pinched dough a little twist.

Note: If you are making buns with more than one filling, you can identify them by placing one type with the pinched side up instead of down and/or making a mark on the top of one type with the wide end of a chopstick dipped in food coloring. (Red is traditional for sweet fillings.)

Serve these soft buns with a delicious savory filling to accompany a simple soup for a company lunch—your guests will be impressed, but you won't be too tired to enjoy their company. They also make great picnic or travel food. The Chinese also make sweet versions of these with sweet red bean, nut, or date fillings. I have not included any sweet fillings, but you can easily devise one from pitted dates cooked to a paste with orange juice, flavored with a little orange rind, peanut butter (or other nut butter), and flaked coconut, or buy Chinese sweet red bean paste.

Sometimes these buns are made with a very puffy baking powder dough, but I prefer a yeast dough—it's not as sweet. This dough can be quickly made in a food processor. It's pliable and easy to work with, and makes a fluffy, soft bread.

If you don't like making yeast dough, or don't have the time to make it, you can use one loaf of commercial, dairy-free frozen white bread dough.

If you prefer to bake the buns rather than steam them, you can use either the homemade or frozen commercial bread dough. If you make the dough yourself, using soymilk instead of most of the water makes a softer dough. (Baking tends to dry the dough out.) The recipe includes directions for this option.

Note: I don't recommend using a whole wheat dough for these buns, as it lacks the delicacy needed and steaming makes the dough taste rather pasty. Do not use whole wheat pastry flour instead of unbleached flour—pastry flour doesn't contain enough gluten for a good yeast dough. You could try a half whole wheat dough and bake rather than steam the buns.

If the buns are to be steamed, either line the steam baskets with a couple of layers of cheesecloth or cut a 3-inch square piece of waxed paper, parchment paper, or oiled brown paper for each bun. Oil one side of the pieces. Place each bun, pinched-side-down, on the cheesecloth or the oiled side of the paper, and place them on the basket with at least an inch between them. Cover with a damp towel, and let them rise for 20 minutes in a warm spot.

If the buns are to be baked, don't use the paper. Preheat the oven to 350°F. Place the buns 2 inches apart on 2 greased and floured cookie sheets. Cover with damp towels and let rise 30 minutes in a warm spot.

Steaming the buns: If your steam baskets stack, you can cook them all at the same time; otherwise you'll have to steam them in 2 batches, or use 2 woks or pots. Place the steamers over boiling water in a large wok or pot. Don't let the water touch them. Cover the wok or pot and steam the buns over high heat for 15 minutes. Make sure the water doesn't boil away during cooking. Serve them hot.

If you make the buns ahead of time, let them cool, then place them in plastic bags. They'll keep 2 or 3 days in the refrigerator or up to 2 months in the freezer. To reheat them, steam frozen buns for 7 minutes or refrigerated buns for 5 minutes.

To bake the buns, brush the tops with plain soymilk, and bake for 20 minutes, or until golden and puffy. Serve hot, or cool and refrigerate or freeze them as for steamed buns. Reheat baked buns in a 350°F oven, 12 minutes if frozen or 10 minutes if refrigerated.

Per bun: Calories 73, Protein 2 g, Fat 1 g, Carbohydrates 14 g

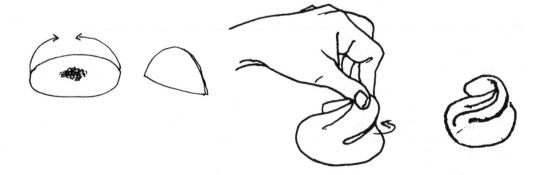

Fillings for Savory Filled Buns (Bao Xian)

VEGETARIAN "BARBECUED PORK" FILLING

Yield: 8 servings

1 tablespoon roasted sesame oil or other oil
1 cup chopped onions
2 cups coarsely chopped Vegetarian "Barbecued Pork"
  (pp. 58-59)
2 tablespoons water
2 tablespoons light soy sauce
1 tablespoon light unbleached sugar
Pinch of white pepper
2 tablespoons cornstarch mixed with 6 tablespoons water
¼ cup chopped green onions

Heat a large heavy wok or skillet over high heat. When it is very hot, add the oil. When the oil is hot, add the onions. Stir-fry the onions for 2 minutes, adding a few drops of water if necessary to keep them from sticking. Add the "Barbecued Pork," water, soy sauce, sugar, and white pepper, and stir well. Add the dissolved cornstarch and stir until it has thickened. Remove from the heat and stir in the green onions. Cool thoroughly before filling the dough.

Per serving: Calories 190, Protein 20 g, Fat 3 g, Carbohydrates 17 g

CURRIED "CHICKEN" FILLING

Yield: 8 servings

2 tablespoons oil
1 cup chopped onions
1 tablespoon curry paste or powder
2 cups Vegetarian Ground "Chicken" (p. 53), steamed and
  crumbled
2 tablespoons dry sherry

If you are in a hurry to cool the fillings, spread them out on a large plate and place the plate in the freezer until the mixture is cool enough to use.

Fillings can be made up to two or three days ahead of time and then refrigerated. Leftover fillings can be spread on Mandarin Pancakes (pp. 87-88), Cornmeal Crepes (p. 90), or flour tortillas for a delicious wrap.

This is probably the most popular filling of all—a guaranteed hit with omnivores and vegetarians alike!

Variation

If you have no Vegetarian "Barbecued Pork" on hand, use 2 cups frozen firm or extra-firm tofu, thawed, squeezed, and crumbled, cooked with 1 recipe of the "Barbecued Pork" sauce (pp. 58-59).

Variations

If you have no vegetarian "chicken" product on hand you can make a good filling with plain textured soy protein granules or crumbled frozen tofu. It will not be quite as good in texture and flavor as the original.

To use the soy protein granules, reconstitute 1½ cups in 1¼ cups boiling water.

Or use 2 cups firm or extra-firm tofu that has been frozen, thawed, squeezed dry, and crumbled.

Mix the reconstituted soy protein or tofu with 2 tablespoons of light soy sauce, 1 tablespoon nutritional yeast, ½ teaspoon onion powder, and ½ teaspoon salt. Make the filling using this mixture instead of the Vegetarian Ground "Chicken."

Use 4 teaspoons of cornstarch instead of 2 tablespoons.

2 teaspoons unbleached sugar
1 cup cold vegetarian broth mixed with 2 tablespoons cornstarch
½ cup chopped green onions

Heat a heavy wok or skillet over high heat. When very hot, add the oil. When the oil is hot, add the onions. Stir-fry the onions, adding a little water as necessary to keep them from sticking, until they are translucent and starting to brown. Add the curry and stir-fry briefly, then stir in the crumbled "ground chicken," sherry, sugar, and broth-cornstarch mix. Stir just until the mixture thickens. Remove from the heat and add the green onions. Cool thoroughly before filling the buns.

Per serving: Calories 130, Protein 13 g, Fat 4 g, Carbohydrates 9 g

GREEN TOFU FILLING

Yield: 8 servings

1 pound dark Chinese greens (see pp. 18-19), or Swiss chard, kale, and/or collard greens, washed, trimmed, and chopped
1 tablespoon oil
1½ cups chopped fresh mushrooms
2 to 4 cloves garlic, crushed
1 tablespoon grated fresh ginger
1 cup mashed medium-firm tofu
1½ tablespoons light soy sauce
1 tablespoon dry sherry
½ teaspoon salt
½ teaspoon unbleached sugar
Pinch of white pepper
1 tablespoon cold water mixed with 1 teaspoon cornstarch
2 tablespoons roasted sesame oil

Steam or microwave the greens until they are tender but still bright green. Cool under cold running water, and squeeze them as dry as you can. Set aside.

Heat a large, heavy wok or skillet over high heat. When it's very hot, add the 1 tablespoon oil. When the oil is hot, add the mushrooms. Stir-fry the mushrooms until they change color and soften. Add the garlic, ginger, and greens, and stir-fry briefly. Add the tofu, soy sauce, sherry, salt, sugar, and white pepper. Stir in the cornstarch mixture and sesame oil; stir for 30 seconds and remove from the heat. Cool thoroughly before filling the buns.

Per serving: Calories 77, Protein 4 g, Fat 2 g, Carbohydrates 7 g

Variations for Green Tofu Filling

For a "meatier" filling, instead of the tofu you can use crumbled leftover "Pork" Balls (pp. 60-61), crumbled, steamed Vegetarian "Ground Pork" (p. 60), or ground flavored seitan of any kind.

FLOWER ROLLS
STEAMED BREAD ROLLS

Yield: 10 rolls

1 recipe dough for Steamed Savory Filled Buns (p. 78) or
  1 pound loaf of commercial, dairy-free, frozen white bread
  dough
Oil for brushing
Optional: **soymilk for brushing rolls if they are baked**

If you are using frozen bread dough, take it out of the package, brush it with oil, cover it with plastic wrap and let it sit at room temperature for about 2 hours, Or thaw it in the microwave according to package directions.

If you are using the homemade dough, let it rise once.

To shape the rolls, roll the dough into an 11 x 15-inch rectangle on a well-floured surface. Brush the dough well with oil. Starting with the long side nearest you, roll the dough up like a jelly roll. Seal the dough and cut it into 10 equal-sized rolls with a sharp knife. With a chopstick, press firmly down in the center of each roll, so that the

These are the Chinese equivalent of dinner rolls, but they are formed into flower shapes and steamed. They are usually served with roast meat and duck in China, but they would be delightful with a savory stew or braised dish.

rolled-up dough inside sort of pops out of either side a little, or "flowers."

Place the rolls in two steam baskets lined with a couple of layers of cheesecloth or cut a 3-inch-square piece of waxed paper, parchment paper, or oiled brown paper for each bun. Oil one side of the pieces. Place each bun, pinched-side-down, on the cheesecloth or the oiled side of the paper and place them in the steam baskets with at least 1½ inches between them. Cover with a damp towel and let them rise for 20 minutes in a warm spot.

If you have to cook one batch of rolls at a time, rather than cooking them all at once in two steamers, or on stackable steamers, cover one batch and let it rise at room temperature; cover the remaining batch with plastic wrap and refrigerate them. When the first batch is half-risen, take the refrigerated batch out. When the first batch of rolls is doubled, place them over boiling water and steam them as directed below. Repeat with the next batch.

To steam the buns, if your steam baskets stack, you can cook them all at the same time; otherwise you'll have to steam them in two batches (as directed above), or use two woks or pots. Place the steamers over boiling water (don't let the water touch) in a large wok or pot, cover the wok or pot and steam them over high heat for 15 minutes. (See pp. about steaming.) Make sure that the water doesn't boil away. Serve them hot.

If the buns are to be baked, don't use the paper. Preheat the oven to 350°F. Place the buns 2 inches apart on 2 greased and floured cookie sheets. Cover with damp towels and let rise 30 minutes in a warm spot.

To bake the buns, brush the tops with plain soymilk and bake for 20 minutes, or until golden and puffy. Serve hot, or cool and refrigerate or freeze them as for steamed buns.

Reheat frozen buns in a 350°F oven for 12 minutes, cold buns for 10 minutes.

Per roll: Calories 116, Protein 3 g, Fat 1 g, Carbohydrates 32 g

DEEP-FRIED DEVILS

Yield: about 30

1 pound commercial dairy-free frozen white or whole wheat bread dough, or 1 recipe dough for Steamed Savory Filled Buns (p. 78)
Oil for deep-frying

If you are using frozen bread dough, take it out of the package, brush it with oil, cover it with plastic wrap, and let it rest at room temperature for about 2 hours. You can also thaw it in the microwave according to package directions.

If you are using the homemade dough, let it rise once.

Roll out the dough to ½ inch in diameter, and cut into sections 5 inches long. Stretch the dough strips out, and place one on top of another, to make pairs of dough strips. Longways, press a chopstick down on each pair, and pull them a bit to elongate them a little more.

Deep-fry in hot oil at 375°F until golden and crispy. (See Chapter XIII about deep-frying.) Don't fry too many at once. They puff up and take very little time to cook. Drain them on paper towels, and serve hot.

Per each: Calories 39, Protein 1 g, Fat 0 g, Carbohydrates 7 g

These crispy fried bread treats are often served at breakfast with Savory Rice Porridge (Congee or Jook, p. 98), but they could also be served with any soup. Because these are fried rather than steamed, a light whole wheat dough will work nicely, if you prefer it.

These scrumptious buns are traditional breakfast or snack breads, eaten with hot soup, hot soymilk (sweet or savory), and pickled vegetables. They also make wonderful receptacles for any sort of stir-fry (especially spicy ones) or vegetarian barbecued "meats" and grilled vegetables.

The dough is unleavened, but the way the dough is folded and layered with a simple roux of oil and flour makes the layers separate and puff up as they bake.

In Northern China, these buns are baked in large, barrel-shaped ovens with a charcoal fire at the bottom. The buns are slapped against the sides of the oven. But an ordinary oven works just fine.

Northern Chinese Sesame Buns

Shao Bing

Yield: 8 buns

2 cups unbleached flour
¼ teaspoon salt
¾ cup boiling water
3 tablespoons raw, hulled sesame seeds

Roux:

1½ tablespoons oil
½ tablespoon roasted sesame oil
¼ teaspoon salt
3 tablespoons unbleached flour

To make the dough, mix the flour and salt in a medium bowl or the bowl of your food processor. If you are making this by hand, stir in the boiling water and then knead on a lightly floured board for 10 minutes. If you are using a food processor, keep the motor running and add the boiling water through the top. When it gathers together in a ball on top of the blade, let it run for 30 more seconds.

Place the dough in an oiled bowl, cover, and let rest for 30 minutes.

To make the roux, heat the oils in a small saucepan or skillet over medium heat. When the oil is hot, stir in the salt and flour with a wooden spoon. Keep stirring constantly until the mixture is caramel colored. Pour onto a dish and refrigerate until it's time to roll out the dough.

1

2

3

Roll out the dough on a floured board into an 8- x 15-inch rectangle. (It's okay if the corners are a bit rounded.) Evenly spread the roux over the dough almost to the edges. Cut the dough into thirds. Stack the pieces, with the roux-coated sides to the inside. Cut the stack into 8 equal pieces. They should be about 2 inches square.

Roll each square into a rectangle about ⅛-inch thick. Fold the long sides of each square into the center, overlapping. Seam-side-up, roll half of the piece of dough ⅛-inch thick. Starting at the thicker (unflattened) end, fold the dough toward the flattened side twice to make a little bun with the flattened part on the bottom.

Note: As you cut, stack, and roll the dough, some of the roux will ooze out the sides. Just pull up the dough and spread the roux toward the inside of the dough.

Sprinkle some sesame seeds on the work surface, and roll each little bun into a 3- x 5-inch rectangle about ¼-inch thick. Place the rectangles, not touching, on ungreased cookie sheets.

Cover the buns and let them rest from 5 to 60 minutes. You can also refrigerate them for up to 24 hours, or freeze them.

Bake at 400°F for 15 minutes, or until golden and puffy. You may need to bake them longer if the dough is cold. To serve, slit 3 sides open and serve hot.

Per bun: Calories 160, Protein 4 g, Fat 5 g, Carbohydrates 24 g

Do give these a try—there's no rising involved, they seem rich but are actually quite low-fat, and they are very impressive to guests.

The buns are best served freshly baked, but they can be covered and reheated later in the day (5 minutes in a 400°F oven). The baked buns can also be frozen for a month.

7

4

5

6

Mandarin Pancakes are also called **Beijing Pancakes, La Ta, or Chinese Tortillas.**

These are very thin, tortilla-like flatbreads. They are cooked in a double layer and then separated before using as a wrapper for grills and stir-fries—a Chinese wrap! Spicy mixtures are particularly good, but you can use these flatbreads instead of rice with almost any Chinese dish. You can substitute very thin, small white flour tortillas, but the Chinese flatbreads are more delicate, and they are very easy to make.

These breads are traditionally served with Peking Duck (see a vegetarian variation, p. 56) and Mu Shu Pork (see Mu Shu Tofu, p. 126).

To reheat, thaw if frozen. Place the pancakes inside a wet, clean tea towel, and steam over simmering water for 5 minutes, or until heated through. They can be kept over steam over low heat for up to an hour. When serving, keep them covered, as they dry out quickly.

Mandarin Pancakes

Yield: 24 pancakes

2 cups unbleached flour
2 tablespoons oil or roasted sesame oil
¾ cup boiling water

Place the flour in a medium bowl, and work in 2 teaspoons of the oil with your fingers. Add the boiling water all at once, and mix with a fork until a ball forms. If some flour remains, add more hot water 1 teaspoon at a time. Knead briefly.

To make in a food processor, mix the flour and 2 teaspoons of the oil in the processor, then add the boiling water through the top while the machine is running. Run until the dough forms a ball, and turn off immediately.

Place the dough in a plastic bag, close it tightly, and let the dough rest for 15 to 30 minutes.

Roll the dough into a 12-inch long log. Cut the log into 12 equal pieces. Keep them covered while you work. For each double pancake, cut one of the pieces exactly in half. Roll each half into a ball, and flatten slightly. With a rolling pin, roll each ball on a very lightly floured surface into a 3-inch circle. Brush a bit of the remaining oil on top of one circle. Place the other circle on top. Roll out the stacked circles from the center to the top edge, rotate a quarter-turn, and roll out the same way again; repeat until you have a 7- to 8-inch round. (It doesn't have to be a perfect circle.) Keep the stacked circles on a lightly floured board or cookie sheet in a single layer, and cover.

To cook the pancakes, heat a large, heavy skillet over medium-high heat. Fry each set of stacked pancakes on the ungreased surface, turning every 15 seconds or so until blistered, parchment-colored, and dry on both sides. Remove from the pan and carefully pull the two halves apart. Stack them fried-side-down on a plate, and keep covered as you cook the rest. Either serve warm, or cool them, wrap airtight, and refrigerate or freeze.

Per pancake: Calories 43, Protein 1 g, Fat 1 g, Carbohydrates 7 g

GREEN ONION PANCAKES

Yield: 8 pancakes

2 cups unbleached flour
1 teaspoon salt
1 cup boiling water
2 tablespoons plus 2 teaspoons roasted sesame oil
1 teaspoon salt
½ cup minced green onions
About 8 teaspoons oil

Place the flour and 1 teaspoon of salt in a medium bowl. Add the boiling water all at once, and mix with a fork until a ball forms. Knead briefly.

To make in a food processor, place the flour and 1 teaspoon salt in the processor bowl, then add the boiling water through the top while the machine is running. Run until the dough forms a ball, and turn off immediately.

Place the dough in a plastic bag and close tightly, or cover the bowl with a wet towel, and let the dough rest for 30 minutes.

Divide the dough into 8 equal pieces, and roll into balls. On a lightly floured surface, roll each ball out into a thin circle. Drizzle each circle with 1 teaspoon of sesame oil, and spread it around the circle with your fingertips to coat the surface. Sprinkle the oiled surface with about ⅛ teaspoon of salt and 1 tablespoon of minced green onions, distributing them evenly over the circle. Roll up each coated circle into a tight "jelly-roll." Flatten this roll slightly with a rolling pin. Roll up each flattened roll into a coil. (They will look sort of like cinnamon buns.) Pinch the edge to seal it. Cover these coils with plastic, and let rest another 30 minutes to relax the dough again.

Place each coil on end and flatten it into a patty, then roll the patty out into a thin pancake again, about 6 inches across.

You can stack the pancakes with a piece of waxed paper between each one.

To cook, heat a heavy 8 or 9-inch skillet, such as cast-iron, over medium-high heat. Drizzle 1 teaspoon of oil into the pan for each pancake, swirling it around the pan. Add 1 pancake to the pan at a

This is a very popular northern Chinese bread, eaten often for breakfast with Savory Rice Porridge (p. 98) or soup. They are usually made very large and cut into wedges, but I prefer to make smaller ones like tortillas—they are easier to handle.

They take a little time to make, but it's mostly resting time to let the dough relax before you roll it out. The dough can be made in a food processor in seconds, and the pancakes cook very quickly. Plan on two 30-minute rest periods, plus another 30 to 45 minutes for the rest of the procedure.

time. Loosen the edges with a spatula. Cover the pan with a lid for 2 minutes. The pancake should puff up a little bit and be golden-brown and crispy on the bottom. Flip it over and cook uncovered for about 2 minutes more. Repeat until all the pancakes are done.

To keep the pancakes warm while you cook, place them on a platter in a 200°F oven with the door slightly open. Try to serve them freshly made, but if you have to make them ahead, store them at room temperature, cooled first, and then placed in a plastic bag. Reheat covered with a lid, on a dry, medium-hot skillet, watching carefully. You just want to heat them, not burn them!

Per pancake: Calories 181, Protein 3 g, Fat 8 g, Carbohydrates 22 g

NORTHERN CHINESE THIN CORNMEAL CREPES

JIAN BIN

Yield: 10 crepes

These unusual pancakes are often carried to the fields spread with bean paste and rolled around green onions for a snack, but they are delicious rolled around any savory stir-fry. These are smaller than they would be made in China, but the delicate cakes are easier to handle when made this size.

1⅞ cups water
1 cup yellow cornmeal
½ cup unbleached flour
½ teaspoon salt

Place all the ingredients in a blender, and blend well to make a batter. Heat a large nonstick electric frying pan or griddle to 400°F. Blend the batter each time before you pour it out, because the cornmeal tends to sink to the bottom.

Pour ¼ cup batter onto the griddle for each cake and let it spread by itself, guiding the batter into a circle shape, if necessary. Cook until the pancakes are dry on the top, then carefully flip the pancakes over with a wide, thin spatula. Cook until crisp on the sides, about 4 minutes total. Remove carefully from the pan. Stack the pancakes on a plate, and cover with a clean tea towel. Serve warm, or wrap in foil and refrigerate until serving time.

If you make these ahead, reheat them by wrapping the stack of crepes in foil and baking in a 350°F oven for 15 minutes.

Per crepe: Calories 70, Protein 2 g, Fat 0 g, Carbohydrates 15 g

The Chinese have cultivated rice for over 5,000 years, from the time when the father of Chinese agriculture, Emperor Shen Nung, held yearly planting ceremonies. Princes and other lower-ranking officials ceremoniously planted the first soy beans, millet, barley, and wheat, but only the emperor sowed the first seeds of sacred rice. Historians believe rice came to China via Java from the swamps of Bengal where it originated. It is believed that the Bengalese learned to cultivate this native plant around 3,000 B.C.

The cultivation of rice made its way throughout Asia, the Middle East, and southern Europe to the Americas. There are now some 7,000 varieties of *Oryza sativa* (common rice) feeding approximately as many of the world's people as does wheat. Rice growing is more labor intensive than growing other grains. However, it requires less processing after harvest, and the total plant is used in making many products. Rice straw is used for rope, baskets, hats, snowshoes, mats, fuel, and papermaking. Rice hulls are used for packing and insulating. Broken rice is used for flour, glue, and paste and to make rice wines and vinegars.

Chapter IX

RICE

"It is in the hand of the farmer that the rice plant grows."

Old Chinese Saying

THE PLACE OF RICE IN CHINESE COOKING

The average Asian eats about 400 pounds of rice a year, which gives you some idea of the importance of rice to the Chinese. "Come eat rice with me" is the most gracious greeting in Chinese hospitality. Instead of asking, "How are you?" as a greeting the Chinese ask, "Have you had your rice today?" Upsetting the rice bowl is believed by some to be an omen of misfortune. To empty a rice bowl deliberately on the ground is a grave insult. An old Chinese proverb claims that a meal without rice is like a pretty girl with only one eye! If you say that you feel hungry half an hour after a Chinese meal, you would probably be advised that you didn't eat enough rice!

Rice is the palette upon which the Chinese diner spreads colorful and flavorful tidbits. Just as the French and Italians revere the bread with which they mop up the juices of a stew and insist that it be of a quality to stand on its own, the Chinese insist on fresh, properly cooked, good-quality rice. Chinese rice is not salted, since it is eaten with relatively salty food.

Leftovers may be used for Sizzling Rice Soup (p. 110) or Fried Rice (p. 95-96), but rice is generally served plain at the center of a

To Wash or Not to Wash?

In many cultures it is considered obligatory to wash the rice to make it less starchy and therefore fluffier and "cleaner" tasting. This may have been due to the talc that used to coat rice to make it look whiter, and because the rice was not always clean in the past. But rice today is not coated and is perfectly clean, so I don't wash it. Nutrients are carried away in the wash water. However, it's up to you.

meal. It may be cooked with some savory foods on top for a quick lunch. Rice porridge (congee or jook) is a common breakfast, lunch or snack all over the Near and Far East. Congee is an English word derived from the Tamil Indian word "kanji" meaning "rice boilings."

Glutinous rice, a sticky variety of rice, is deemed to be especially nourishing for new mothers and invalids and is used in dumplings and stuffings.

Rice flour is used to make dumpling wrappers, noodles, and some desserts, particularly in southern China where wheat products are not so common.

TYPES OF RICE USED IN CHINESE COOKING

American Chinese cooking expert and restaurant owner Barbara Tropp wrote in her book *Mastering the Art of Chinese Cooking* (William Morrow & Co., N.Y., 1982) that, while Chinese-Americans prefer long-grain rice, the Chinese prefer shorter grain (pearl) rice. I have not encountered this opinion anywhere else. This does give you permission, though, to use short-grain rice with Chinese meals if you prefer. Since the majority opinion seems to go with long-grain rice, that's what I'm recommending for everyday cooking. The following are some types of rice used in Chinese cooking.

Long-Grain White Rice

This is often called Carolina or patna rice and is readily available almost everywhere. Although this may be culinary heresy, you could use an aromatic rice, such as Thai jasmine rice, or Indian basmati, if you prefer. Basmati is less polished than other white rice, so it is a little more nutritious.

Short-Grain White Rice

If you prefer this type, use pearl rice, Japanese Kokuho Rose, Blue Rose, or even Italian arborio rice (which is actually a medium grain). Short-grain white rice is used for Savory Rice Porridge (p. 98) and Rice Crusts (p. 94).

Brown Rice (Long and Short Grain)

Brown rice has the bran intact. It is available in natural food stores and most supermarkets. It takes about twice as long to cook as white rice, although it will cook more quickly if soaked first.

Glutinous, "Sweet," or Sticky Rice

This rice has no gluten in it, but the name refers to the sticky texture it has when cooked. I am particularly fond of this type of rice. The people of Laos, Cambodia, and Vietnam eat more sticky rice than the Chinese, but it is used in Chinese cooking for dim sum treats such as Lotus-Wrapped Savory Rice Packages (p. 96), and Savory Rice Porridge (p. 98). The flour is used in dumplings, desserts, and noodles.

You can find brown glutinous rice, but it is used infrequently. Cook as for the white variety, but use 2½ cups water instead of 2¼ cups and cook twice as long, or until tender. Make sure you soak it the full 8 hours first.

BASIC STEAMED CHINESE LONG-GRAIN WHITE RICE

Yield: 1 cup (will feed 2 to 3 people)

1 cup long-grain white rice
1½ cups water

Use a pot that is at least double the amount of rice and water you are using, but not so large that you end up with nothing but crust on the bottom. The pot should have a heavy bottom and a tight-fitting lid.

Place the water and rice in the pot, and bring it to a boil over high heat. When it boils, turn it down to low, cover, and cook for 15 to 20 minutes, without lifting the lid or stirring. Turn off the heat and let the rice rest for at least 5 minutes or up to 30 minutes. Fluff with a fork and serve.

Variations

Brown Rice: Whether you use short or long-grain brown rice, soak the rice in the cooking water from 1 to 12 hours. If you soak it for at least 8 hours, it should take only 20 to 25 minutes to cook.

Use an extra 1 tablespoon water per cup of rice used. Cook exactly as in the basic steamed recipe, but cook rice soaked for only 1 hour or so for 45 minutes, or until tender.

Using an Electric Rice Cooker

These devices are very popular in Asia, but I must confess that I don't have one. I have always made rice successfully in a saucepan with a tight fitting lid. Electric rice cookers are convenient, cook rice well (including brown rice), and keep it warm. Just follow the directions for your cooker.

Note: Always cook at least 1 cup of rice at a time.

Rescuing a Pot of Burnt Rice

Place a slice of bread on the surface of the rice, cover the pot, and let stand for 10 minutes or so. Discard the bread, which should absorb most of the burnt smell. Scrape the rice out of the pot, being careful not to disturb the burnt portion on the bottom.

Reheating Rice

Place the rice in a heat-proof bowl, a sieve, colander, or steamer. Place this about 2 inches above simmering water in a pot. Cover the pot and steam for 10 minutes.

Or place the rice in a microwave-proof bowl, cover it with waxed paper, and microwave on high for about 2 minutes for 1 to 2 cups.

Short-grain White Rice: I make it exactly the same way as long-grain rice.

Parboiled or "Converted" Rice: Use 1⅞ cups water per cup of rice, and cook for 20 to 25 minutes. Otherwise prepare it as directed in the basic steamed recipe. This will make a drier rice than the Chinese are accustomed to, but it is a bit more nutritious than regular white rice.

White Glutinous "Sticky" Rice: Soak 1½ cups white glutinous rice in 2¼ cups water for 1 hour. Bring the rice and soaking water to a boil in a medium-sized, heavy-bottomed pot with a tight fitting lid. When it comes to a boil, cover it, turn the heat to low, and steam for 35 minutes. Remove the pan from the heat, and let it rest for at least 5 minutes.

Brown Glutinous "Sticky" Rice: Cook the same as for white glutinous rice, but use 2½ cups water. Soak for 8 hours. Cook for 60 minutes, or until tender.

RICE CRUSTS

Yield: 4 servings

Rice crusts are crispy, golden fried pieces of steamed rice that are essential for dramatic Sizzling Rice Soup (p. 110) or can be used as a base for savory stir-frys.

1 cup cooked short-grain white rice cooled for 5 minutes

Spread the rice ¼ inch thick on an oiled cookie sheet, pat down firmly, and cut into 2-inch squares. Bake at 350°F for about 30 minutes until firm and dry. Don't let it brown.

The cooled rice crusts can be kept in a plastic bag in the refrigerator for a couple of weeks.

Just before serving, deep-fry the rice crusts in oil heated to 375°F until they are puffed and golden. Drain on paper towels and serve immediately.

Per serving: Calories 40, Protein 1 g, Fat 0 g, Carbohydrates 9 g

Basic Fried Rice

Yield: 6 servings

Scrambled Tofu:

½ pound medium-firm or firm tofu, drained and crumbled

2 tablespoons nutritional yeast flakes

2 teaspoons soy sauce

¼ teaspoon turmeric

¼ teaspoon onion powder

Salt and pepper to taste

1½ tablespoons oil

1 cup shredded canned or homemade Chinese-style seitan, *or*

 Commercial marinated or baked tofu, *or*

 Slivered vegetarian "ham" or "Canadian back bacon"

1½ cups fresh bean sprouts or finely shredded napa or savoy cabbage

 Or 1½ cups mixture of:

 ½ large green or red bell pepper, chopped, and ½ cup thawed frozen petit pois (baby peas), or thawed frozen peas and carrots

4 cups cold cooked white or brown long-grain rice

Optional: 1 cup sliced mushrooms, zucchini, cucumber, or shredded lettuce

2 large green onions, chopped

½ tablespoon roasted sesame oil

1 teaspoon salt

Pepper to taste

To make the Scrambled Tofu, mix the crumbled tofu with the other scramble ingredients. Heat a lightly-oiled nonstick skillet over high heat. Add the tofu and keep turning it with a spatula until it turns a bright scrambled egg color and dries out to your satisfaction. Set aside.

Rice is normally eaten plain in China, but occasionally a savory or fried rice dish will be made with leftover rice and other bits and pieces. This type of dish—a dish of the poor—was made popular in Chinese restaurants in North America. Like chop suey and the flat egg foo yung omelets in brown sauce, fried rice is really a Chinese-American dish, rather than a Chinese dish. However, it is well loved and can be very delicious.

Savory fried rice does not need to be greasy. It should be seasoned with salt or just a little light soy sauce—most American versions are too heavy on the soy sauce. You can use the suggestions I have made in the recipe, or change it to suit what you have on hand.

Fried rice invariably contains scrambled egg, which I have replaced with scrambled tofu. The rice should not be freshly made but cold so that it is a bit dry.

Yanchow Fried Rice

This version of fried rice is the only one that is served as part of a party menu and comes from the famous river port on the Yangtze River. It generally contains shrimp, but this is a vegetarian version.

Make the Basic Fried Rice on pp. 95-96, using bean sprouts instead of cabbage, and using red pepper instead of peas and/or carrots. Add the mushrooms and 1 cup of slivered zucchini. Use Chinese canned or homemade "mock abalone" (p. 46) or homemade Seitan "Seafood" (p. 45) for the protein. Or use vegetarian "scallops" from a can.

One of my fondest memories from meat-eating days is eating savory lotus-leaf "tamales" as we shopped the crowded Sunday streets of Vancouver's Chinatown for vegetables and Asian specialties. When I became a vegetarian, I vowed to produce a meatless version that brought back those memories. If I'd only known how easy that would be, I would have done it years ago!

To fry the rice, heat a large heavy wok over high heat. When it's very hot, add the oil. When the oil is hot, add the seitan or tofu and the vegetables. Stir-fry for several minutes, or until the cabbage starts to wilt. Add the rice, breaking up the clumps with your fingers. Add the sesame oil and salt and pepper, and keep turning the rice with a spatula until the rice is hot. Dump in the Scrambled Tofu and stir-fry until everything is well-mixed and hot. Taste for salt and pepper and serve immediately.

Per serving: Calories 190, Protein 10 g, Fat 4 g, Carbohydrates 26 g

LOTUS-WRAPPED SAVORY RICE PACKAGES

"CHINESE TAMALES"

Yield: 6 servings

1½ cups uncooked glutinous "sticky" white rice, soaked 1 to 8 hours in 2¼ cups cold water

Filling Ingredients:

2 (10-ounce) cans vegetarian "roast duck" braised gluten (mun chai'ya), *or* about 2 cups chopped Braised Chinese Seitan (p. 46)

10 to 12 medium-sized dried Chinese mushrooms, soaked in hot water for 20 to 30 minutes until soft, stems discarded, and chopped

1 medium carrot, scrubbed and finely diced

2 tablespoons chopped vegetarian "ham" or "Canadian back bacon"

1 tablespoon dry sherry

1 tablespoon light soy sauce

½ tablespoon minced fresh ginger

½ tablespoon minced garlic

1 teaspoon roasted sesame oil

Rice Flavoring:

2 tablespoons light soy sauce

1 tablespoon dry sherry

1 tablespoon roasted sesame oil

½ teaspoon salt

3 lotus leaves, soaked for 1 hour in enough hot water to cover, then drained, wiped dry, and cut in half

Roasted sesame oil for brushing the leaves

White string or twine

Bring the rice and soaking water to a boil in a heavy-bottomed medium pot with a tight fitting lid. Turn the heat to low, and cook for 35 minutes. Set aside.

If using the canned vegetarian "roast duck," place it in a colander and rinse it well. Chop the vegetarian "roast duck" or braised gluten into small chunks.

In a large wok or heavy skillet, stir-fry the filling ingredients together over high heat until they are well-mixed and fragrant. Remove from the heat. Add the cooked rice and the rice flavorings and mix well.

Brush the insides of the lotus leaf halves with roasted sesame oil. Pile ⅙ of the filling in the middle of each leaf, and press it together well. Fold the edges of the leaf in to make a tight package. Tie each package with white string or twine. Place the packages on an oiled plate or steam basket, and steam for 15 minutes over plenty of boiling water.

Remove the string or twine before serving the packages. They are good hot or at room temperature.

Per serving: Calories 227, Protein 19 g, Fat 3 g, Carbohydrates 27 g

Savory Rice Bowls

Yield: 2 servings

Make 1 cup of the Basic Steamed Chinese White Long-Grain Rice on p. 93. After you turn down the heat under the boiling rice, wait until the bubbles disappear. Place about 1 cup of any Chinese savory mixture on top, cover, and steam for 15 to 20 minutes.

Lotus-Wrapped Savory Rice Packages are wonderful snack or celebration food, and very easy to prepare.

I particularly like the flavor of the vegetarian "roast duck" braised gluten, which you can find in cans in Asian grocery stores.

You can also use any other type of canned Chinese braised gluten, even the "abalone style." Rinse it well before using.

The dried lotus leaves lend a particular flavor and aroma to these savory packages. It is often suggested that aluminum foil or cooking parchment be used instead, but I think it's worth your while to find lotus leaves. They are cheap, store for ages, and are easy to find in any Chinese or Asian grocery store.

The savory rice bowl is a popular dish for a quick lunch or supper. It is steamed rice with a savory mixture cooked on top of it. Often this is leftover meat, Chinese sausage or ham, or eggs with a few mushrooms.

My Chinese cooking mentor Benjamin Lee used to fondly describe his mother's congee—a simple, comforting dish which is usually served at breakfast, but also makes a light supper. Serve with Green Onion Pancakes (pp. 88-89) or Deep-Fried Devils (pp. 85-86) for a light meal.

Brown rice is not traditional, but it gives you the whole grain cereal feeling that many people prefer. (Don't use raw brown rice—it takes a *long* time to cook to the porridge stage.)

Condiments

- any chopped seasoned seitan (gluten), textured soy protein, or tofu
- slivers of dried soaked Chinese mushrooms
- slivers of soaked yuba (bean curd skin)
- roasted chopped peanuts or cashews
- steamed, braised, or stir-fried chopped Chinese greens (pp. 18-19), or Swiss chard, kale, or collard greens
- slivered vegetarian "ham"
- Vegetarian Chinese "Sausage" pp. 52-53

Savory Rice Porridge

Congee or Jook

Yield: 4 to 6 servings

6 to 8 cups low-salt "chicken-style" vegetarian broth (some vegetarian broth powders are less salty than cubes or pastes)
½ cup uncooked short-grain white rice, or a mixture of ½ cup short-grain and ½ cup glutinous white rice, or 1½ cups cooked short-grain brown rice
1 teaspoon grated fresh ginger
3 to 4 tablespoons chopped green onions
Salt and pepper to taste
Optional: **1 piece dried orange or tangerine peel, softened in water, minced, or ½ teaspoon freshly grated orange peel**

Garnishes: **Offer these for each diner to use as desired.**
  Chopped fresh cilantro
  Chopped Chinese preserved turnip (very salty)
  A drizzle of roasted sesame oil
  Light soy sauce
  Vinegar or hot sauce
  Fermented bean curd (doufu-ru, see pp. 28-29)

In a medium pot combine the broth, rice, ginger, and optional tangerine or orange peel. Bring the rice to a boil, then simmer on low, uncovered, for about 1½ hours, or until the mixture is like a thin porridge. Add more water or broth if it gets too thick.

Note: The amount of broth depends on how thick you prefer the porridge. You can start out with 6 cups and add more later if it's not enough, or start out with 8 cups and cook it down more if it's too liquidy for you.

Taste for salt and pepper. Don't add too much salt if your condiments are salty. Ladle the porridge into soup bowls and top with any condiments you are using, plus the green onions and cilantro, if you are using it.

Per serving: Calories 227, Protein 19 g, Fat 3 g, Carbohydrates 27 g

An excellent place to start cooking Chinese is with noodles and soups, both of which which cross all kinds of cultural barriers. In Northern China, noodles made from wheat flour are as common as the rice bowl of the South (where rice-flour noodles are often served). Noodles are frequently served in broth, with just a few condiments, as a whole meal, or a snack.

Clear or light soups are often sipped as a beverage during a Chinese meal. Heartier soups may be eaten as a savory dish with rice. There may even be more than one soup served during a meal! Dumplings are often served in soup, as well as noodles.

Many of the following recipes are quick and easy to make. They are light but filling, making them ideal homecooked meals-in-a-bowl for hectic modern lifestyles.

Simple Chinese noodle dishes can be made by serving cooked hot or cold noodles in a little broth with one of the dipping sauces on pp. 116-120. The Spicy Peanut Dipping Sauce is particularly good.

Chapter X

NOODLES, SOUPS, AND SAUCES

"Drink and eat moderately and carefully and garden vegetables can be like feasting on rich delicacies."

From *Master Chu's Mottoes for Guiding Families*, Ching Dynasty

Chinese Noodles and North American or Vegan Substitutes

Chinese Name	Description	Substitute
gan mian or ji mian	plain thin (flour and water)	spaghettini or Japanese soba
mian xian	very thin (flour and water), Amoy-style	vermicelli, Japanese soba, or cappellini
la mian or long xu mian	very fine "pulled" noodles	angel hair pasta (capelli d'angelo)
bai mian	flat (flour and water)	fettuccine* or linguine
dan mian	thin, straight egg (may be in "clusters")	spaghettini or Japanese soba
dan mian qui (chow mein noodles)	thin egg noodle "clusters"	vermicelli, capellini or spaghettini soba,
mi fen or mee-fun, ngunsi-fun, or lai-fun	thin rice noodles	rice or Italian vermicelli or capellini
ho-fun	wide, flat rice noodles	linguine or the wider flat Thai or Vietnamese "rice stick" noodles
fen si, fen szu, fun-see, or sai fun	thin mung bean or pea starch noodle	cellophane, bean thread, glass, shining, jelly, silver threads, or transparent noodles; or rice vermicelli

Note: *The best type of fettuccine for Chinese cooking is the thinner style which is packaged in a box rolled up and dried in little "nests." DeCecco is a widely-available, good-quality brand.*

In this recipe, developed for an article I wrote for *Vegetarian Times* magazine (June 1995), I use soy flour as part of the flour, and water as the liquid. The protein, fats, and lecithin in the soy flour act as tenderizers, coating the gluten in the wheat flour. The golden color of the soy flour also lends a pleasant color.

It is possible to make noodles using only flour and water, but they don't hold up as well or have as much flavor.

Using Pasta Machines for Chinese Noodles

If you own an Italian pasta maker, you can use it to make fresh Chinese-style noodles and wonton wrappers.

Experienced pasta makers choose the inexpensive roller-type, hand-cranked machine. There are electric roller-types, but they are more expensive and I don't see the point—it's not that hard to crank the hand-driven ones. Kids love to help with this!

Extruder machines for making pasta used to be all the rage. Now most of them languish in garages, for the simple reason that they produce inferior

HOMEMADE NOODLES AND WONTON WRAPPER DOUGH

Makes a generous 1 pound of fresh noodles or 90 to 100 wontons

1⅔ cups unbleached white flour, or 1 cup unbleached white flour and ⅔ cup whole wheat flour

½ cup full-fat soy flour

(If you are making dough for wontons (pp. 75-76), add 1 tablespoon oil to the dough, to make it more flexible.)

⅔ cup water

Optional: **½ to ¾ teaspoon salt**

Unbleached flour for rolling

Cornstarch for dusting

To make the dough by hand, mix the flour, soy flour and salt in a medium-sized bowl. Pour in the water and stir with a fork until the dough comes together in a ball. Knead the dough on a lightly-floured surface for about 10 minutes, or until the dough is smooth. Place the dough in a plastic bag, and let it rest for at least 10 minutes.

You can also knead the dough, especially larger amounts, in a heavy-duty kitchen machine with a dough hook, instead of by hand.

To make the dough in a food processor, mix the flour, soy flour and salt in a dry processor bowl, then add the water through the top with the motor running. Process for about 30 seconds, or until a smooth ball forms. The dough may seem a bit sticky, but you'll be flouring it as you work. Place the dough in a plastic bag, and let it rest for at least 10 minutes.

To make the dough in a bread machine, place the wet and dry ingredients in the bread mixing basket according to the directions for your machine, and turn it on for the dough cycle. Unplug the machine when it finishes kneading. Lightly oil the dough, place it in a plastic bag and refrigerate for at least half an hour. The dough gets warm in a bread machine.

To roll and cut the dough by hand, divide the dough into eighths, keeping the portion you aren't working with in the plastic bag.

Roll each piece out on a floured surface into a rectangle ⅛-inch thick (or whatever thickness you wish), flouring as you go to prevent sticking. Hang the rolled-out portions of dough over the backs of chairs or on a pasta rack to dry for 20 to 30 minutes before cutting. Humidity makes the dough harder to roll out.

Dust the dough well with cornstarch, and roll each portion up loosely like a little jelly roll. If the portions seem too long, you can cut them in half. Cut them into the desired widths (⅛ inch to ¼ inch) with a sharp knife. Shake the noodles out and spread them on cookie sheets sprinkled with cornstarch.

To roll and cut with a hand-crank pasta machine or electric pasta-rolling machine, divide the dough into eighths, keeping the portions you aren't working with in the plastic bag. Flour the dough well and run it through the first setting of the machine. Now, flour it lightly again, fold it into thirds, and run it through the first setting again. Do this until the dough looks smooth. Then flour the dough and run it through each successive setting twice, until it is the desired thickness.

I like the noodles best at the third-to-the-last setting, number 5, on my machine, and the second-to-the-last setting, number 6, for wonton wrappers. This is pretty standard for the inexpensive hand-roller machines. The very expensive ones are better-aligned, so you can more easily use the last, very thin, setting, if you wish.

Hang the rolled-out dough to dry as instructed above. Dust each portion of dough well with cornstarch. If the portions seem too long, cut them in half and run through the cutters with the desired width. Spread the noodles out on cookie sheets sprinkled with cornstarch.

If you are going to use the noodles within 4 hours, cover the cookie sheets with a towel. Otherwise, you can place them in a plastic bag or rigid container and refrigerate them for up to 3 days. (See sidebar, p. 102, for freezing and drying instructions.)

To cook fresh noodles, have your sauce, soup, or stir-fry ready, and use 4 to 6 quarts of boiling, salted water in a large pot over high heat. Do not thaw frozen noodles. Shake off any excess cornstarch, drop the noodles in the boiling water, and stir gently with a long fork or spaghetti rake. Cover the pot and remove the cover as soon as the water returns to a boil. Count from the second the water comes to a boil. Be vigilant! Very fine noodles take only about 5 pasta. Most Chinese noodles are rolled or pulled. (Spaghetti is an extruded pasta.)

Never wash your pasta machine or get it wet! I just shake it and brush it with a clean pastry brush. Store it in dry plastic bags. When first using a new machine, throw away the first piece of dough, after rolling it through the rollers several times.

Note: The amount of salt in noodle dough is a matter of taste. Eggs contain sodium, so eggless noodles can taste flat without a bit of salt. I have made the salt optional; however, I add it myself.

Making Wrappers for Wontons

Do not allow strips of rolled-out dough to dry out. Cover them with a damp tea towel while you work. Do not allow tears in the dough or the filling will seep out. If you find a tear, fold it up and pass it through the rollers again. Roll the dough out as thinly as your machine will allow, about a sixteenth of an inch (second-to-last setting for most inexpensive machines). The strips should be about 3 inches wide by 3 inches long.

Storing, Freezing and Drying Homemade Noodles

If you plan to refrigerate or freeze fresh noodles, let them dry on the cookie sheets for at least 15 minutes, or up to 4 hours, then place them in plastic bags or rigid containers. Refrigerate them for up to 3 days, or freeze them for up to 2 months.

Drop frozen noodles into boiling water, and cook just until the noodles float, then drain and serve immediately.

If you want to dry your homemade noodles, dry them for a minimum of 24 hours on the cookie sheets. When you are sure that the noodles are dry all the way through, you can store them in metal cookie tins or rigid plastic storage containers for about a month. Dried homemade noodles take only a few seconds longer to cook than fresh.

I prefer freezing because the noodles are more like the fresh product. But I usually make noodles fresh, because they're a treat and don't really take very long to make, once you get the hang of it.

seconds, thicker noodles take about 15 seconds. Very soft noodles may need to be removed as soon as the water comes to a boil again. Thoroughly dried or frozen noodles may take somewhat longer, but test them 1 minute after the second boil. Some recipes for cooking fresh noodles tell you to cook 1 to 3 minutes—this amount of time is counted from the moment the noodles are dropped into the pot, not from the second boil. Otherwise, the noodles would be overcooked.

Drain the noodles. Serve immediately. Some cooks drain them over the serving bowl so that the hot water heats the bowl.

CHINESE NOODLE "PANCAKE"

JINN MEIN

Yield: 4 to 6 servings

1 to 1¼ pounds fresh Chinese flour and water thin noodles (gan mian, ji mian, or mian xian), or fresh egg-free Italian tagliarini (flat, fresh, thin noodles)
1 tablespoon roasted sesame oil
½ teaspoon salt
2 to 4 tablespoons oil for frying or baking

Cook the fresh noodles in a large pot of boiling water until just tender (see pp. 101-102). Drain and toss with the salt and sesame oil.

To pan-fry the noodle "pancake," you must cook the noodles in 2 batches, or use 2 pans at one time. Heat 2 tablespoons of the oil in a 10-inch, heavy skillet over medium heat. When it's hot add half of the cooked, seasoned noodles, and pat them down into an even layer that fills the pan. Press down with a spatula on the noodles occasionally as they cook. When the bottom is firm and golden-brown (about 10 minutes), turn the "pancake" carefully and cook until the other side is golden-brown. If you are cooking the other half, repeat the process and keep the cooked "pancake" in a 200°F oven.

To oven-fry the "pancake," heat the oven to 500°F. While it heats up, heat a 14-inch round pizza pan or a 10- x 15-inch rimmed cookie sheet in the oven. Pour 2 tablespoons oil into the hot pan, coating it all over. Spread all of the cooked noodles in an even layer to cover the bottom of the pan. Bake on the bottom rack of the oven for 25 to 30 minutes, or until the "pancake" is crispy and golden. If it browns too much on the bottom, turn it over.

Cut the "pancake" into wedges or squares, and top with a savory stir-fry.

Per serving: Calories 335, Protein 13 g, Fat 11 g, Carbohydrates 46 g

Chinese Nood cake" makes a wonderful change from rice or plain noodles as an accompaniment to a flavorful stir-fry. Use fresh noodles for the best results.

Vegetable-Noodle Salad with Sesame

Yield: 8 servings

1 pound plain, thin flour and water noodles (gan mian, ji mian, or mian xian, extra-thin Amoy-style flour and water noodles), or spaghettini, vermicelli, or cappellini (thin Italian pasta)

Dressing:

7 tablespoons light soy sauce

¼ cup roasted sesame oil

3½ tablespoons dark unbleached sugar

3 tablespoons black vinegar or balsamic vinegar

3 tablespoons water

1 tablespoon grated fresh ginger

2 teaspoons salt

1 teaspoon chili garlic paste

1 to 2 cloves garlic, crushed

2 bunches green onions, chopped

¼ cup toasted sesame seeds

1 pound lightly cooked fresh or frozen whole small green beans or asparagus, cut into 2-inch lengths or broccoli flowerettes, thinly sliced

This is a very easy and delicious salad, adapted from a recipe in Deborah Madison's *Vegetarian Cooking for Everyone*, Broadway Books, N.Y., 1997. I frequently take this salad to potlucks and invariably have several requests for the recipe.

Variations for Vegetable-Noodle Salad with Sesame

You can substitute other vegetables if you don't have the ones I suggested.

Instead of adding the optional Breast of Tofu "Chicken" or vegetarian "ham," you could use one of the following:

- leftover deep-fried or oven-fried tofu

- deep-fried or oven-fried "chiken brest" (pp. 172-173)

- chunks made from textured soy protein

- canned vegetarian "roast duck" or other Chinese canned "mock meat"

- any homemade "mock meat" from Chapter VI

Optional: **1 red bell pepper, sliced**

Optional: **Slivers of crispy Breast of Tofu "Chicken," vegetarian "ham," or "Canadian back bacon"**

Cook the noodles in a large pot of boiling water until tender. Drain well. Mix the dressing ingredients together well, pour over the noodles, and toss well.

Add the green onions, sesame seeds, vegetables, and any optional ingredients, and toss well. Store in the refrigerator but bring to room temperature before serving.

Per serving: Calories 300, Protein 11 g, Fat 10 g, Carbohydrates 40 g

DAN DAN NOODLES

Yield: 2 servings

4 ounces thin rice noodles, or 6 ounces spaghettini or Japanese soba noodles

1½ cups hot vegetarian broth

2 tablespoons peanut butter

"Meat" Sauce:

1 tablespoon oil

1 medium onion, chopped

4 dried Chinese black mushrooms, soaked in hot water for 20 to 30 minutes, stems discarded, and sliced

2 cloves garlic, minced

Optional: **1 tablespoon chopped Sichuan pickled vegetables**

⅓ cup textured soy protein granules soaked in ¼ cup boiling water, or ½ cup vegetarian hamburger crumbles

1 tablespoon light soy sauce

1 tablespoon brown bean paste or light miso

1 teaspoon chili garlic paste
½ tablespoon cornstarch mixed with 2 tablespoons cold water

2 tablespoons chopped green onion
1 tablespoon roasted sesame oil

Boil the noodles in plenty of water until tender. (Rice noodles cook in only 2 to 3 minutes.) Drain them in a colander.

Mix the hot broth with the peanut butter. Keep warm.

Heat a wok or heavy skillet over high heat. When it's hot, add the oil. When the oil is hot, add the onion, mushrooms, garlic, and pickled vegetables, if using. Stir-fry until the onions soften, adding a bit of water as necessary to prevent scorching. Add the textured soy protein, soy sauce, brown bean paste, and chili paste. When it bubbles, stir in the cornstarch mixture, and stir until thickened. Remove from the heat.

Run hot water over the noodles, drain, and divide them between 2 heated soup bowls. Heat the broth if necessary, and pour over the noodles. Divide the sauce evenly between the two bowls, top with the chopped green onion and drizzle with the sesame oil. Serve immediately.

Per serving: Calories 510, Protein 15 g, Fat 19 g, Carbohydrates 65 g

Dan dan noodles are a common street-food dish in Sichuan province—quick, hearty, and satisfying. There are many versions, but they usually consist of some sort of spicy meat sauce with peanuts or sesame paste. You can use wheat or rice noodles.

Allergy Note

If you are allergic to peanuts, use Chinese sesame paste or tahini instead of peanut butter. Chinese sesame paste is roasted, and tahini is not.

SHANGHAI NOODLES

Yield: 4 servings

7 ounces flat Chinese flour and water noodles (bai mian), or
    8 ounces fettuccine or linguine
2 teaspoons oil
6 dried Chinese black mushrooms, soaked in hot water for 20 to
    30 minutes, stems discarded, and sliced
1 cup sliced fresh mushrooms
2 cloves garlic, minced
4 cups sliced Chinese greens (pp. 18-19) or savoy cabbage, kale,
    or collard greens, or a mixture

This is a wonderful "meal in a bowl."

About 2 cups Braised Chinese Seitan (p. 46), Red-Braised Seitan (p. 47), or reconstituted textured soy protein chunks, deep-fried or oven-fried (pp. 172-173)

Seasoning Sauce:

3 tablespoons light soy sauce plus 1 tablespoon vegetarian stir-fry "oyster" sauce (p. 116) or brown bean sauce

1½ tablespoons Chinese black vinegar or balsamic vinegar

1 teaspoon roasted sesame oil

¼ teaspoon white pepper

2 green onions, chopped

Boil the noodles in plenty of boiling water until tender. Drain and set them aside in a colander.

Heat a heavy wok or skillet over high heat. When very hot, add the 2 teaspoons oil. When the oil is hot, add the dried and fresh mushrooms and garlic. Stir-fry for 2 minutes.

Add the greens and stir-fry until they just wilt. Add a dribble of water if necessary to keep them from sticking.

Add the noodles, seitan or soy protein chunks, and the seasoning sauce ingredients. Toss the mixture well to combine and heat through. Serve immediately, sprinkled with the green onions.

Per serving: Calories 371, Protein 34 g, Fat 6 g, Carbohydrates 44 g

Stir-Fried Savory Noodles and Vegetables

Chow Mein

Yield: 4 servings

8 ounces plain, thin flour and water noodles (gan mian or ji mian), or extra-thin Amoy-style flour and water noodles (mian xian), or thin Italian pasta (spaghettini or vermicelli)

1 tablespoon roasted sesame oil

Cooking Sauce:

2 tablespoons light soy sauce

2 tablespoons vegetarian stir-fry sauce "oyster" sauce (p. 116)

¼ cup water

¼ teaspoon white pepper

Stir-Fried Vegetables:

1½ tablespoons oil

2 cups slivered any style Chinese gluten (seitan) or extra-firm tofu tossed with 1 to 2 tablespoons vegetarian stir-fry "oyster" sauce (p. 116)

1 medium onion, cut into 6 sections, layers separated

2 cloves garlic, minced or crushed

1 teaspoon grated fresh ginger

2 stalks celery, sliced diagonally into ½-inch lengths

4 cups thinly sliced vegetables (such as broccoli, napa cabbage, mushrooms, bell peppers, snow peas, or green beans)

4 green onions, chopped

Cook the noodles in a large pot of boiling water until tender. Drain the noodles in a colander placed over another pot to catch the boiling water. Toss the drained noodles with the roasted sesame oil, and place the colander over the pot of hot water, covering the noodles, to keep them warm while you make the stir-fry.

Combine the cooking sauce ingredients, and set aside.

Heat a large wok or heavy skillet over high heat. When it's very hot, add the 1½ tablespoons oil. When the oil is hot, add the seitan, onion, garlic, and ginger. Stir-fry until the onion begins to turn translucent, and the seitan is browned a little. Add the celery and other vegetables, and stir-fry for a few minutes until the vegetables are just crisp-tender. (Add the quick-cooking vegetables, such as snow peas, last, to avoid over-cooking.)

Add the cooking sauce and cook just until it boils. Place the warm noodles on a heated platter, and pour the stir-fried vegetables and sauce evenly over the surface of the noodles. Sprinkle the green onions on top, and serve immediately.

Per serving: Calories 312, Protein 28 g, Fat 9 g, Carbohydrates 29 g

There are many variations of this wonderful noodle dish—a meal in itself. This one is not only very easy, but not as oily as some of the noodle dishes one is served in restaurants. Many North Americans think that chow mein noodles are deep-fried, but "chow" means "stir-fry."

If you prefer, you can use reconstituted flavored soy protein chunks or cutlets, cut into slivers, or the Breast of Tofu "Chicken" (p. 43), instead of the seitan or tofu.

This recipe makes an excellent basic broth or stock. It is inexpensive, and you can control the amount of salt. You can make large quantities of it once a month, if you wish, and freeze it in 1- or 2-cup quantities, or in ice cube trays. (Pop them out into plastic bags when they are solid.) The cubes contain about 2 tablespoons of broth.

Amounts and types of vegetables don't have to be exact, but I like lots of onions, garlic, celery, and carrots. For a brown stock, you can roast the vegetables at 400°F for 45 minutes. For variety, you can use the outside leaves of organic lettuce, or any other vegetables except those of the cabbage family and beets. Soybean sprouts are often used in Chinese vegetarian stock. Some cooks use potatoes, or potato peelings, but this doesn't make a clear stock.

When the broth is finished, it should taste good enough to drink as a hot beverage. If it tastes a bit flat, and you've added enough salt, try adding about ¼ cup of light miso or Chinese brown bean sauce, some Marmite or other yeast extract, some

HOMEMADE VEGETARIAN BROTH

Yield: 3 quarts

1 tablespoon oil
2 large onions or 4 leeks, coarsely chopped
4 carrots, scrubbed and chopped
2 large stalks celery with leaves, diced
Optional: **1 or 2 whole heads of garlic, cloves separated and**
   smashed with a knife (no need to peel)
¼ cup dry sherry for deglazing pan
3 quarts (12 cups) water (some of this can be the cooking water
   from cooking whole soybeans, if you like—in that case, don't
   use the soybean sprouts)
4 cups fresh soybean sprouts
1 bunch green onions, chopped
1½ ounces dried Chinese black mushrooms
4 (¼-inch) slices fresh ginger, crushed
Optional: **2 teaspoons Sichuan peppercorns**

Heat a large heavy pot and add the oil. When the oil is hot, add the onions, carrots, celery, and garlic, and cook until the onions have softened and started to brown. If you want a browner stock, allow the vegetables to brown a bit more. Add a little water or dry sherry as you stir them, to keep them from sticking.

If using the wine, pour it in and deglaze the pan. Stir to scrape up any brown bits. Add the water, mushrooms, ginger, salt, and peppercorns and bring to a boil. Cover and simmer for about 2 hours. Strain through a sieve, discarding the vegetables; then strain again with cheesecloth lining the sieve. The broth will keep about a week in covered jars in the refrigerator. After that time, boil it again for a few minutes, bottle and refrigerate again, or freeze it.

Per cup: Calories 81, Protein 4 g, Fat 2 g, Carbohydrates 10 g

"Meatball" or "Chicken" Ball Soup

Yield: 4 to 6 servings

Soup:

6 cups vegetarian broth
1 cup fresh (or thawed frozen), snow peas, green beans, or
carrots, diagonally sliced, or frozen petit pois (baby peas)
4 large fresh mushrooms, thinly sliced
2 tablespoons light soy sauce
1 tablespoon grated fresh ginger
1 tablespoon dry sherry
Salt to taste

½ recipe Pork "Balls" or "Chicken" Balls, steamed, and, if you
prefer, deep-fried as directed in the recipes

Bring the soup ingredients to a boil in a large pot. Simmer just until the vegetables are crisp-tender. Taste for salt.

Add the "meatballs" and cook for 1 minute to heat, then serve immediately. If left too long in the broth, the "meatballs" may fall apart.

Per serving: Calories 85, Protein 8 g, Fat 1 g, Carbohydrates 8 g

Boiled Dumplings in Soup

Yield: 8 to 10 servings

12 cups vegetarian "chicken-style" broth
2 tablespoons grated fresh ginger
½ cup chopped green onions
Optional: **¼ cup chopped fresh cilantro**
½ recipe Northern-Style Boiled Dumplings (pp. 73-74), boiled
and drained

Bring the broth to a boil in a large pot, along with the ginger, green onions, and cilantro. As soon as it boils, add the cooked dumplings, reduce to a simmer, then remove from the heat. Carefully ladle the soup and dumplings into bowls, and serve.

Per serving: Calories 99, Protein 4 g, Fat 0 g, Carbohydrates 18 g

light soy sauce, a little nutritional yeast, some leftover dried mushroom soaking water, and/or even a couple of commercial vegetarian broth cubes.

To make broth quickly, pressure cook it for 20 to 30 minutes.

Vegetarian Broth or Stock

There are many excellent vegetarian broth cubes, pastes, powders, and ready-made vegetarian stocks. Their quality has improved greatly over the years. It is easy to find vegetarian broths made without MSG and preservatives. Some are made from organic ingredients. Try different brands from natural food stores and supermarkets. Brands vary from region to region. Check the labels carefully, and taste test them all. Some will have a more "chickeny" flavor, which is suitable for Chinese cooking.

To make commercial broth taste more authentically Chinese, I usually make it a little weaker and then flavor it with a little soy sauce and dry sherry.

The broth from soaking dried Chinese black mushrooms makes an excellent addition to broth, giving it rich flavor, so don't discard it. It can be frozen.

Sizzling Rice Soup

Yield: 4 servings

Serve this for company! The fried rice crusts sizzle loudly and dramatically when you pour the hot soup over them. Do this at the table for maximum effect.

Oil for frying
6 cups vegetarian broth
6 ounces Chinese broccoli or other Chinese greens (pp. 18-19), or Swiss chard, kale, or collard greens, washed, trimmed and sliced
2 medium carrots, thinly sliced or julienned
6 dried Chinese black mushrooms, soaked in hot water for 20 to 30 minutes until soft, stems discarded, and sliced
½ cup frozen petit pois (baby peas)
½ cup sliced celery
3 ounces firm tofu, diced
3 tablespoons dry sherry
½ teaspoon salt
¼ teaspoon white pepper
1 cup reconstituted soy protein chunks (p. 50-51)
¼ cup cornstarch or water chestnut flour
½ recipe Rice Crusts (p. 94)

Heat oil for deep-frying in a wok or heavy frying pan to 375°F. (See Chapter XIII about deep-frying.)

Meanwhile, heat the soup broth in a large pot over high heat. Add all of the other soup ingredients, except the textured soy protein chunks, cornstarch, and rice crusts.

While this simmers, roll the the soy protein chunks in the cornstarch to coat, and deep fry. When they are golden and crispy, drain them on paper towels on a cookie sheet, and place in a 200°F oven.

Immediately deep-fry the rice crusts a few at a time until they are puffed and golden brown. Drain them on the cookie sheet with the soy protein chunks. As soon as they are done, add the soy protein chunks to the soup. Carry the soup to the table, distribute the fried rice crusts evenly among four large soup bowls, and ladle the hot soup over the rice crusts.

Per serving: Calories 198, Protein 10 g, Fat 1 g, Carbohydrates 31 g

Baby Bok Choy, Mushroom, and Deep-Fried Tofu Soup

Yield: 4 servings

9 (1½-inch) cubes of commercial tofu, or triangles of Oven-Fried
   Tofu (p. 175)
1 tablespoon oil
1½ pounds baby bok choy, washed, dried, and trimmed
6 dried Chinese black mushrooms, soaked in hot water for 20 to
   30 minutes until soft and stems discarded (save soaking
   water)
1 cup sliced fresh white or brown mushrooms
5 cups light vegetarian broth
2 tablespoons light soy sauce
2 tablespoons dry sherry
2½ cups cooked plain, thin flour and water noodles (gan mian
   or ji mian), or spaghettini
Roasted sesame oil

This makes a wonderful light lunch.

If you are using commercial fried tofu, pour boiling water over it, and let it stand for a few minutes. Drain and squeeze out as much water and oil as you can, and cut the cubes in half. If you are using the Oven-Fried Tofu, cut the triangles in half.

Heat a large wok or heavy pot over high heat. When hot, add the oil. When the oil is hot, add the bok choy and mushrooms. Stir-fry for 2 to 3 minutes. Add the remaining ingredients including the mushroom soaking water and the tofu. Let it simmer for a few minutes until everything is hot.

Serve immediately and pass the sesame oil to sprinkle over each serving.

Per serving: Calories 296, Protein 15 g, Fat 8 g, Carbohydrates 36 g

HOT AND SOUR SOUP

Yield: 4 to 6 servings

This popular soup is easy to make at home, and it's great for cold-sufferers!

Variations

If you want a "meatier" soup, you can add some slivers of vegetarian "ham" or "Canadian back bacon," or any leftover "mock meat" (see Chapter VI).

Although the soup is good without them, tree ear fungus and "golden needles" are traditional ingredients.

In place of the preserved and pickled vegetables, you can use 4 ounces of sauerkraut with ½ teaspoon chili garlic paste and 1 to 2 tablespoons rice, cider, or white wine vinegar. You may need a little vinegar anyway, if the pickled vegetables don't add enough sour taste to the soup.

6 ounces medium-firm tofu, cut into ½-inch cubes

2 ounces Sichuan preserved vegetables, cut into slivers

2 ounces Chinese pickled vegetables, cut into slivers

½ cup thawed frozen petit pois (baby peas), or a loose cup of fresh or thawed frozen, snow peas, trimmed if necessary

Optional: ½ cup sliced fresh mushrooms (button, shiitake, or oyster)

½ ounce dried tree ear fungus, soaked in hot water for 20 to 30 minutes until soft, stems discarded, and chopped

½ ounce "golden needles" (dried tiger lily buds), soaked in hot water for 20 to 30 minutes until soft, stems discarded, and chopped

3 dried Chinese black mushrooms, soaked in hot water for 20 to 30 minutes until soft, stems discarded, and slivered (save soaking water)

4 cups vegetarian broth (including mushroom soaking water)

2 green onions, chopped

1 tablespoon grated fresh ginger

2 tablespoons dry sherry

1 to 2 tablespoons light soy sauce

Optional: Sprinkling of ground Sichuan pepper

Julienne strips of carrot or other vegetable

1 tablespoon cornstarch dissolved in 1 tablespoon cold water

1 teaspoon roasted sesame oil

In a medium pot, place all of the ingredients, except the dissolved cornstarch and sesame oil. Bring to a boil, turn down the heat and simmer for about 2 minutes. Add the dissolved cornstarch. Bring to a boil, stirring until it has thickened slightly and is clear. Stir in the sesame oil, and serve immediately.

Per serving: Calories 80, Protein 4 g, Fat 2 g, Carbohydrates 8 g

CHINESE VEGETARIAN NOODLES IN SOUP

Yield: 4 servings

½ pound dry thin Amoy-style flour and water noodles (mian xian) or vermicelli, cappellini, or Japanese soba noodles

4 cups vegetarian broth

5 large dried Chinese black mushrooms, soaked in hot water for 20 to 30 minutes until soft, stems discarded, and thinly sliced (save soaking water)

6 fresh mushrooms, sliced

½ medium onion, thinly sliced

1 stalk broccoli, (peel the bottom part) thinly sliced

½ cup thinly sliced commercial baked marinated tofu or cooked Breast of Tofu "Chicken" (p. 43) or other cooked savory tofu

1 tablespoon light soy sauce

1 teaspoon unbleached sugar

1 teaspoon cornstarch dissolved in 1 tablespoon cold water

4 teaspoons roasted sesame oil

Cook the noodles in boiling water until tender. Drain and set aside.

Heat the broth and mushroom soaking water in a large pot. Add the dried mushrooms, fresh mushrooms, onion, and broccoli. Simmer until the broccoli is crisp-tender.

Add the tofu, soy sauce, and sugar. Taste for salt. Stir in the dissolved cornstarch.

Run very hot water over the noodles in a colander. Divide the noodles evenly between 4 large soup bowls. Ladle the broth, vegetables, and tofu evenly over the noodles. Drizzle 1 teaspoon sesame oil over each bowl just before serving.

Per serving: Calories 304, Protein 12 g, Fat 2 g, Carbohydrates 56 g

This recipe is merely a guide, because you can use various kinds of vegetables and protein in it. Substitute snow peas or napa or savoy cabbage for the broccoli, if you like, or use leftover textured soy protein chunks instead of the tofu.

It's a common dish in China on the streets, in restaurants, and at home. We have it when we're craving something warm, savory, and simple.

How to Eat Noodles in Soup

The Chinese way to eat noodles in soup is to hold the bowl in one hand and move the noodles from bowl to mouth with chopsticks held in the other hand. You drink the broth straight from the bowl. Westerners can use a fork to eat the noodles, leaning slightly over the bowl, and drink the broth with a spoon.

Homestyle Tofu and Spinach Soup

Yield: 4 servings

This is one of the most common homemade Chinese soups—quick and easy to make, nutritious and cheap. It seems that everyone's mother has her own recipe!

5 cups good vegetarian broth
1½ pounds fresh spinach, cleaned and trimmed
2 ounces bean thread noodles (fen si, cellophane noodles, or pea-starch noodles), cut in 3-inch lengths and soaked in hot water to cover for 5 to 10 minutes
8 ounces medium-firm tofu, cubed
3 tablespoons dry sherry
2 tablespoons light soy sauce
2 teaspoons light unbleached sugar

Heat the broth in a medium soup pot or large wok over high heat. Add the spinach and cook for 2 minutes. Drain the noodles, and add to the soup. Cook for 2 minutes. Add the remaining ingredients and cook just enough to heat the tofu. Serve immediately.

Per serving: Calories 173, Protein 9 g, Fat 2 g, Carbohydrates 23 g

Tofu, "Ham," Spinach, and Mushroom Soup

Yield: 8 servings

A thick and tasty soup that can be thrown together quickly.

Variation

For a full meal soup, add 6 ounces thin, dried Chinese wheat noodles or spaghettini.

1 (10-ounce) package whole frozen spinach, thawed, squeezed dry, or 1 pound fresh spinach, washed, dried, and trimmed
8 cups vegetarian broth
8 medium dried Chinese black mushrooms, soaked in hot water for 20 to 30 minutes until soft, stems discarded, and sliced (save the soaking water)
1 pound medium-firm tofu, cut into ½-inch cubes
2 cups sliced white mushrooms
½ cup slivered vegetarian "ham" or "Canadian back bacon"
2 tablespoons light soy sauce
1 tablespoon cornstarch dissolved in 1 tablespoon cold water
Freshly-ground white or black pepper to taste
2 teaspoons roasted sesame oil

Coarsely chop the spinach.

Bring the broth and mushroom soaking water to a boil in a large pot. Add all of the ingredients except the cornstarch, pepper, and sesame oil. Return to a boil, then stir in the cornstarch mixture, and simmer over medium heat for 3 to 4 minutes. Add the pepper, drizzle with sesame oil, and serve.

Per serving: Calories 114, Protein 8 g, Fat 4 g, Carbohydrates 10 g

VELVET CORN SOUP

Yield: 4 servings

6 to 7 ounces firm tofu
1 tablespoon vegetarian stir-fry sauce "oyster" sauce (p. 116)
½ tablespoon oil
4 cups vegetarian broth
1 (14- to 15-ounce) can creamed corn
1 cup frozen petit pois (baby peas)
1 tablespoon light soy sauce
Optional: **1 tablespoon soy "bacon" chips, or 2 tablespoons chopped vegetarian "ham" or "Canadian back bacon"**
White pepper, to taste
1 tablespoon cornstarch dissolved in 1 tablespoon cold water
1 teaspoon roasted sesame oil

Cut the tofu into very small dice or thin slivers, and toss with the stir-fry sauce. Heat a large, heavy wok or skillet over high heat. When it's hot, add the oil. When the oil is hot, add the tofu. Turn the heat down to medium-high, and stir-fry for several minutes. Don't brown the tofu, just let the sauce be absorbed by it. Set the tofu aside.

In a medium pot or saucepan, mix the broth, creamed corn, peas, soy sauce, and soy "bacon" or "ham," if you're using it. When it comes to a boil, turn the heat down to a simmer, and cook gently until the peas are barely tender. Add the tofu, white pepper, and dissolved cornstarch while stirring. Simmer until the soup thickens, then drizzle the sesame oil on top and serve.

Per serving: Calories 179, Protein 8 g, Fat 5 g, Carbohydrates 25 g

Corn is not the first thing that comes to mind when you think of Chinese cooking, but when it was imported from the Americas, the Northern Chinese took to it readily. This soup, which often contains chicken or crab in its nonvegetarian incarnation, is extremely popular, even at formal banquets, but it's quick and simple to make.

Note: The creamed corn contains no dairy ingredients.

Chinese oyster sauce is a favorite flavoring—thick, rich-tasting, and slightly sweet. Fortunately, there are commercial vegetarian versions available, made with mushrooms instead of oysters. Various brands are labeled "vegetarian stir-fry sauce," "mushroom oyster sauce," or "vegetable mushroom sauce." Whichever you buy, check the label to make sure that the ingredient list does not contain oysters or oyster extract. ("Oyster-flavored sauce," by the way, **does** contain oysters.) Also make sure the sauce is dark brown and very thick. Some "stir-fry" sauces are nothing more than flavored soy sauce. It will be obvious that this is not what you are looking for when you shake the bottle and find it contains a thin liquid.

Vegetarian "oyster" sauce is inexpensive, and I highly recommend that you locate a source for it and have it on hand for Chinese cooking—you will use it often. It keeps indefinitely unopened, or refrigerated after opening. I use it frequently to coat plain tofu for use as a

VEGETARIAN STIR-FRY "OYSTER" SAUCE

Yield: about ½ cup

1 mushroom broth cube
½ cup boiling water
2 tablespoons brown bean sauce
1 generous tablespoon dark unbleached sugar
1 teaspoon cornstarch dissolved in 1 teaspoon cold water

Dissolve the broth cube in the boiling water. Mix with the brown bean sauce and sugar, and heat to boiling. Add the dissolved cornstarch and stir until thickened. Cool and store in a covered jar in the refrigerator.

Per tablespoon: Calories 14, Protein 1 g, Fat 0 g, Carbohydrates 2 g

SPICY DIPPING SAUCE

Yield: about ¾ cup

½ cup light soy sauce
¼ cup rice, cider, or white wine vinegar
2 teaspoons roasted sesame oil
2 teaspoons grated fresh ginger
1 teaspoon dark unbleached sugar
Optional: **Pinch of dried red chili flakes, or ⅛ teaspoon chili garlic paste**

Mix all of the ingredients in a bowl. This can be made ahead of time.

Per 2 tablespoons: Calories 38, Protein 1 g, Fat 0 g, Carbohydrates 9 g

Plum Sauce from Canned Fruit

Yield: about 4 cups

1 cup canned halved and pitted red plums in juice
1 cup canned halved and pitted apricots in juice
½ cup drained roasted red peppers or pimientos from a jar
1 cup light unbleached sugar
½ cup plum jam
2 tablespoons light soy sauce
½ cup rice, cider, or white wine vinegar
1 tablespoon grated fresh ginger
1 teaspoon minced garlic
¼ teaspoon freshly ground white pepper
Optional: **1 teaspoon five-spice powder**
½ teaspoon ground cinnamon
½ teaspoon cumin
½ teaspoon powdered mustard
¼ teaspoon dried red chili flakes

Place all of the ingredients in a blender, and blend until smooth. Place the blended mixture in a medium non-aluminum pot, and bring to a boil over medium-high heat, stirring often with a wooden spoon. Cover, turn down the heat to low, and simmer for 20 minutes, stirring occasionally. Pour the hot sauce into 4 sterilized half-pint canning jars to within ½ inch of the rim. Wipe the rims with a clean cloth. Seal the jars with new lids and rings. Water-bath can by boiling in a kettle of boiling water, on a rack, with the water 2 inches above the level of the jars, for 15 minutes. Remove the jars from the kettle, and let them cool completely. Test the lids for a seal before removing the rings.

Note: This recipe needs to be canned by the water-bath canning method. Please consult a book on canning.

Per 2 tablespoons: Calories 35, Protein 0 g, Fat 0 g, Carbohydrates 9 g

chicken substitute in stir-fries and fried dishes, and also as a seasoning in sauces.

The brand I use is Lee Kum Kee Vegetarian Stir-Fry Sauce (Mushroom Flavored), from Hong Kong. It is made from essence of shiitake mushrooms. This company makes a number of other Chinese sauces and condiments which are widely available in North America. If your Asian grocery store or large supermarket carries the Lee Kum Kee brand of regular oyster sauce or other condiments, they can probably order the Vegetarian Stir-Fry Sauce.

If you can't locate this important condiment in your area, perhaps you can stock up on it when you visit a large city with Asian grocery stores. Otherwise see p. 185 for a list of mail-order websites.

If you cannot buy it, it's easy to make an acceptable substitute, but you need mushroom broth cubes. I have only used Hugli brand mushroom broth cubes, a Swiss brand, but you can experiment with other brands.

QUICK AND EASY PLUM SAUCE

Yield: ¾ cup

This is easy to make on the spur of the moment. It's especially good if you have your own home-made jam and chutney.

½ tablespoon light unbleached sugar
½ tablespoon rice, cider, or white wine vinegar
½ cup plum jam (any kind)
¼ cup finely-chopped sweet chutney

Let the sugar dissolve in the vinegar. (You can heat it if you want to speed this up.) Then mix all the ingredients together.

Per 2 tablespoons: Calories 35, Protein 0 g, Fat 0 g, Carbohydrates 9 g

BLACK BEAN DIPPING SAUCE

Yield: about ⅞ cup

This is a great dipping sauce for Northern-Style Boiled Dumplings (pp. 73-74).

6 tablespoons water or mushroom soaking water
¼ cup fermented black beans, minced
2 tablespoons light soy sauce
2 tablespoons dry sherry
2 tablespoons roasted sesame oil
4 teaspoons unbleached sugar
2 cloves garlic, crushed
½ teaspoon dried red chili flakes

Mix all of the ingredients together in a bowl. This can be made ahead of time.

Per 2 tablespoons: Calories 64, Protein 2 g, Fat 5 g, Carbohydrates 4 g

DUCK SAUCE

Yield: about ⅞ cup

½ cup water
4 tablespoons brown bean sauce
4 tablespoons light unbleached sugar
2 tablespoons roasted sesame oil

Mix the ingredients in a small saucepan. Stir over high heat until the sugar is dissolved, and the mixture has thickened to your liking. Chill the mixture before serving.

Per 2 tablespoons: Calories 72, Protein 1 g, Fat 5 g, Carbohydrates 7 g

Although many recipes for "Duck sauce" call for plum sauce or hoisin sauce, the traditional sauce in China is made with brown or yellow bean paste (p. 14). Serve this with Buddha's Roast "Duck" (p. 56).

SWEET-AND-SOUR DIPPING SAUCE

Yield: about ¾ cup

½ cup cold vegetarian broth
3 tablespoons unbleached sugar
3 tablespoons rice, cider, or white wine vinegar
1 tablespoon light soy sauce
1 tablespoon ketchup or tomatoey chili sauce
1 tablespoon cornstarch
Optional: **½ teaspoon chili garlic paste, or a dash of cayenne**

Mix the ingredients in a small saucepan, and stir over high heat until thickened.

Per 2 tablespoons: Calories 34, Protein 0 g, Fat 0 g, Carbohydrates 8 g

This is a good sauce to serve with Shanghai Spring Rolls (p. 63-65).

SPICY PEANUT SAUCE

Yield: about 1 cup

¼ cup natural peanut butter
2 tablespoons roasted sesame oil
2 tablespoons dark or mushroom soy sauce
2 tablespoons Chinese black vinegar or balsamic vinegar
6 to 8 tablespoons water (depending on the thickness you like)
4 teaspoons unbleached sugar
1 teaspoon chili garlic paste
Salt to taste
2 teaspoons minced garlic
2 tablespoons chopped green onion

Use this as a dipping sauce for Steamed Spring Rolls (pp. 63-65) or as a sauce for cold noodles.

Allergy Note

If you have a peanut allergy, you can substitute any other roasted nut butter for the peanut butter.

Place the peanut butter in a small mixing bowl. Stir in the sesame oil. When it's smooth, stir in the rest of the ingredients, except the garlic and green onions. Use 6 tablespoons water at first, then add more if it's too thick for your liking. Taste for salt. You can refrigerate this for several hours before serving. Sprinkle with the garlic and green onion just before serving.

Per 2 tablespoons: Calories 88, Protein 3 g, Fat 7 g, Carbohydrates 4 g

Hot Mustard

Chinese hot mustard, which is often served with dim sum and dumpling dishes, along with a dish of chili garlic paste, is made simply by mixing powdered mustard with equal parts cold water. The English type of mustard powder, such as Colman's, is the best type to use. Do not use prepared mustard—you must use powdered mustard.

Soy-Vinegar Dipping Sauce is an all purpose sauce for dumplings, and can also be used on noodles.

SOY-VINEGAR DIPPING SAUCE

Yield: about ⅔ cup

¼ cup light or dark soy sauce
¼ cup vinegar (with light soy sauce, use rice, cider, or white wine vinegar; with dark soy sauce, use Chinese black vinegar or balsamic vinegar)
2 tablespoons roasted sesame oil
2 teaspoons sugar

Mix all of the ingredients together in a bowl.

Per 2 tablespoons: Calories 66, Protein 1 g, Fat 5 g, Carbohydrates 4 g

Stir-frying (or "chowing," from the Chinese term "chao") is probably the most widely-used and widely-known Chinese cooking technique. It is an ancient technique, devised to save fuel and time. The traditional cooking vessel, the wok, was devised as a wide-mouthed, shallow cone, with a curved base that could fit snugly inside of a charcoal stove or brazier with a circular opening in the top. This type of stove and cooking vessel is used all over Asia and India.

Stir-frying is basically a technique for fast-frying or sautéing small pieces of food in a little oil over fierce heat ("Big Heat" in Chinese). The ingredients are tossed continuously for a few minutes, so that they cook evenly all over. The average stir-fry dish takes 3 to 5 minutes to actually cook. It's a great way to showcase very fresh vegetables.

I recommend using expeller-pressed Asian peanut oil for stir-frying. It is a fragrant, tasty, healthy oil high in monounsaturated fats. It stands up well to high temperatures. (See p. 16 about vegetable oils and p. 169 about oils for frying.)

I sometimes use a little roasted sesame oil for stir-frying, even though most Chinese cooks would consider this heretical. Because it is expensive, sesame oil is usually added to dishes after cooking for flavor and to add shine. However, when you are using a very small amount of oil for low-fat cooking, you want to make every fat gram count in terms of flavor, and roasted sesame oil is long on flavor.

A wok is the best implement to stir-fry in, but, if you don't have one see pp. 33 for alternatives.

It's easy to learn to stir-fry—most of the work is in the preparation.

HERE ARE SOME THINGS TO REMEMBER

Before you begin to cook, you must assemble all of your ingredients—you won't have time to cut or mix anything when you are in the middle of stir-frying! Slice, dice, chop, marinate, mix everything first, and arrange it within an arm's reach of the stove. If you are doing more than one stir-fry dish, do one at a time, and arrange all of the ingredients for each dish on a separate tray or counter, so you don't mix them up.

Do not double or triple stir-fry recipes. If you need to cook more, do it in batches—it goes very fast. Stir-frying too much at a time may cause foods to stew.

Chapter XI

STIR-FRIED DISHES

"Variation of texture runs like a minor theme throughout the whole of Chinese gastronomy."

Hsiang Ju Lin and
Tsiufeng Lin,
Chinese Gastronomy

Before you start this chapter, read the section about equipment on pp. 31-37. You will find information about types of stoves and pots for stir-frying, how to season, cook in, clean, and store a wok, and how to use a Chinese cleaver.

"Dry-Frying"
The Low-Fat Alternative

Chinese cooks sometimes use a method called "dry-frying," which is like stir-frying, but in a hot wok with no oil, or just a tiny bit. If you are on a low-fat regimen, you might like to convert your stir-fry recipes to this method. A good example of this is the Pineapple Sweet and Sour on pp. 133-134.

Heat the wok until it is very hot. If you like, add a teaspoon of roasted vegetable oil. (It gives you the most flavor for the least fat grams.) Stir-fry the same as described in this section, but if the food sticks, add a few drops of water, wine, or broth, just enough to keep the food moving—not enough to stew the ingredients. This method is not quite as tasty as stir-frying with some oil, but it works very well with strongly-seasoned dishes.

Use the hottest coil on your electric stove. (One is usually hotter than all the others.) To adjust the heat while stir-frying on an electric burner, just slide the pan off and on the burner.

If you have a gas stove, your maintenance person may be able to raise the flame for you on one burner, so that it will go as high as it can while still remaining blue.

Place your serving plate in an oven on low heat to keep it warm—you don't want the food to cool before you get it to the table.

Have your rice cooked first. Leave the lid on to keep it warm.

WHEN YOU BEGIN TO STIR-FRY

Heat your dry, clean wok or skillet over high heat until it is very hot before adding the oil. To test for the "big heat," sprinkle a few drops of water in the pan. They should dance around and evaporate immediately.

Add the oil (usually 1 to 3 tablespoons) and swirl it around.

Let the oil heat up until it's very hot, but not smoking. Test the heat of the oil by adding a tiny piece of food to it. If it sears immediately, it's hot enough.

If you need to add more oil during the cooking process, dribble it down the side of the wok, so that it heats up before it hits the food. Keep the heat high the whole time unless indicated.

You must have firm control of the wok. Use an oven mitt to grasp the handle if it's metal, and stir-fry with the other hand.

Add the "aromatics," "fragrant ingredients," or flavoring agents to the hot oil. These are usually onion, ginger, or garlic or a combination. Lower the heat or slide the pan off the heat so that they do not burn. Stir them for just a few seconds until the fragrance has "exploded," as the Chinese say.

Turn up the heat or slide the pot back on the burner, and add your marinated or coated protein, if you are using it—tofu, seitan or gluten, or textured soy protein. If the protein is juicy, it should be drained and coated in cornstarch before adding to the pan. Don't cook more than 1 cup at a time. If you have more, do it in batches. Stir-fry briskly with a wok spatula, tossing with an over-and-under motion constantly, until the food browns. Sometimes the protein is removed and added back to the pan later—sometimes it is left in. The recipe will tell you what to do.

Use firm or extra-firm tofu for stir-frying. You can also use deep-fried or oven-fried tofu in stir-fries.

Add vegetables a handful at a time. First add the ones that take the longest time to cook (the reconstituted dried mushrooms and tougher vegetables), then the green leafy or more fragile vegetables, and end with the ones that take the least time to cook, such as bean sprouts.

Vegetables should be as dry as possible, so that they won't stew.

Very firm vegetables, such as carrots, may be partially cooked ahead of time (steamed or microwaved). After partially cooking, they should be plunged immediately into ice-cold water to stop the cooking process and preserve their bright colors.

Toss and turn the vegetables until they are lightly cooked. *Never* overcook. Remember, they will cook a little bit more during the last part of the process, and even more in the residual heat after cooking. The vegetables should be "crisp-tender," or tender with just a hint of crispness on the inside, and bright in color. Discoloration or faded color is a sign of overcooking.

However, do not undercook the vegetables either. In some Western restaurants, cooks seem to think the vegetables in a stir-fry should be almost raw. I find this is very annoying.

Add liquid ingredients and seasonings, such as wine, soy sauce, etc. Unless you particularly want a lot of "gravy" to go on noodles or to add to a meal largely made up of rice, don't use much liquid. If you are adding the protein back to the pan, do it now.

Last of all, add the thickening agent, if one is being used. (In some regions of China, thickeners are not used.) This is usually cornstarch dissolved in water. Sometimes more seasonings are added to this mixture. Stir it until it thickens. It should be velvety-smooth.

Slide the food onto your heated serving platter or bowl, and serve immediately. Diners should be ready and waiting at the table.

Note: The most important caveat of Chinese cuisine is to buy the freshest vegetables you can, preferably in season. This is doubly important for vegetables in a stir-fry, where they are just barely cooked.

Note: To make the vegetables glisten attractively, drizzle a small amount of fragrant roasted sesame oil over the finished dish. Don't do this to every dish or you risk making everything taste the same.

Take any of the stir-fried dishes in this chapter which involve vegetables, and just leave out the protein ingredient, and you have a vegetable dish. Add more vegetables, or some mushrooms, if that seems appropriate.

However, if your menu needs a simple vegetable dish, a clean-tasting Cantonese-style stir-fry seasoned lightly with salt, sugar, oil, and sometimes wine, can't be beat—especially when the vegetables are fresh and in season.

Anything from asparagus and brussels sprouts to carrots, to green beans, to zucchini can be cooked this way. You can cook one kind of vegetable or combine two, three, or more. If you cook more than one, try to have some contrasting colors, such as broccoli and red peppers, or green beans with carrot slices.

Vegetables take differing amounts of time to cook. Bean sprouts and snow peas, for instance, take very little time—just a minute or two. Read about stir-frying on pp. 121-123.

BASIC STIR-FRIED CHINESE VEGETABLES

Yield: 4 servings

2 tablespoons oil

1 pound fresh vegetables, cut into small pieces

½ teaspoon salt

1 teaspoon sugar

Optional: **1 teaspoon grated ginger**

Optional: **1 or more cloves garlic, chopped**

Optional: **1 teaspoon sesame oil**

Heat a large wok or heavy skillet over high heat. When it's very hot, add the oil. When the oil is hot, add the vegetables, salt, and sugar and any optional ingredients, except the soy sauce or vegetarian "oyster" sauce and sesame oil. Stir-fry quickly over high heat until the vegetables are just "crisp-tender." If the vegetables are very dry, or are firm and have not been pre-cooked, or they are sticking, add a little water just a tablespoon at a time, while you stir-fry. Avoid getting them too wet or they will stew.

As soon as the vegetables are perfectly cooked, add soy sauce or vegetarian "oyster" sauce if you like, and toss well. Add salt to taste and the sesame oil. Place the vegetables on a heated platter, and serve immediately.

Per serving: Calories 95, Protein 2 g, Fat 7 g, Carbohydrates 6 g

STIR-FRIED CHINESE BROCCOLI

GAI LAN

Yield: 4 servings

1 pound Chinese broccoli (gai lan)
2 tablespoons oil
½ teaspoon salt
1 teaspoon sugar
1 tablespoon soy sauce or vegetarian stir-fry "oyster" sauce
(p. 116)

Clean and trim the broccoli of old, tough leaves. Blanch the whole stalks in boiling water until the stems are just crisp tender. Drain and immerse them in very cold water to stop the cooking. Drain well and pat dry with a towel.

Heat a large wok or heavy skillet over high heat. When it's very hot, add the oil. When the oil is hot, add the broccoli, along with the salt and sugar. Stir-fry for about 2 minutes, then add the soy sauce, and toss well. Add more salt to taste. Arrange the stalks neatly on a heated platter, and serve immediately.

Per serving: Calories 97, Protein 2 g, Fat 7 g, Carbohydrates 6 g

Note: Very firm vegetables can be blanched in hot water or steamed or microwaved until they are just partially-cooked, then plunged into icy water to stop further cooking. This makes the stir-frying go faster and makes it possible to cook firm vegetables at the same time as more tender or fragile vegetables.

Chinese broccoli is one of my favorite vegetables of all time. Read more about this delicious and very nutritious vegetable on p. 19.

Although I give you some optional ingredients and flavor variations, keep in mind that the taste of the vegetable should come through. This is not meant to be a highly-spiced dish, nor is it meant to have a sauce.

**Variations for
Stir-Fried Chinese
Broccoli**

Instead of the salt, use 1 tablespoon light soy sauce; or ½ tablespoon salted or fermented black beans, chopped; or 1 tablespoon vegetarian stir-fry "oyster" sauce (p. 116).

You can add a few sliced rehydrated dried Chinese black mushrooms or fresh mushrooms. To add onion, cut a small peeled onion into 6 wedges, then separate the layers. You can also add a bit of dried red chili flakes or chili garlic paste, for a spicy dish. Just a few slivers of vegetarian "ham" or "Canadian back bacon" can add flavor.

Mu Shu Tofu

Yield: 4 servings

Mu Shu Pork is traditionally served with Mandarin Pancakes (p. 87-88), thin Chinese wheat flour "tortillas." Here, tofu stands in for the pork and the scrambled eggs or omelet that is added to the dish. If you prefer, you can use about 1½ cups of commercial seitan or homemade Braised Chinese Seitan (p. 46), Red-Braised Seitan (p. 47), cut into slivers, You can also substitute slivers of reconstituted flavored cooked textured soy protein chunks or cutlets (pp. 50-51) for the tofu slivers, and just use the tofu for the scrambled part.

You need a few traditional Chinese dried ingredients for this dish—dried mushrooms, "golden needles" (dried tiger lily buds), and tree ear fungus. It's a fun and casual dish for company.

Note: You will need a total of 12 ounces firm tofu for this dish.

4 to 5 medium dried Chinese black mushrooms
½ ounce dried "golden needles" (tiger lily buds), p.20
½ ounce tree ear (black) fungus (wood ear), p. 22

Scrambled Tofu:

6 ounces firm tofu
2 tablespoons nutritional yeast flakes
1 tablespoon light soy sauce
¼ teaspoon turmeric
¼ teaspoon onion powder
⅛ teaspoon garlic granules

Slivered Tofu:

6 ounces firm tofu
1 tablespoon roasted sesame oil
2 cloves garlic, chopped
4 green onions, shredded

Sauce:

2 tablespoons light soy sauce
1 tablespoon brown or yellow bean sauce
1 tablespoon dry sherry
1 tablespoon mushroom soaking broth
1 teaspoon unbleached sugar

24 Mandarin Pancakes (pp. 87-88)

In separate bowls, soak the dried mushrooms, "golden needles," and tree ear fungus in boiling water for 20 minutes. When they are soft, drain them. Discard the mushroom stems, cut the hard tips off the "golden needles," and cut everything into slivers.

Mash 6 ounces of the tofu with a fork along with the nutritional yeast, 1 tablespoon soy sauce, turmeric, onion powder, and garlic granules. Scramble or stir-fry the mashed tofu in a nonstick pan over high heat, turning with a spatula constantly, until it resembles scrambled eggs; set aside.

Cut the remaining 6 ounces of tofu into thin slivers. Heat a large wok or heavy skillet over high heat until it's very hot. Add the sesame oil. When the oil is hot, add the tofu slivers and stir-fry until they start to brown. Add the garlic, green onions, slivered mushrooms, "golden needles," and tree ear fungus. Stir-fry for a few more minutes. Add the sauce ingredients and toss well. Add the scrambled tofu and mix.

Serve with Mandarin pancakes. Each diner places a bit of the mu shu mixture on a pancake, rolls it up, and eats it with their hands.

Per serving: Calories 402, Protein 15 g, Fat 14 g, Carbohydrates 51 g

Stir-Fried "Eggs," Tofu Scramble,
or Authentic Foo Yung

Yield: 2 servings

Scramble:

6 ounces firm tofu
2 tablespoons nutritional yeast flakes
1 tablespoon light soy sauce
Optional: **1 tablespoon dry sherry**
½ tablespoon roasted sesame oil
¼ teaspoon turmeric
¼ teaspoon onion powder
⅛ teaspoon garlic granules
Freshly ground pepper to taste
½ tablespoon oil

Vegetables:

½ tablespoon oil
½ medium red bell pepper, seeded and sliced
½ medium green bell pepper, seeded and sliced
1 medium onion, thinly sliced
½ cup sliced celery

Egg foo yung in China is basically a scrambled (or stir-fried) egg dish with vegetables and other condiments added. I use tofu for a vegan version. It makes a great light meal with rice or Chinese breads at any time of the day and is a good way to use up leftover odds and ends.

Stir-fried eggs are usually served with soy sauce and sesame oil on the side, but occasionally with a sweet-and-sour sauce or vegetarian stir-fry "oyster" sauce (p. 116).

Variations for Foo Yung

You can add a few tablespoons of chopped vegetarian "ham" or "Canadian back bacon," if you like, or some leftover steamed or browned Vegetarian Ground "Pork," (pp. 60-61), or Vegetarian Chinese "Sausage" (p. 52). You can also use ground Braised Chinese Seitan (p. 46) or Red-Braised Seitan (p. 47).

You can substitute other vegetables for the ones I called for—frozen petit pois (baby peas); cucumber; zucchini; fresh tomato; green onions; mushrooms; pre-cooked cauliflower; bean sprouts; thawed frozen corn or canned corn kernels; frozen peas and carrots; diced carrots—to name but a few possibilities.

Stir-Fried "Chicken" and Bell Peppers is an easy-to-make, delectable family dish. Firm or extra-firm tofu coated with vegetarian stir-fry "oyster" sauce makes a wonderful vegetarian "chicken" at a moment's notice.

1 large clove garlic, minced
2 tablespoons light soy sauce
½ teaspoon light unbleached sugar

With a fork, mash together all the "scramble" ingredients, except the ½ tablespoon oil, until well mashed and mixed.

Scramble or stir-fry the mashed tofu mix with the ½ tablespoon of oil in a nonstick pan over high heat. Turn with a spatula constantly until it resembles scrambled eggs, and set aside.

Heat a large wok or heavy skillet over high heat. When it's very hot, add the second ½ tablespoon oil. When the oil is hot, add the vegetables and stir-fry until they wilt, about 3 minutes. Add the soy sauce and sugar. Toss in the scrambled tofu, and stir-fry briefly just to mix and heat. Taste for seasoning, adding salt, pepper, soy sauce, or sesame oil as your taste dictates. Serve hot.

Per serving: Calories 242, Protein 13 g, Fat 14 g, Carbohydrates 16 g

Stir-Fried "Chicken" and Bell Peppers

Yield: 2 to 4 servings

6 to 7 ounces firm or extra-firm tofu
1 tablespoon vegetarian stir-fry "oyster" sauce (p. 116)

Cooking Sauce:

1 tablespoon water
2 teaspoons light soy sauce
1 teaspoon cornstarch
½ teaspoon light unbleached sugar
½ teaspoon salt

½ tablespoon oil
1 teaspoon grated fresh ginger
½ large green bell pepper, seeded and cut into strips
½ large red bell pepper, seeded and cut into strips

Cut the tofu into ¼-inch slices, and then into ½-inch-wide strips. Place in a bowl with the stir-fry sauce.

In a separate bowl, mix the cooking sauce ingredients, and set aside.

Heat a large wok or heavy skillet over high heat. When it's very hot, add the oil. When the oil is hot, add the tofu and ginger. Stir-fry for a couple of minutes over high heat. Add the peppers and stir-fry a couple of minutes more. Add the cooking sauce and stir until thickened. Serve immediately.

Per serving: Calories 104, Protein 5 g, Fat 7 g, Carbohydrates 5 g

Stir-Fried "Chicken" and Snow Peas

Yield: 3 to 4 servings

6 to 7 ounces firm or extra-firm tofu, cut into ½-inch cubes
1 tablespoon vegetarian stir-fry "oyster" sauce (p. 116)
2 teaspoons light soy sauce
2 teaspoons dry sherry
2 teaspoons cornstarch
Dash of white pepper
1 tablespoon oil

Cooking Sauce:
½ cup water
1 tablespoon dry sherry
1 tablespoon light soy sauce
1 tablespoon vegetarian stir-fry "oyster" sauce (p. 116)
1 tablespoon cornstarch
1 teaspoon roasted sesame oil
¼ teaspoon light unbleached sugar

Vegetables:
1 clove garlic, minced

Variation

You can use 2 green peppers, seeded and cut into 1-inch squares, or 1½ cups julienned zucchini instead of the snow peas in this Cantonese favorite.

4 medium dried Chinese black mushrooms, soaked in hot water
  for 20 to 30 minutes until soft, stems discarded, and thinly
  sliced (save soaking water)
½ cup sliced canned bamboo shoots or sliced celery
½ pound fresh or frozen snow peas, trimmed and stringed
Optional: ½ cup toasted cashews or blanched almonds

Mix the tofu cubes with the first tablespoon of "oyster" sauce, the
2 teaspoons each soy sauce, sherry, and cornstarch, and the pepper.
Set aside while you prepare the vegetables.

In a separate bowl, mix the cooking sauce ingredients, and set aside.

Heat a large wok or heavy skillet over high heat. When it's hot, add
the oil. When the oil is hot, add the tofu and garlic, and stir-fry until
the tofu begins to brown. Add the mushrooms, bamboo shoots, and
snow-peas. Stir-fry for about 2 minutes, adding drops of water if
the mixture begins to stick. Add the cooking sauce and stir until it
bubbles and thickens. Stir in the nuts, if you are using them. Serve
immediately.

Per serving: Calories 150, Protein 6 g, Fat 8 g, Carbohydrates 12 g

SICHUAN "BEEF" AND BROCCOLI

Yield: 4 to 6 servings

2 cups reconstituted textured soy protein chunks (see pp. 50-51)
  mixed with 2 tablespoons dark or mushroom soy sauce, or
  Chinese-Style "Beefy" Seitan (pp. 48-49), cut into slivers
1 teaspoon cornstarch
1 tablespoon cooking oil
6 cloves garlic, minced or crushed
1 bunch broccoli (stalks peeled), cut into thin slices
  (about 6 cups)
1 to 2 large onions, each cut into 6 wedges, layers separated
2 tablespoons water
Optional: 1 large red bell pepper, seeded and cut into 1-inch
  squares

Cooking Sauce:

1 tablespoon rice, cider, or white wine vinegar

1 tablespoon chili garlic paste

½ tablespoon light unbleached sugar

1 cup light vegetarian broth

1 tablespoon cornstarch mixed with 2 tablespoons cold water

Mix the soy protein chunks with the 1 teaspoon cornstarch. Heat the oil in a nonstick wok or large skillet over high heat. Add the garlic and soy protein chunks. Stir-fry until the soy protein chunks are browned. Remove from the pan and set aside.

Combine the cooking sauce ingredients in a bowl, and set aside.

Add the broccoli, onions, bell peppers, and 2 tablespoons water to the pan. Cover and cook for 2 to 3 minutes until the broccoli is just crisp-tender. Add a little more water if necessary.

Add the soy protein chunks back to the pan, along with the cooking sauce. Stir until the sauce is thickened, and serve immediately.

Per serving: Calories 113, Protein 8 g, Fat 3 g, Carbohydrates 14 g

"BEEF" AND BROCCOLI IN VEGETARIAN "OYSTER" SAUCE

Yield: 4 to 6 servings

2 cups Chinese-Style "Beefy" Seitan chunks (pp. 48-49), cut into slivers, or 2 cups reconstituted textured soy protein chunks (see pp. 50-51), mixed with 2 tablespoons dark or mushroom soy sauce, cut into slivers

1 teaspoon cornstarch

1 tablespoon oil

1 large clove garlic, minced or crushed

1 thin slice ginger, minced

1 bunch broccoli, stalks peeled and cut into small pieces

1 large onion, cut into 6 wedges, layers separated

This was one of the first Chinese dishes that I learned to make many years ago from Benjamin Lee, a fellow student at Langara College in Vancouver. I used to make him Italian food and he, in return, would teach me some Chinese dishes. I'll bet he'd enjoy this vegetarian version just as well!

Variation
"Beef" and Broccoli in Black Bean Sauce

Omit the "oyster" sauce. Increase the ginger to 1 minced teaspoon, and the garlic to 2 minced teaspoons. Mash the ginger and garlic with 2 tablespoons of fermented black beans on a small plate with the back of a fork. Stir-fry the mixture with the seitan, as instructed. Add 3 tablespoons dry sherry along with the broth.

This Cantonese recipe is more traditional than the pineapple version that follows, but they are both delicious.

Note: Both the seitan and soy protein chunks can be prepared ahead of time.

3 to 4 tablespoons vegetarian stir-fry "oyster" sauce (p. 116)
Pinch of salt
Pinch of sugar
½ cup cold water or light vegetarian broth mixed with a scant
    tablespoon cornstarch

Mix the seitan with the 1 teaspoon cornstarch. Heat a large wok or heavy skillet over high heat. When hot, add the oil. When the oil is hot, add the garlic, ginger, and the seitan. Stir-fry until the seitan is browned. Remove from the pan and set aside.

Add the broccoli, onion, and add 2 tablespoons water to the pan. Cover and cook for 2 to 3 minutes until the broccoli is just crisp-tender. Add a little more water if necessary.

Add the seitan or soy protein back to the pan, along with the remaining ingredients. Stir until the sauce is thickened, and serve with steamed rice.

Per serving: Calories 203, Protein 28 g, Fat 3 g, Carbohydrates 15 g

CRISPY "PORK" WITH SWEET-AND-SOUR SAUCE

Yield: 4 servings

Cooking Sauce:

3 tablespoons tomato sauce, or 1½ tablespoons water plus
    1½ tablespoons tomato paste
2 tablespoons cider, rice, or white wine vinegar
2 tablespoons light unbleached sugar
1 tablespoon light soy sauce
1 tablespoon dry sherry
¾ cup water

1 tablespoon oil
1 large onion, cut into 6 wedges, layers separated
1 large red bell pepper, seeded and cut into 1-inch squares
1 clove garlic, chopped
1 teaspoon grated fresh ginger

½ cup sliced water chestnuts (preferably fresh), or 1 large stalk celery, cut into ¼-inch-thick slices

¼ cup frozen petit pois (baby peas) thawed in hot water and drained

1 tablespoon cornstarch dissolved in 2 tablespoons cold water

24 pieces deep-fried seitan (p. 44), or about 2 to 3 cups reconstituted and deep-fried or oven-fried textured soy protein chunks or small cutlets (pp. 50-51)

In a bowl, mix the cooking sauce ingredients, and set aside.

Heat a large wok or heavy skillet over high heat. When it's very hot, add the oil. When the oil is hot, add the onion, pepper, garlic, and ginger. Stir-fry until the onion starts to turn translucent, adding a few drops of water if necessary, to prevent sticking.

Add the water chestnuts, peas, and cooking sauce. Bring to a boil, then stir in the thickener. Stir until it thickens and quickly add the fried seitan. Stir well and serve immediately.

Per serving: Calories 178, Protein 14 g, Fat 3 g, Carbohydrates 21 g

Pineapple Sweet and Sour

Yield: 6 servings

1 large onion, cut into 8 wedges, layers separated

1 clove garlic, minced

1 teaspoon grated fresh ginger

1 (19-ounce) can unsweetened pineapple chunks and their juice

1 green bell pepper, seeded and cut into 1-inch squares

1 red bell pepper, seeded and cut into 1-inch squares

⅓ cup light unbleached sugar

¼ cup rice, cider, or white wine vinegar

¼ cup ketchup

1 tablespoon light soy sauce

3 cups commercial or homemade (p. 174) deep-fried tofu squares or triangles (cut the triangles in half)

2 tablespoons cornstarch dissolved in 2 tablespoons cold water

Pineapple Sweet and Sour is a restaurant favorite that is a cinch to make at home. This recipe is an example of "dry-frying" or stir-frying without oil, which makes a lighter dish when you are using a deep-fried product as the protein.

For a lower-fat dish, you can use oven-fried tofu or oven-fried reconstituted textured soy protein chunks.

Variations for Pineapple Sweet and Sour

In place of the deep-fried tofu you can also use one of the following:

- 1 recipe Oven-Fried Tofu (p. 175), cut in half or thirds (can be made ahead)

- 3 cups Deep-Fried Seitan pieces (p. 44) (can be made ahead)

- 2 cups button or halved fresh shiitake mushrooms, batter-fried just before adding to the sauce. (See pp. 171-173 about batter frying.)

- 2 cups dry textured soy protein chunks or small cutlets (pp. 50-51)

If you use the textured soy protein chunks, preheat the oven to 400°F. Simmer the chunks in enough boiling water to cover them for 10 to 15 minutes until they are tender. Drain well and pat dry. Roll them in Seasoned Flour (p. 49) and follow the directions for oven-frying on p. 172. If you don't object to a little extra oil, you can deep-fry the pieces instead (see Chapter XIII).

This is one of my family's all-time favorites. It is an adaptation of a Cantonese dish usually made with chicken. You can make almost any Chinese chicken-breast stir-fry vegetarian by substituting an equal amount of extra-firm tofu for the boneless chicken breast.

Heat a large wok or heavy skillet over high heat. When it's very hot, add the onion, garlic, and ginger, and dry-fry, adding sprinkles of water as necessary to prevent sticking. Keep the vegetables moving at all times.

When the onion begins to get slightly translucent, add the pineapple, peppers, sugar, vinegar, ketchup, and soy sauce. When this comes to a boil, add the tofu and the dissolved cornstarch. Cook over high heat until the sauce thickens and the tofu is heated through. Serve immediately.

Per serving: Calories 217, Protein 10 g, Fat 5 g, Carbohydrates 32 g

Asparagus Tofu with Black Bean Sauce

Yield: 4 servings

Cooking Sauce:
½ cup cold water or light vegetarian broth
1 tablespoon light soy sauce
1 tablespoon cornstarch
½ teaspoon light unbleached sugar

12 to 14 ounces extra-firm tofu, cut into slivers
2 teaspoons dry sherry
1 teaspoon water
1 teaspoon cornstarch
1 teaspoon light soy sauce
1 tablespoon oil
2 cloves garlic, minced or crushed
2 teaspoons fermented black beans, mashed with a fork
1 pound asparagus, trimmed and cut diagonally into 1-inch
    pieces
1 medium onion, cut into 6 wedges, layers separated
2 tablespoons water

Combine the cooking sauce ingredients in a bowl, and set aside.

Mix the tofu slivers with the sherry, 1 teaspoon water, 1 teaspoon cornstarch, and 1 teaspoon soy sauce in a bowl.

Heat a large wok or heavy skillet over high heat. When it is hot, add the oil. When the oil is hot, add the garlic and fermented black beans. Stir-fry for a few seconds, then add the marinated tofu. Stir-fry for 3 minutes, then remove to a bowl.

Add the asparagus and onion to the pan, and stir-fry for 30 seconds. Add the 2 tablespoons water to the pan, cover, and cook for 2 minutes. Remove the cover, add the tofu mixture and cooking sauce. Stir-cook until the sauce has thickened. Serve immediately with rice.

Per serving: Calories 160, Protein 9 g, Fat 8 g, Carbohydrates 12 g

SICHUAN KUNG PAO "CHICKEN"

Yield: 4 servings as a main dish

12 to 14 ounces firm or extra-firm tofu, cut into small strips
1 tablespoon light soy sauce
2 teaspoons cornstarch
⅛ teaspoon white pepper
1 tablespoon oil
4 green onions, cut diagonally into ¾-inch pieces
2 teaspoons minced garlic
1 tablespoon chili garlic paste
1 red bell pepper, seeded and cut into ¾-inch squares
1 tablespoon brown bean paste
½ cup cold vegetarian broth
1 tablespoon cornstarch
1 teaspoon light unbleached sugar
1 cup unsalted roasted peanuts or cashews, chopped

Mix the tofu with the soy sauce, 2 teaspoons cornstarch, and white pepper.

Variations

Instead of the asparagus, use 1 pound broccoli flowerettes, cut very thinly, or fresh or frozen snow peas or snap peas with edible pods. You may have to cook the broccoli for 1 or 2 minutes longer than the asparagus, but it should be just crisp-tender. You may also have to add ½ cup broth.

Variation
Asparagus "Beef" with Black Bean Sauce

Substitute about 2 cups of slivered Chinese-Style "Beefy" Seitan (pp. 48-49) for the tofu.

Any dish labeled "kung pao" is spiced with chili paste and garlic and stir-fried with nuts—and is bound to be delicious!

**Variations for
Sichuan Kung Pao
"Chicken"**

In place of the tofu strips use Breast of Tofu "Chicken," (p. 43) cut into small strips, or 2 cups soy protein chunks which have been reconstituted in a "chickeny" broth (see pp. 50-51).

This is a very simple homestyle dish from Northern China, where leeks are frequently used. It is a great winter meal. This was adapted from a recipe in Ken Hom's *Vegetarian Cookery*, BBC Books, London, 1995.

Heat a wok or heavy skillet over high heat. When hot, add the oil. When the oil is hot, add the tofu and stir-fry until lightly browned. Add the green onions, garlic, and chili garlic paste. Stir-fry for 1 minute.

Add the bell pepper and brown bean paste. Stir-fry for 2 minutes.

Stir the broth, 1 tablespoon cornstarch, and sugar together, and add to the pan. Stir until thickened. Sprinkle the peanuts on top, and serve immediately.

Per serving: Calories 337, Protein 15 g, Fat 23 g, Carbohydrates 13 g

Stir-Fried Tofu with Leeks

Yield: 4 servings

Cooking Sauce:
4 teaspoons chili garlic paste
1½ tablespoons dark soy sauce
1 tablespoon dry sherry
½ to 1 cup light vegetarian broth

1 tablespoon oil
**12 ounces leeks, well-cleaned, tough leaves discarded, and
    shredded with a sharp knife (white and green parts)**
3 cloves garlic, minced
**12 to 14 ounces firm tofu made into Oven-Fried Tofu (p. 175), or
    sliced into small triangles and pan-fried in 2 tablespoons hot
    oil until golden on both sides**

Combine the cooking sauce ingredients in a bowl, and set aside.

Heat a large wok or heavy skillet over high heat. When it's hot, add the oil. When the oil is hot, add the leeks and garlic. Stir-fry for about 3 minutes.

Add the tofu and the cooking sauce, and cook 3 more minutes. Serve immediately.

Per serving: Calories 175, Protein 8 g, Fat 7 g, Carbohydrates 14 g

Red Pepper Tofu

Yield: 4 servings

12 to 14 ounces firm or extra-firm tofu, cut into ½-inch cubes
3 tablespoons vegetarian stir-fry "oyster" sauce (p. 116)

Cooking Sauce:

⅓ cup vegetarian broth
6 tablespoons dry sherry
6 tablespoons light soy sauce
2 tablespoons rice, cider, or white wine vinegar
3 tablespoons light unbleached sugar
4 teaspoons chili garlic paste

1 tablespoon oil

Vegetables:

2 tablespoons minced garlic
4 stalks celery, diagonally sliced ¼ inch thick
1 large red bell pepper, seeded and thinly sliced
1 medium onion, thinly sliced

4 teaspoons cornstarch dissolved in 2 tablespoons water
⅓ cup chopped toasted walnuts, almonds, or cashews

This is a colorful and spicy dish which can stand on its own with some steamed rice and simple braised greens. It can also be a lovely addition to a festive meal. It is one of our favorites.

Mix the tofu cubes thoroughly with the vegetarian stir-fry sauce in a bowl, and let stand while you prepare the other ingredients.

Mix the cooking sauce ingredients in a pitcher, and set aside.

Heat a large wok or heavy skillet over high heat. When hot, add the oil. When the oil is hot, add all of the vegetables. Stir-fry over high heat for about 1 minute. Add the tofu and stir-fry 1 minute more. Stir the cooking sauce and pour it into the pan. Bring to a boil, then simmer for 3 minutes over medium-high heat. Add the dissolved cornstarch and stir over high heat until the sauce thickens.

Pour onto a heated platter or shallow serving bowl, and top with the toasted nuts. Serve immediately.

Per serving: Calories 365, Protein 12 g, Fat 12 g, Carbohydrates 26 g

Stir-Fried Peas and Tofu

Yield: 4 to 6 servings

Children enjoy this mild Cantonese-style dish, made with ingredients that you probably always have in the house.

12 to 14 ounces extra-firm tofu
1 tablespoon light soy sauce
1 tablespoon dry sherry
1 teaspoon cornstarch
1 tablespoon oil
1 teaspoon minced fresh ginger
2 cups frozen petit pois (baby peas)
1 cup light vegetarian broth
3 tablespoons light soy sauce
1 teaspoon light unbleached sugar
4 teaspoons cornstarch dissolved in 2 tablespoons cold water

Cut the tofu into thin slices, and then cut the slices into little squares. Toss the tiny squares in a bowl with the 1 tablespoon soy sauce, sherry, and 1 teaspoon cornstarch.

Heat a large wok or heavy skillet over high heat. When hot, add the oil. When the oil is hot, add the marinated tofu. Stir-fry until the tofu browns a little.

Add the ginger, peas, broth, soy sauce, and sugar. Simmer until the peas are just tender, then add the dissolved cornstarch. Stir over high heat until thickened, and serve immediately.

Per serving: Calories 159, Protein 9 g, Fat 6 g, Carbohydrates 16 g

Harvest Moon Stir-Fry

Yield: 4 to 6 servings

Cooking Sauce:

1 cup cold vegetarian broth

1½ tablespoons cornstarch

1 tablespoon light soy sauce

1 tablespoon vegetarian stir-fry "oyster" sauce (p. 116)

½ tablespoon chili garlic paste

½ tablespoon roasted sesame oil

1 tablespoon oil

4 cloves garlic, minced

1 tablespoon minced fresh ginger

½ pound fresh brussels sprouts, cut in half

2 large carrots, peeled and cut into ¼-inch-thick rounds

¼ cup water

½ pound fresh button mushrooms, cut in half

¾ teaspoon salt

¾ teaspoon light unbleached sugar

1 large onion, cut into 6 wedges, layers separated

1 large red, orange, yellow, or green bell pepper, seeded and cut into 1-inch squares

This spicy stir-fry of fall vegetables contains carrot rounds that mimic the full harvest moon and other round vegetables, such as brussels sprouts and onions.

Mix the cooking sauce ingredients in a bowl, and set aside.

Heat a large wok or heavy frying pan over high heat. When it is hot, add the oil. When the oil is hot, add the garlic and ginger, and stir-fry for a few seconds. Add the brussels sprouts, carrots, and water. Stir-fry for 1 minute. Cover and cook over high heat for 1 minute.

Add the mushrooms, cover, and cook for 1 minute. Add the salt, sugar, onion, and bell pepper, and stir-fry uncovered for 1 minute. Cover and cook 1 more minute. Add the cooking sauce and stir over high heat until the sauce has thickened. Serve immediately.

Per serving: Calories 109, Protein 2 g, Fat 4 g, Carbohydrates 14 g

Stir-Fried Vegetarian "Duck"
with Chili, Bell Pepper, and Black Beans

Yield: 2 to 4 servings

Ridiculously easy to make, with outstanding flavor and appearance.

1 (10-ounce) can vegetarian "roast duck" braised gluten (mun chai'ya), rinsed, drained, and cut into small chunks, or 6 ounces extra-firm tofu cut into ½-inch chunks and mixed with 1 tablespoon vegetarian stir-fry "oyster" sauce (p. 116)
1 tablespoon cornstarch
1 tablespoon oil

Vegetables:

½ large red bell pepper, seeded and cut into ½-inch squares
½ large green bell pepper, seeded and cut into ½-inch squares
4 green onions, cut into 1-inch lengths
2 cloves garlic, minced
1 tablespoon fermented black beans
¼ teaspoon dried red chili flakes

Cooking Sauce:

½ cup vegetarian broth
1 tablespoon dry sherry
1 tablespoon light soy sauce
1 teaspoon light unbleached sugar
1 teaspoon cornstarch dissolved in 1 tablespoon cold water

Mix the gluten with the 1 tablespoon cornstarch. Heat a large wok or heavy skillet over high heat. When hot, add the 1 tablespoon oil. When the oil is hot, add the gluten and brown in the hot oil.

Immediately add the bell peppers, onions, garlic, fermented black beans, and chili flakes. Stir-fry for 2 or 3 minutes. Add the cooking sauce ingredients, except for the dissolved cornstarch. Heat to boiling. Stir in the dissolved cornstarch, and stir until thickened. Serve immediately.

Per serving: Calories 128, Protein 5 g, Fat 6 g, Carbohydrates 8 g

CHILI GREEN BEANS

Yield: 4 servings

**1 pound small fresh green beans, trimmed, or frozen small
  whole green beans**
1 tablespoon oil
2 cloves garlic, crushed
½ teaspoon dried red chili flakes
2 tablespoons light soy sauce
½ teaspoon light unbleached sugar
1 teaspoon roasted sesame oil

This is a marvelously simple way to prepare green beans, whether fresh or frozen.

If you are using fresh beans, blanch them for about 2 minutes in boiling water, then drain and place them in cold water. If using frozen beans, thaw them in a colander by running hot water over them. Drain the beans well. *Do not use frozen cut beans for this dish.*

Heat a large wok or heavy skillet over high heat. When it's hot, add the oil and turn the heat down to medium. Add the garlic and chili flakes, and stir-fry for a minute. Add the green beans, soy sauce, and sugar, and turn up the heat to high. Stir-fry for 3 to 5 minutes until the beans are done. Sprinkle with the sesame oil and serve. These beans are also excellent when served at room temperature.

Per serving: Calories 82, Protein 2 g, Fat 5 g, Carbohydrates 8 g

ZUCCHINI WITH GINGER

Yield: 4 servings

1 tablespoon oil
1 pound medium zucchini, cut into ¼-inch slices
1 tablespoon grated fresh ginger
½ cup vegetarian broth
2 teaspoons light soy sauce
1 tablespoon dry sherry
1 teaspoon roasted sesame oil

Zucchini is not a Chinese vegetable, but its delicate flavor and texture adapts well to mildly flavored stir-fries.

Heat a large wok or heavy skillet over high heat until very hot, then add the oil. When the oil is hot, add the zucchini and ginger. Stir-fry for 1 minute. Add the broth, soy sauce, and sherry. Stir-fry over high heat until the broth cooks down a bit and the zucchini is crisp-tender. Remove from the heat, sprinkle with the sesame oil, and serve.

Per serving: Calories 62, Protein 1 g, Fat 4 g, Carbohydrates 3 g

Sichuan Spicy Tangerine "Chicken"

Yield: 4 servings

Dried tangerine peel is a common ingredient in Sichuan cooking. Here I use fresh rind. You can substitute ordinary orange peel successfully too.

3 tablespoons dry sherry
2 tablespoons light soy sauce
12 ounces firm or extra-firm tofu, cut into ½-inch dice, or 2 cups textured soy protein chunks or cutlets which have been reconstituted in a "chickeny" broth, and cut into ½-inch pieces
½ cup flour

Sauce:

2 tablespoons oil
½ teaspoon dried red chili pepper flakes
Optional: **¼ teaspoon crushed Sichuan pepper**
1 heaping tablespoon freshly grated tangerine or orange peel (orange part only—preferably organic)
1 tablespoon rice, cider, or white wine vinegar
1 cup vegetarian broth

Toss the sherry and soy sauce with the tofu, and let marinate for at least 10 minutes.

Toss the marinated tofu in the flour, reserving the extra marinade.

Heat a large wok or heavy skillet over high heat. When it's hot, add 1 tablespoon of the oil. When the oil is hot, add half the floured tofu cubes. Stir-fry until they are fairly crisp and browned. Remove them from the pan, add the second tablespoon of oil, let it heat, and cook the remaining tofu the same way.

Add the first batch of tofu back to the pan, along with the pepper flakes, Sichuan pepper, and tangerine peel. Stir-fry for a minute, then add the vinegar, remaining marinade, and broth. Cook over high heat until most of the broth evaporates. Serve hot.

Per serving: Calories 199, Protein 8 g, Fat 10 g, Carbohydrates 14 g

Spicy "Pork," Greens, and Onions

Yield: 2 to 4 servings

Cooking Sauce:

⅓ cup water or vegetarian broth

2 tablespoons light soy sauce

1 tablespoon light unbleached sugar

1 tablespoon rice, cider, or white wine vinegar

1 tablespoon dry sherry

2 teaspoons cornstarch

1½ cups slivered Braised Chinese Seitan (p. 46) or Red-Braised Seitan (p. 47) or slivered reconstituted textured soy protein chunks (pp. 50-51)

1 teaspoon cornstarch

1 tablespoon dry sherry

1 tablespoon oil

1 large onion, thinly sliced

2 cloves garlic, minced

1 teaspoon grated fresh ginger

¼ to ½ teaspoon dried red chili flakes

2 to 3 cups thinly sliced Chinese greens (pp. 18-19), or Swiss chard, kale, or collards

This easy dish makes an excellent filling for Mandarin Pancakes (pp. 87-88) or for the Northern Chinese Sesame Buns (pp. 85-87).

Mix together the cooking sauce ingredients, and set aside.

Toss the seitan with the 1 teaspoon cornstarch and 1 tablespoon sherry.

Heat a large wok or heavy skillet over high heat. When the pan is hot, add the oil. When the oil is hot, add the seitan and stir-fry rapidly until it begins to brown. Add the onion, garlic, ginger, and chili flakes, and stir-fry until the onion begins to soften, adding a few drops of water as necessary to prevent sticking.

Add the greens and stir-fry until they begin to wilt. Add the cooking sauce and stir until the mixture thickens. Serve immediately.

Per serving: Calories 222, Protein 22 g, Fat 5 g, Carbohydrates 20 g

STIR-FRIED "CHICKEN" AND MUSHROOMS IN VEGETARIAN "OYSTER" SAUCE

Yield: 4 servings

2 cups thinly-sliced extra-firm tofu or Breast of Tofu "Chicken" (p. 43)
1 very small onion, chopped
2 tablespoons light soy sauce
2 tablespoons water
1 tablespoon cornstarch
1 tablespoon oil
1 clove garlic, minced
½ pound fresh mushrooms, sliced
½ cup vegetarian broth
2 tablespoons vegetarian stir-fry sauce "oyster" sauce (p. 116)
1 teaspoon light unbleached sugar

In a medium bowl, combine the tofu, onion, soy sauce, water, and cornstarch. Let stand while you prepare the other ingredients and heat the pan.

This is a vegetarian adaptation of one of the first Chinese dishes I cooked on a regular basis. It is a very luxurious-tasting dish.

Variations

In place of the tofu you can also use canned vegetarian braised gluten (seitan) "roast duck" (mun chai'ya), or "chickeny" reconstituted textured soy protein chunks.

Heat a large wok or heavy skillet over high heat. When it is very hot, add the oil. When the oil is hot, add the tofu mixture and stir-fry for 2 to 3 minutes. Add the garlic and mushrooms, and stir-fry again for 2 to 3 minutes. Add the broth, stir-fry sauce, and sugar. Stir and let the dish boil briefly until the sauce thickens. Serve immediately.

Per serving: Calories 177, Protein 11 g, Fat 8 g, Carbohydrates 11 g

Stir-Fried "Beef" with Peppers and Tomatoes

Yield: 4 servings

Cooking Sauce:

½ cup vegetarian broth

1 tablespoon cold water mixed with ½ tablespoon cornstarch

½ tablespoon dry sherry

½ tablespoon light unbleached sugar

2 cups thinly sliced Chinese-Style "Beefy" Seitan pieces (pp. 48-49)

3 tablespoons light soy sauce

1 tablespoon water

1 tablespoon dry sherry

½ tablespoon cornstarch

2 cloves garlic, minced or crushed

2 tablespoons oil

2 large green bell peppers, seeded and cut into 1-inch squares

2 large tomatoes, cut into 6 to 8 wedges each

Freshly ground pepper to taste

In a medium bowl, combine the seitan with the soy sauce, water, sherry, and cornstarch. Stir in the garlic.

My old school friend Benjamin Lee from Vancouver, B.C. taught me this dish years ago. I had never had tomatoes in Chinese food, and this dish was a revelation.

Variation for Stir-Fried "Beef" with Peppers and Tomatoes

In place of the fresh tomatoes, use 14 ounces whole good quality plum tomatoes, drained. Split them in half and place on a cookie sheet. Broil 3 to 4 inches from the heat until they begin to char. Turn over and repeat on the other side.

Heat a large wok or heavy skillet until very hot over high heat. Add 1 tablespoon of the oil. When the oil is hot, add the bell peppers. Stir-fry several minutes until the peppers are beginning to char and are almost tender. Remove the peppers from the pan.

Raise the heat to high again, and add the remaining tablespoon of oil. When the oil is hot, add the seitan (reserving the marinade), and stir-fry over high heat until it begins to brown a bit. Add the peppers, remaining marinade, tomatoes, and ground pepper, and stir-fry until the tomatoes are heated through.

Add the cooking sauce and cook over high heat until it thickens. Serve immediately.

Per serving: Calories 179, Protein 19 g, Fat 7 g, Carbohydrates 9 g

HUNAN TOFU WITH FRESH GARLIC

Yield: 2 to 4 servings

This delectable dish is made with foods that most vegetarians have in the refrigerator all the time—tofu, celery, carrots, green peppers—so it's a good "fall-back" dish.

6 to 7 ounces extra-firm tofu
1 teaspoon light soy sauce
1 teaspoon dry sherry
1 teaspoon cornstarch
1 tablespoon oil
2 tablespoons minced fresh garlic
½ large green pepper, seeded and cut into squares
½ cup diced celery
2 carrots, scrubbed or peeled and thinly sliced on the diagonal
½ cup vegetarian broth
1 tablespoon dry sherry
2 tablespoons light soy sauce
2 teaspoons cornstarch dissolved in 2 tablespoons cold water

Cut the tofu into ¾-inch squares, ¼ inch thick. Mix the squares in a bowl with the 1 teaspoon soy sauce, 1 teaspoon sherry, and 1 teaspoon cornstarch.

Heat a large wok or heavy skillet over high heat until very hot. Add the oil. When the oil is hot, add the tofu. Stir-fry until it starts to brown. Add the garlic, pepper, celery, and carrots, and stir-fry for 3 to 5 minutes. Add the broth and cook for 1 minute. Add the 1 tablespoon sherry, 2 tablespoons soy sauce, and the dissolved cornstarch, and stir until it thickens. Serve immediately.

Per serving: Calories 138, Protein 6 g, Fat 7 g, Carbohydrates 10 g

STIR-FRY WITH GREENS, MUSHROOMS, AND CURRIED SEITAN

Yield: 4 servings

Cooking Sauce:

1 cup vegetarian broth

2 tablespoons dry sherry

2 tablespoons light soy sauce

2 teaspoons light unbleached sugar

2 teaspoons oil

2 medium onions, cut into 6 wedges, layers separated

4 cloves garlic, minced

12 medium dried Chinese black mushrooms, soaked in hot water for 20 to 30 minutes until soft, stems discarded, and slivered

8 cups thinly sliced dark Chinese greens (pp. 18-19), or Swiss chard, kale, or collards

2 small cans seitan, or ½ recipe Curried Braised Chinese Seitan (p. 47)

2 teaspoons cornstarch dissolved in 2 tablespoons cold water

Combine the cooking sauce ingredients in a bowl, and set aside.

If you have some canned or homemade Chinese curried braised seitan in the house, this is a simple, fast, and delicious meal when served with rice.

Heat a large wok or heavy skillet over high heat. When hot, add the oil. When the oil is hot, add the onions, garlic, and mushrooms. Stir-fry until the onion starts to soften a bit, adding a few drops of water if necessary to prevent sticking.

Add the greens and stir-fry briefly. Add the cooking sauce and seitan, and bring to a boil. Stir in the dissolved cornstarch as soon as the greens wilt. Stir until the sauce thickens, and serve immediately.

Per serving: Calories 226, Protein 15 g, Fat 3 g, Carbohydrates 31 g

FRESH SPINACH STIR-FRIED WITH FERMENTED BEAN CURD (DOUFU-RU)

Yield: 4 servings

Doufu-ru (see pp. 28-29) is an acquired taste, but it is used so subtly in this very common home-style dish that your guests will be puzzling over the delicious seasoning.

1 tablespoon oil
6 cloves garlic, chopped
1 pound fresh spinach, washed, drained, trimmed, and thickly sliced
2 teaspoons white fermented bean curd (doufu-ru)
¼ cup vegetarian broth
2 teaspoons light soy sauce
1 teaspoon roasted sesame oil

Heat a wok or heavy skillet over high heat. When it's hot, add the oil. When the oil is hot, add the garlic and stir-fry for a few seconds. Quickly add the spinach, and then the fermented bean curd and broth. Toss until the spinach wilts, mixing the fermented bean curd around well. Add the soy sauce and sesame oil, and serve immediately.

Per serving: Calories 74, Protein 3 g, Fat 3 g, Carbohydrates 4 g

Although most Westerners associate stir-fried foods with Chinese cuisine, the Chinese use a wide variety of methods. Braising, stewing, and steaming are three low-fat methods that are often used, especially in Northern cooking and during the winter. Braising, stewing, or simmering are divided into two categories in Chinese cooking.

In the "Shao" method, the food is cut, sometimes marinated, browned in oil to seal in the juices and give it rich color, and then placed in a heavy pot or casserole with the braising liquid and seasonings. The food is simmered until tender, and the liquid is reduced to a sauce, just like a western-style stew. Sometimes a thickener is added at the end.

In the "Lu" method, a rich cooking liquid is prepared, and the food is placed in it unseared and is then slowly cooked. The cooking liquid is often saved and used again, though this is not as common in vegetarian cooking. The traditional "red-cooking" lu mixture is water or broth with soy sauce, wine, sugar, star anise or five spice, and tangerine peel. Tofu and seitan can be "red-cooked," but I find the method too strong for the delicate taste of tofu. Try the Red-Braised Seitan on p. 47.

There are beautiful and inexpensive Chinese pots made especially for these cooking methods. Although they are not a necessity, you might like to consider adding one or two to your kitchen. Here is a rundown of Chinese clay pots, and substitutes for them.

CHINESE CLAY AND CERAMIC COOKING POTS

It is not necessary to own Chinese cooking pots for stews and braises, but it will be hard to resist purchasing a couple of Chinese clay and ceramic cooking pots if you shop in an Asian cookware or grocery store. These pots are handsome, cheap, and versatile. They were designed to be used over fires and charcoal braziers and are good-looking enough to come to the table. They adapt well to modern cooking methods and can be used in other styles of cooking as well as Asian.

These pots must be handled with care. Do not heat an empty pot. Apply heat gradually and avoid sudden temperature changes. Avoid placing a hot pot on a cold or damp surface. Use a minimum of detergent when cleaning them.

Chapter XII

BRAISED, STEAMED, AND STEWED DISHES

"If you like good food, cook it yourself."

Li Liweng

Note: European-style clay pots or roasters are not suitable alternatives to Chinese clay pots. They are meant for very slow oven roasting, something unheard of in China.

SANDPOTS

These extremely inexpensive bisque-colored pots are made from a special type of clay that can withstand intense temperatures, so they can be used in the oven and over direct heat. The exterior is unglazed and looks rough and sandy; the interior is glazed dark brown. They come with a lid and one or two handles. Wire is often wrapped around the outside to conduct heat more easily. They range from individual serving size to 5 quarts, and can be squat with sloping sides, or tall and bulbous. Check for cracks before buying.

Some cooks recommend soaking the pot in water for an hour before use, but this isn't necessary if you heat the pot slowly. Always use a heat diffuser ("flame tamer") on electric burners, and also on gas burners if there is no wire wrap on the pot. To use in the oven, place in a *cold* oven and then turn on the heat.

Sandpots are traditionally used for long-simmering stews, braises, casseroles, and rice.

A Western alternative would be any heavy casserole or Dutch oven, such as cast-iron, enameled cast-iron or aluminum, anodized aluminum (like Calphalon), magnalite roasters, or Corning Ware casseroles.

YUNNAN POTS

These are unglazed red clay steam pots with a cone-shaped spout in the center, named for the province in southern China. These ruggedly handsome pots are used for wet steaming. The covered clay steamer is placed in or over boiling water, in a larger pot. If placed in the water, some of the water will be drawn up through the spout to mix with the juices of the food. This is particularly good for soups. You may see western versions of this pot made by enterprising potters, decorated with beautiful glazes. You can steam puddings, cakes, and fruit compotes in these pots too.

If you don't have a Yunnan pot, use an uncovered bowl in a steamer. There are also ceramic English steamed pudding molds that have a cone-shaped spout in the middle. They work perfectly.

GLAZED CERAMIC STEAMING BOWLS

These bowls are used for steaming and soup-making. The covered bowl is set in a pot of water, and the food cooks in its own juices. The bowls can also be used in the oven (start in a cold oven), resulting in a more browned product. You could even use the bowl for baked beans. The bowls are very decorative, usually either with a plain dark brown glaze, or white with blue trim. They are usually 6 or 7 inches in diameter and can hold 1½ to 2 quarts.

An alternative would be any glazed covered casserole.

CABBAGE AND TOFU SANDPOT

Yield: 4 servings

1 pound napa or savoy cabbage

1 tablespoon oil

1 teaspoon salt

1 teaspoon unbleached sugar

12 ounces Oven-Fried Tofu (p. 175) or Homemade Deep-Fried Tofu (pp. 174-175), diced

¼ pound carrots, peeled and roll-cut (see p. 37)

2 tablespoons light soy sauce

2 tablespoons dry sherry

1 teaspoon roasted sesame oil

This is a very simple, homey dish, made with common winter ingredients.

Separate the cabbage leaves, stack them, and thickly slice.

Heat a large wok or heavy skillet over high heat until very hot. Add the oil. When the oil is hot, add the cabbage with the salt and sugar, and stir-fry for a couple of minutes. Transfer the cabbage to a Chinese sandpot, a cast-iron pot, or something similar. Top with the tofu, carrots, soy sauce, and sherry. Cover and bring to a boil. Reduce the heat and simmer for about 15 minutes until the carrots are tender. Drizzle the sesame oil over the top before serving.

Per serving: Calories 152, Protein 8 g, Fat 8 g, Carbohydrates 9 g

Vegetarian Yunnan Pot

Yield: 4 servings

This is a delicious noodle hotpot that makes a versatile and filling lunch. The recipe is long only because there are so many choices! It's a great vegetarian recipe to try in your Yunnan pot, if you have one. Most of the recipes you will see for Yunnan pots contain meat or chicken. If you don't have a Yunnan pot, just use a ceramic bowl.

Variations

In place of the 8 "pork" balls you can use one of the following:

- 1 recipe Oven-Fried Tofu (p. 175)

- 8 large homemade or commercial deep-fried tofu cubes or triangles

- 1 packed cup any kind of home-prepared or Chinese canned gluten (seitan) product (see Chapter VI)

1 tablespoon oil

Vegetables:

¼ pound napa or savoy cabbage, cut into thick slices

1 carrot, scrubbed and thinly sliced on the diagonal

6 medium dried Chinese black mushrooms, soaked in hot water for 20 to 30 minutes until soft, stems discarded, and sliced

2 cloves garlic, chopped

1 tablespoon grated fresh ginger

8 Lion's Head Deep-Fried "Pork" Balls (½ recipe, pp. 157-159), browned as directed in the recipe

1½ to 2 cups cooked plain thin flour and water noodles (gan mian, ji mian, or bai mian), or spaghettini, soba noodles, fettuccine, or linguine

2 large green onions, cut into 1-inch lengths

Cooking Sauce:

⅓ cup water, vegetarian broth, or mushroom soaking water

2 tablespoons vegetarian stir-fry "oyster" sauce (p. 116)

2 teaspoons light soy sauce

1 teaspoon cornstarch dissolved in 1 tablespoon cold water

2 teaspoons roasted sesame oil

Heat a large heavy skillet or wok over high heat. When very hot, add the oil. When the oil is hot, add the cabbage, carrot, mushrooms, garlic, and ginger. Stir-fry constantly until the cabbage starts to wilt. Scrape the vegetables into the bottom of your Yunnan pot or a ceramic bowl that will hold all of the ingredients with some room to spare. Top the vegetables with the protein of your choice, then the cooked noodles, then the green onions. Mix the cooking sauce ingredients together, and pour over the top. Place the Yunnan pot on a trivet or a can in a pot, or fit it into the top of a pot with water in it. (The pot should sit above the water. If it is in the water, too much water might come up through the spout into the food.) Cover the Yunnan pot with its fitted lid.

If you are using a ceramic bowl, place the bowl on a trivet in a large pot with enough water to come 1 or 2 inches up the sides of the bowl. Don't cover the bowl itself, but cover the pot.

Bring the water to a boil. Steam for 30 to 45 minutes over fairly rapidly boiling water, adding more water as necessary. (Keep an eye on it so that the water doesn't boil away.) The cabbage should be tender, but not mushy.

Drizzle with the sesame oil, and serve immediately.

Per serving: Calories 217, Protein 11 g, Fat 4 g, Carbohydrates 31 g

Sandpot Tofu with "Meats"

Yield: 4 to 6 servings

1 tablespoon oil

About 6 ounces commercial seitan, cut into small chunks, or Braised Chinese Seitan (p. 46) or Red-Braised Seitan (p. 47)

2 ounces dried yuba (bean curd skin sticks), soaked in warm water for 10 minutes, then drained and cut into 1-inch pieces

6 dried Chinese black mushrooms, soaked in hot water for 20 to 30 minutes until soft, stems discarded, and sliced (save soaking water)

2 slices vegetarian "ham" or "Canadian back bacon," cut into ½-inch slices

1 pound medium-firm tofu, cut into ½-inch cubes

4 green onions, diagonally sliced

3 slices fresh ginger

Mushroom soaking water plus enough vegetarian broth to make 2 cups

2 tablespoons dry sherry

2 tablespoons light soy sauce

1 tablespoon vegetarian stir-fry "oyster" sauce (p. 116)

Salt and freshly ground pepper to taste

4 to 6 teaspoons roasted sesame oil

• 2 cups oven-fried or deep-fried reconstituted textured soy protein chunks or small cutlets (pp. 50-51)

In place of the flour noodles you can use rice noodles such as ho-fun, Thai or Vietnamese "rice stick" noodles.

Bean curd or tofu "hot-pots" often contain various meats and fresh or dried seafood. These are rich-tasting winter dishes. Here is a vegetarian version which will warm you just as well. You can substitute baked or fried seitan balls, plain or braised (p. 44), or canned vegetarian "roast duck" gluten (mun chai'ya) for the braised seitan, if you like.

Heat a wok or medium heavy saucepan over high heat. When it's hot, add the oil. When the oil is hot, add the seitan and yuba. Stir-fry for 2 to 3 minutes. Add everything except the salt, pepper, and sesame oil. Bring to a boil, turn down the heat, cover, and simmer for about 10 minutes. Taste for salt and pepper.

Serve hot in bowls with steamed rice, drizzling a teaspoon of sesame oil over each serving.

Per serving: Calories 329, Protein 33 g, Fat 15 g, Carbohydrates 13 g

Buddha's Delight

Lo Han Vegetarian Dish or
Eight Treasure Vegetarian Dish

Yield: 4 servings

This is sometimes the only vegetarian dish on the menu in Chinese restaurants. It can be extremely simple or composed of many ingredients. The "eight treasures" refer to 4 fresh ingredients and 4 dried.

You can leave out the tofu and substitute baked or fried seitan balls, plain

8 dried Chinese black mushrooms
½ ounce dried "golden needles" (dried tiger lily buds), p. 20
½ ounce dried tree ear (black) fungus (wood ear), p. 22
2 ounces dried yuba (bean curd sticks)
2 tablespoons oil
½ pound medium-firm or firm tofu, cut into ½-inch cubes
4 ounces fresh mushrooms, sliced
½ pound napa or savoy cabbage, sliced
2 cups almost any fresh vegetable, such as broccoli, cauliflower, snow peas, green beans, bean sprouts, carrots, etc., cut into bite-size pieces if necessary
Mushroom soaking liquid plus enough vegetarian broth to make 2 cups
¼ cup light soy sauce
2 tablespoons dry sherry
1 tablespoon vegetarian stir-fry "oyster sauce" (p. 116)
1 teaspoon sugar
2 tablespoons grated fresh ginger
2 tablespoons chopped green onions
1 teaspoon roasted sesame oil

In separate bowls, soak the dried mushrooms, "golden needles," and tree ear fungus in enough boiling water to cover while you prepare the other ingredients.

Break the yuba sticks into manageable pieces, and soak for 10 minutes in warm water. When they have softened, drain them, and cut into 1-inch pieces.

Cut and discard the stems off the soaked mushrooms. Slice the mushrooms. Cut the hard tips off the "golden needles," and cut them in half. Coarsely chop the tree ear fungus.

Heat a wok over high heat. When hot, add the oil. When the oil is hot, add the tofu and bean curd sticks. Fry until they start to change color. Add the soaked dried ingredients, fresh mushrooms, and other vegetables except snow peas and the green onions. Stir-fry for a few minutes. Add the remaining ingredients except snow peas, green onions, and sesame oil. Simmer for about 5 minutes. Add snow peas, if using, and cook 3 minutes. Sprinkle with the green onions and sesame oil, and serve with hot rice.

Per serving: Calories 259, Protein 14 g, Fat 14 g, Carbohydrates 14 g

or braised (p. 44). Or you can use Oven-Fried Tofu (p. 175), or homemade or commercial deep-fried tofu, chunks of homemade or commercial seitan, or any vegetarian "mock meat," "roast duck," or "mock abalone" (see Chapter VI). Some sliced bamboo shoots and/or diced celery can also be added.

Hunan-Style "Duck" Curry

Yield: 4 servings

1 tablespoon oil

1 to 2 cans vegetarian "roast duck" braised gluten (seitan) (mun chai'ya), rinsed and cut into 1-inch pieces

3 tablespoons curry paste or powder

2 tablespoons minced garlic

2 teaspoons grated fresh ginger

½ teaspoon chili garlic paste

1 large green pepper, cut into 1-inch squares

¼ to ½ pound mushrooms, halved (use ½ pound if you only use 1 can of "duck")

1 large onion, peeled, cut into 6 wedges, layers separated

2 cups vegetarian broth

¼ cup light soy sauce

This is an excellent winter dish. It has all the flavor of a long-cooked stew, but is quick to make. The Chinese generally use an oil-based curry paste, which can be found in most Asian grocery stores. Daw Sen brand from Calcutta is good. A good-quality curry powder will also do.

Curry is not a Chinese ingredient, but was adopted in some areas where there was trade with India. Chinese curry dishes are generally eaten in the winter.

Variation

If you have no vegetarian "duck," substitute about 2 cups textured soy protein chunks which have been reconstituted in a chicken-like broth.

A fabulous way to cook fresh green beans as a side dish. Out of season, you can use the whole small frozen green beans.

¼ cup dry sherry

2 tablespoons cornstarch dissolved in 2 tablespoons cold water

Heat a large wok or heavy skillet over high heat. When it's very hot, add the oil. When the oil is hot, add the seitan, curry, garlic, ginger, and chili paste. Stir-fry for 1 to 2 minutes, then add the green pepper, mushrooms, and onion. Stir-fry for another 2 minutes.

Add the broth, soy sauce, and sherry. Cover, turn the heat down to medium-low, and simmer for 10 minutes. Stir in the dissolved cornstarch, turn the heat up to high, and stir until it has thickened.

Per serving: Calories 184, Protein 19 g, Fat 3 g, Carbohydrates 13 g

GREEN BEANS WITH GARLIC

Yield: 4 servings

2 tablespoons oil

3 cloves garlic, crushed or minced

Optional: **1 tablespoon minced fresh ginger**

1 pound fresh or frozen green beans (thawed if frozen), trimmed and left whole, or cut into 2-inch lengths

4 teaspoons light soy sauce

1 teaspoon light unbleached sugar

1 tablespoon dry sherry

Optional: **1 tablespoon toasted sesame seeds**

Heat a large wok or heavy skillet over medium heat. When it's hot, add the oil. When the oil is hot, add the garlic and ginger, and stir-fry for a couple of minutes until it starts to change color; do not brown. Add the green beans and toss well. Turn up the heat to high, and cook for about 2 minutes. Add the soy sauce and sugar, and stir-fry for 2 minutes. Add the sherry. Reduce the heat to medium, and cook, uncovered, for about 10 minutes. Stir occasionally until the beans are tender. Add a little bit of vegetarian broth if the beans appear to be too dry. Serve hot, room temperature, or cold as a salad. Top with the toasted sesame seeds, if you like.

Per serving: Calories 107, Protein 2 g, Fat 7 g, Carbohydrates 9 g

VEGETARIAN "LION'S HEAD" BRAISED "PORK" BALLS WITH CABBAGE

Yield: 4 servings

"Lion's Head" "Pork" Balls:

1 cup textured soy protein granules

¾ cup boiling water

2 tablespoons light soy sauce

Optional: **2 tablespoons dry sherry**

¾ cup mashed medium-firm tofu, or ½ (12.3-ounce) package extra-firm silken tofu, mashed

1 tablespoon grated fresh ginger

1 tablespoon roasted sesame oil

2 tablespoons vegetarian stir-fry "oyster" sauce (p. 116)

1½ tablespoons cornstarch

½ cup pure gluten powder (vital wheat gluten)

2 tablespoons oil

Vegetables and Broth:

1 pound napa or savoy cabbage

1½ cups "chicken-style" vegetarian broth

2 tablespoons light soy sauce

½ tablespoon light unbleached sugar

½ tablespoon cornstarch dissolved in 2 tablespoons cold water

Optional: **2 tablespoons dry sherry**

Optional: **6 dried Chinese black mushrooms, soaked in hot water for 20 to 30 minutes until soft and stems discarded**

Optional: **1 carrot, peeled and cut into thin "fingers"**

Optional: **Handful of snow peas**

In a medium bowl, soak the textured soy protein in the boiling water, 2 tablespoons light soy sauce, and 2 tablespoons sherry until it has cooled off.

This is one of the most popular home-cooked dishes in China. It's an especially good winter dish, and all you need to serve with it is lots of rice.

Add the tofu to the soy protein along with the ginger, sesame oil, stir-fry sauce, and cornstarch. Mix well. Add the gluten powder. Make sure that the mixture is thoroughly cool before you add the gluten powder, or the mixture will be stringy when cooked. Mix well again, then form the mixture into 16 balls.

Heat a large skillet over medium-high heat. When it's hot, add the oil. When the oil is hot, add the balls and brown until they are golden on all sides. Handle gently. Turn the heat down if the balls brown too fast. Drain the balls on paper, and set aside.

Shred the cabbage and place in the bottom of a heavy cooking pot or Chinese sandpot. Mix the broth, 2 tablespoons light soy sauce, sugar, dissolved cornstarch, and 2 tablespoons sherry. Pour this over the cabbage, and bring to a boil. Place the "pork" balls on top of the cabbage, not in the broth. (They will fall apart if they are cooked in the broth.) Add the mushrooms and/or carrot at this point. Cover and turn the heat down to medium-low. Simmer the mixture for 15 minutes. Add the snow peas and cook for 5 more minutes. Serve hot with steamed rice.

Per serving: Calories 321, Protein 30 g, Fat 12 g, Carbohydrates 17 g

SICHUAN TOFU

Yield: 6 servings

Cooking Sauce:

¼ cup dry sherry

2 tablespoons chili garlic paste

2 tablespoons light soy sauce

1 teaspoon fermented black beans, mashed with a fork

1 tablespoon oil

6 large dried Chinese black mushrooms, soaked in hot water for 20 to 30 minutes until soft, stems discarded, and chopped

6 green onions, cut into short lengths

1½ pounds medium-firm tofu, cut into ½-inch cubes

2 teaspoons cornstarch dissolved in 4 tablespoons cold mushroom soaking water

Optional: **Roasted ground Sichuan peppercorns to taste**

Combine the cooking sauce ingredients in a bowl, and set aside.

Heat a large wok or heavy skillet over high heat. When it's hot, add the oil. When the oil is hot, add the mushrooms and onions. Stir-fry for a couple of minutes, then add the tofu and cooking sauce. Stir-cook for 3 to 4 minutes. Add the dissolved cornstarch and stir over high heat to thicken. Sprinkle with the Sichuan pepper, and serve with rice, hot Mandarin Pancakes (pp. 87-88), or wheat tortillas.

Per serving: Calories 141, Protein 9 g, Fat 7 g, Carbohydrates 7 g

If you like hot foods, you'll love this simple, super-fast dish. Serve with rice or noodles and steamed or stir-fried vegetables, or as part of a larger Chinese meal.

Sichuan peppercorns have a distinctive flavor. Look for them in natural food stores, Asian grocery stores, or the Asian section of large supermarkets. Toast them in a hot, dry skillet until they are aromatic, then grind in a blender or spice grinder and store airtight.

Braised Tofu with Chinese Black Mushrooms

Yield: 4 servings

A richly satisfying dish—the mushrooms are utterly delicious when cooked this way.

½ tablespoon oil

2 green onions, cut into 1-inch lengths

10 dried Chinese black mushrooms, soaked in hot water for 20 to 30 minutes until soft, stems discarded, and cut in half (save soaking water)

Braising Liquid:

1 cup vegetarian broth

¼ cup of the mushroom soaking water

1½ tablespoons light soy sauce

1 teaspoon vegetarian stir-fry "oyster" sauce (p. 116)

½ tablespoon dry sherry

½ teaspoon light unbleached sugar

12 to 14 ounces Oven-Fried Tofu (p. 175)

½ teaspoon cornstarch dissolved in ½ tablespoon cold water

1 teaspoon roasted sesame oil

Heat a large wok or heavy skillet over high heat. When it's hot, add the ½ tablespoon oil. When the oil is hot, add the green onions and soaked mushrooms, and stir-fry for 30 seconds. Add the braising liquid ingredients, and bring to a boil. Add the tofu and let the mixture boil until it reduces by half, about 5 to 10 minutes. Add the dissolved cornstarch and stir until it thickens. Stir in the sesame oil.

Per serving: Calories 135, Protein 8 g, Fat 6 g, Carbohydrates 8 g

MAPO DOUFU

Yield: 4 to 6 servings

Cooking Sauce:

1½ cups water

¼ cup light soy sauce

4 teaspoons chili garlic paste, or 2 crumbled dried hot red chili
peppers

1 cup dried textured soy protein granules soaked 5 minutes in
⅞ cup boiling water

2 teaspoons dry sherry

2 teaspoons soy sauce

2 teaspoons hoisin sauce

½ tablespoon oil

2 teaspoons minced garlic

4 teaspoons minced fresh ginger

1 pound medium-firm tofu, cut into ½-inch cubes and placed in
a colander to drain

4 green onions, thinly sliced

4 tablespoons cornstarch mixed with 4 tablespoons cold water

Combine the cooking sauce ingredients in a bowl, and set aside.

Mix the soaked textured soy protein with the sherry, 2 teaspoons
soy sauce, and hoisin sauce. Set aside.

Heat a large wok or heavy skillet over high heat. When it's hot, add
the oil. When the oil is hot, add the garlic and ginger and stir-fry
briefly. Add the textured soy protein mixture, and stir-fry for 2 minutes. Add the tofu and cooking sauce, and simmer for 3 minutes.

Add the green onions and the cornstarch mixture, and stir over
high heat until thick and bubbly. Serve immediately.

Per serving: Calories 174, Protein 16 g, Fat 6 g, Carbohydrates 13 g

This is a very easy, fam-
ily-style, spicy Chinese
dish which can be served
with rice or noodles and
steamed or stir-fried vegetables, or as part of a
larger Chinese meal.
Instead of the traditional
ground pork or hamburg-
er often used in North
America, I use textured
soy protein.

HUNAN HOT AND SOUR VEGETARIAN "DUCK"

Yield: 4 servings

Canned vegetarian "roast duck," made from wheat gluten, is delicious in this tangy, saucy dish.

2 (10-ounce) cans vegetarian "roast duck" gluten (seitan) (mun chai'ya)
1 tablespoon oil
1 small green pepper, seeded and cut into 1-inch squares
½ cup sliced celery
½ cup thinly sliced carrots
1 tablespoon fermented black beans, mashed with a fork
½ tablespoon minced garlic
1 tablespoon grated fresh ginger
1 teaspoon chili garlic paste
1 cup vegetarian broth
2 tablespoons light soy sauce
2 tablespoons rice, cider, or white wine vinegar
2 tablespoons dry sherry
1 teaspoon cornstarch, dissolved in 1 tablespoon cold water

Rinse the gluten in a colander, and cut it into bite-size pieces. Heat a large wok or heavy skillet over high heat until very hot. Add the oil. When the oil is hot, add the gluten and stir-fry for a couple of minutes. Add the vegetables, black beans, garlic, ginger, chili garlic paste, and broth. Boil for 1 minute. Add the soy sauce, vinegar, and sherry, turn down the heat, and simmer for 4 to 6 minutes. Add the dissolved cornstarch and stir until thickened. Serve immediately.

Per serving: Calories 141, Protein 18 g, Fat 3 g, Carbohydrates 7 g

Spicy Sichuan Eggplant

Yield: 4 servings

Cooking Sauce:

1 cup vegetarian broth

¼ cup chopped green onions

2 tablespoons light soy sauce

2 tablespoons rice, cider, or white wine vinegar

1 tablespoon dry sherry

1 tablespoon chili garlic paste

1 teaspoon light unbleached sugar

2 pounds small Asian eggplants, cut into strips about ¾ inch thick

½ tablespoon oil

1 tablespoon minced fresh garlic

2 tablespoons minced fresh ginger

2 teaspoons cornstarch dissolved in 2 tablespoons cold water

Combine the cooking sauce ingredients in a bowl, and set aside.

Preheat the broiler. Place the eggplant strips on nonstick or lightly greased cookie sheets. Broil 3 to 4 inches from the heat until browned; turn over and brown the other side. The insides should be soft. Set aside. (An alternative method of cooking the eggplant would be pan-frying. See directions on p. 172.)

Heat a large wok or heavy skillet over high heat. When it's hot, add the oil. When the oil is hot, add the garlic and ginger, and stir-fry for a few seconds. Add the broiled eggplant strips and cooking sauce. Mix well and cook over high heat for 2 minutes. Stir in the dissolved cornstarch, and stir until thickened.

Per serving: Calories 98, Protein 2 g, Fat 2 g, Carbohydrates 18 g

This is one of the most delicious eggplant dishes in the world! I have eliminated the deep-frying but not the flavor.

Note: If you can't find the small Asian eggplants, use the large variety, but peel them. If you're not sure how fresh the eggplant is, salt the strips and let them drain in a colander for 30 minutes. Rinse them well and dry before cooking.

Spicy Potatoes, Chinese-Style

For each person, cut a peeled medium potato into ½-inch dice. Add it to a hot nonstick skillet with ½ onion, chopped, 1 clove garlic, minced, and 2 green onions, diced. Stir-fry for a few minutes, until the mixture starts to brown. Add ½ cup water or vegetarian broth, and a teaspoon each of soy sauce and chili garlic paste. You could also add ½ teaspoon vinegar, if you like. Cover and simmer for 5 minutes, or until the potatoes are tender. Taste for salt and pepper. Sprinkle with a little roasted sesame oil.

SIZZLING TOFU AND MUSHROOM STEW

Yield: 3 to 4 servings

This is a very quick and easy Chinese hotpot dish, containing ingredients most of us have around all the time.

10 ounces extra-firm tofu, cut into ¾-inch cubes

Tofu Marinade:

1 tablespoon light soy sauce
1 tablespoon minced ginger
1 tablespoon dry sherry
½ tablespoon roasted sesame oil
1 teaspoon cornstarch
½ teaspoon light unbleached sugar
Dash of white pepper

1 tablespoon oil

Vegetables:

1 tablespoon oil
2 cloves garlic, minced
1 medium onion, thinly sliced
4 large fresh mushrooms, sliced
¼ cup frozen petit pois (baby peas)
1 cup vegetarian broth

1 tablespoon water
1 tablespoon light soy sauce
1 tablespoon dry sherry
½ tablespoon cornstarch

1 green onion, chopped

Mix the tofu cubes with the marinade ingredients, and marinate at least 20 minutes, while you prepare the other ingredients, and put on some rice to cook.

Heat a large wok or heavy frying pan over high heat. When it's hot, add 1 tablespoon oil. When the oil is hot, add the tofu and marinade. Stir-fry until the marinade is absorbed, and the cubes are glazed. Set aside.

In the same pan, or in a 1 quart or larger clay pot with wire, heat the second tablespoon of oil over high heat. (Use a heat diffuser under the clay pot.) When the oil is hot, add the garlic and onion, and stir-fry until the onion wilts. Add the mushrooms, peas, tofu cubes, and broth. Bring to a boil, cover, and simmer for about 3 minutes.

Combine the water, 1 tablespoon light soy sauce, 1 tablespoon dry sherry, and ½ tablespoon cornstarch, and add to the pan. Stir until the broth has thickened. Sprinkle with the green onions, and serve hot.

Per serving: Calories 204, Protein 8 g, Fat 13 g, Carbohydrates 11 g

Steamed Tofu with Spicy Bean Paste Sauce

Yield: 2 to 4 servings

16 ounces medium-firm tofu

Cooking Sauce:

1 tablespoon oil

1 generous tablespoon chopped green onions

½ tablespoon minced fresh ginger

½ tablespoon minced garlic

1½ tablespoons Sichuan hot bean paste or sauce, or brown bean paste with chili garlic paste added to taste

2 tablespoons plus 2 teaspoons light soy sauce

⅔ cup vegetarian broth

1 generous teaspoon cornstarch dissolved in 1 tablespoon cold water

½ tablespoon roasted sesame oil

Optional: **1 tablespoon chopped fresh cilantro**

Cut the tofu into 4 squares. Steam the squares over boiling water for 10 minutes.

This is a homestyle Chinese dish which you would probably not encounter in a restaurant. It makes a wonderful light meal with rice and some greens.

While the tofu steams, prepare the sauce. It goes very fast, so have everything chopped and measured. Heat a wok or heavy skillet over high heat. When it's hot, add the oil. When the oil is hot, add the green onion, ginger, garlic, and bean paste. Stir for 10 seconds. Add the soy sauce and broth, and bring to a boil. Stir in the dissolved cornstarch, and add the sesame oil. Take the pan off the heat.

Drain the tofu in a colander. Cut the drained squares into 1-inch squares, and arrange them neatly on a heated serving plate. Pour the sauce over the squares, and sprinkle with the cilantro.

Per serving: Calories 192, Protein 12 g, Fat 13 g, Carbohydrates 5 g

It seems a bit strange to be doing a whole chapter on fried foods, when most of my cookbooks have been low-fat or ultra-low-fat! However, there are some dishes in Chinese cuisine that are most tasty when deep-fried, or have a deep-fried ingredient as the main component. Deep-frying is one of the most common cooking techniques in Chinese cooking because it can be done quickly in a wok over one burner, and so conserves fuel.

Some people object to deep-fried foods because the fat can be damaged to such an extent that it can cause the formation of free radicals or become carcinogenic. I do not recommend consuming fried foods often. However, deep-fried foods can be an occasional treat without compromising your health as long as you use mostly monounsaturated oil with a high smoking point (read on), use a thermometer and monitor the temperature of the oil constantly so that it never goes higher than 400°F, and *never* reuse frying oil.

Deep-fried foods are usually served in small amounts as part of a larger meal made up of steamed, braised, and stir-fried foods, so the Chinese are able to eat them regularly and not compromise their health or their ability to maintain a healthy weight.

When deep-frying is done properly, very little of the oil is actually absorbed by the food, and the food inside is cooked quickly in its crisp coating, preserving nutrients. If fried foods are greasy, then they have not been cooked properly. It is also important to remember that fat takes a longer time to digest than carbohydrates or proteins, because the enzymes which digest them are in the intestines, not the stomach. Therefore, they make you feel full for a longer time. If you overeat fried foods, this fullness is likely to feel like indigestion. This is another good reason to limit your intake of fried foods.

"Deep-frying" is often actually what is known as "shallow-frying," or frying in only an inch or two of oil. This works well with small pieces of food. Another way of frying which uses a minimum of oil is the pan-frying method, described in the recipe for Breast of Tofu "Chicken" (crispy slices) on p. 43.

Obviously, I am not advocating a switch to deep-fried foods, or promoting fried onion rings and French fries as part of your vegetable quota! But they can be enjoyed on occasion without guilt.

Chapter XIII

DEEP-FRIED OR OVEN-FRIED DISHES

"Good cooking does not depend on whether the dish is large or small, expensive or economical. If one has the art, then a piece of celery or salted cabbage can be made into a marvellous delicacy; whereas if one has not the art, not all the greatest delicacies and rarities of land, sea, or sky are of any avail."

Old Chinese Saying

Allergy Note

I realize that peanut allergies are serious and possibly life-threatening, so, if you have a peanut allergy, substitute another oil where I suggest peanut oil.

CAUTION!

Do not heat oils to the smoking point—the smoke can be carcinogenic. Always use an overhead exhaust fan and/or leave some windows open when you fry, anyway.) Buy a deep-fat thermometer and keep the temperature below 400°F.

The alternative modern, low-fat method—oven-frying—is sometimes acceptable. (I have indicated when either can be used.) Oven-frying is very useful for making a crisp tofu which can be used in place of deep-fried tofu.

Deep-Frying 101

Deep-frying is defined as cooking food in hot fat or oil. The extreme heat firms and seals the surface instantly, trapping air and moisture inside. The moisture steams the food inside and keeps it moist and tender. The outside turns crisp and brown—a very appetizing combination if done right. Although the technique seems quite simple, there are some things to learn before attempting to fry foods.

What kind of oil should be used? The whole subject of healthy oils becomes more and more complicated as time goes on—that's why I prefer to use as little oil as possible in my everyday cooking. Good oils are not cheap—especially if they are organic. Deep-frying takes more oil than you would normally use, and you should discard it after one use. These are all good reasons for making deep-fried foods only an occasional treat.

I don't use solid fats like animal fats or hydrogenated vegetable shortenings, or palm or coconut oils. They are all saturated fats which cause free radicals to form, which can cause arterial damage.

At the other end of the spectrum are polyunsaturated fats. These oils stay transparent and flowing even when chilled. Safflower oil is the most unsaturated oil, followed by sunflower, corn, soy, and cottonseed. Polyunsaturated fats were promoted for many years when doctors became aware of the dangers of saturated fats. Now we know that polyunsaturates have dangers of their own.

To quote Dr. Andrew Weil in his book *Natural Health, Natural Medicine* (Houghton Mifflin Company, Boston, 1990), "Points of unsaturation in fatty acid chains are unstable and vulnerable to attack by oxygen, especially if fats are heated in the presence of air or left standing exposed to air. The products resulting from these oxidation reactions are highly reactive molecules that can damage DNA and other vital components of cells. Diets high in polyunsaturates increase the risk of cancer, speed up aging and degeneration of tissues, and may aggravate inflammatory disease and immune-system disorders." Dr. Weil is talking about free radical damage.

To reduce those health risks, reduce the total amount of fat that you eat, and when you do eat it, use monounsaturated oils. Olive, canola, and peanut oils fall into this category. These oils, used in moderation, do not appear to increase risk of cardiovascular disease, nor do they oxidize rapidly to become carcinogenic.

You want to use a vegetable oil with a high smoking point, because most foods are fried at temperatures between 350°F to 400°F. When a fat or oil reaches the point of smoking, "breakdown" products are already forming. Not only can this cause a disagreeable odor and taste, it can cause the food to be less digestible and create carcinogens. Corn, cottonseed, soy, canola, and peanut oil all have smoking points well above 400°F. Since only canola and peanut oil are sufficiently monounsaturated and have a high smoking point as well, they are the first choices for deep-frying and for stir-frying (which uses intense heat). When you deep-fry in a wok, or shallow-fry, you will be using smaller amounts of oil than you would when deep-frying in a kettle or electric deep-fryer.

Cold or expeller-pressed oils are too expensive for deep-frying if you are on a budget since you are going to discard the oil after frying once. Organic oils are even more expensive. For your occasional deep-frying, you may choose to use commercial supermarket brands of peanut or canola oil. Asian expeller-pressed peanut oils are not cheap, nor are they necessarily organic (it's hard to tell), but they are delicious and far less expensive than many natural foods brands of expeller-pressed oils, so that may be a compromise.

Make sure to buy cold or expeller-pressed oils from a store with a good turnover. Old oils can be rancid. If the oil tastes unpleasant, or produces a burning sensation at the back of your throat when swallowed, it's probably rancid. Rancid oil is not only unpleasant-tasting, it can be full of carcinogens. Oils should be stored in a cool place, preferably in glass bottles, protected from heat, light, and air. Read more about vegetable oils on p. 16.

WHY YOU SHOULD NOT REUSE OIL

Although many cooks save oil to be used again, this is false economy. Dr. Andrew Weil cautions against reusing oil that has been

Broiling or Grilling as an Alternative to Frying

I use this method most often with vegetables, instead of deep-frying them before adding to a recipe. A good example of this method is the Spicy Sichuan Eggplant (p. 163). If you have an indoor grill or a gas barbecue, follow the directions that come with your appliance, placing the food 3 or 4 inches above the heat source. I don't have either, so I use the broiler of my electric range.

I place the pieces of vegetable on an oiled cookie sheet and place the food 3 to 4 inches under the heating element. It's usually not necessary to oil the vegetables, but you can spritz them with a little oil from a pump-sprayer, if you like. Expeller-pressed Asian peanut oil gives the best flavor. Cook the food until it is beginning to char a little, then turn it over and cook it on the other side.

Twice-Frying

This is a favorite Chinese *and* French way of frying foods. Twice-frying allows foods to be pre-cooked and turn out crispy. (This is the authentic way to make French fries very crisp.) First, the food is fried at 350°F until it is pale golden. It is removed and drained on paper. This can be done early on the day it is to be served.

Then, just before serving, the oil is heated to 400°F. (Make sure to use peanut or canola oil for this.) The pre-fried food is added to the hot oil and fried again until crisp and golden brown. It is then drained and served immediately. The second frying actually decreases the amount of oil that is absorbed.

Shallow-Frying

This is virtually the same thing as deep-frying, except that it is usually done in 1 to 1½ inches of oil in a deep frying pan, skillet, sauté pan, or "chicken fryer," so this method conserves oil.

heated to high temperatures. Even though the oil may look all right, the more it is heated, the more oxidation and creation of free radicals. Therefore, oil should be discarded after each use.

WHAT FOODS CAN BE DEEP-FRIED AND HOW SHOULD THEY BE PREPARED?

Almost any vegetarian food can be fried. In most cases, the food should be cut into small pieces so that the insides cook in the short time it takes to brown the outside. Also, the shorter the frying time, the less fat is absorbed. However, vegetarian proteins, such as tofu, textured soy protein, and seitan, are all cooked already, so you could fry large pieces of these foods without having to worry about the insides being raw.

Foods should be more or less the same size, so that they will cook in the same amount of time. Foods should be as dry as possible before they are fried. Surface moisture will make the hot oil foam and it might bubble over the sides of the pan. Very moist foods should be coated with flour, cornstarch, or water chestnut flour (which makes a very crispy product) before frying, or before being coated with batter. If foods are fried without a coating, this is called "dry-frying"; if they are coated with flour, starch, or batter, it is called "wet-frying."

Although vegetarian proteins can be fried without a coating, vegetables should be coated with flour, Seasoned Flour (p. 49), cornstarch, water chestnut flour, or batter to form a casing that holds juices in.

DO YOU NEED ANY SPECIAL EQUIPMENT FOR DEEP-FRYING?

For the cooking vessel, Chinese cooks use their trusty woks, and so do I. You can buy fancy electric deep-fryers with baskets in them. They have the advantage of electric temperature control but, on the other hand, they take a large amount of oil. It's also just another gadget to take up space in your cupboard. (There are small ones available. If you fry a lot, you might like to invest in one. Make sure that it shows the temperature.) I prefer not to use a deep heavy pot or kettle, just because it uses up so much oil.

Another alternative would be a deep electric skillet with an electric temperature control. It will take less oil, if the surface is not too wide. This is good for shallow-frying and pan-frying. An electric wok is great for deep-frying, in terms of both temperature control and conservation of oil. They are not generally recommended for stir-frying because most can't generate the intense heat that is needed.

If you do not have a thermostatically-controlled electric pan, then you will need a deep-frying thermometer with a clamp to hold it to the side of the pot. The little dial-type ones are usually not long enough to fit comfortably in a wok, so try to get the mercury-tube type.

Oven mitts are a must for handling hot pans. Other implements that you will need are tongs for lifting large pieces of food out of the fat; a slotted spoon for lowering foods into the oil and removing them, or a wire skimmer for the same purpose; and paper towels for draining food on. (I use ones made with recycled paper.) You can use brown paper bags, but they aren't as absorbent as paper towels. Some woks come with a wire drainer that hangs over one side of the wok, so that you can lift foods onto it to drain and stay hot at the same time.

WHAT IF YOU DON'T HAVE A THERMOMETER?

Well, I recommend that you get one as soon as you can; they aren't expensive. If you can't wait, though, drop a 1-inch cube of bread in the oil. If it browns in 40 seconds, the oil is about 375°F. If it browns in 20 seconds, it's too hot. If it takes 60 seconds, the oil is 350°F, too cool for most frying.

ARE THERE ANY SPECIAL TIPS FOR SAFETY?

Once you have begun frying, you need to pay close attention. *Don't try to do two things at once.* Plan not to have any distractions. If you have little children, someone else should be nearby to deal with their needs.

If using an electric pan, make sure the cord is intact and is out of the way. Make sure that the pan is steady. Try to use a back burner on a stove. Keep little children well away while you are frying, and place any handles where they will not be bumped or can easily be reached by children.

If you watch the temperature with a thermometer, or if it is electronically controlled, there should be no chance of fire. However, if the pan should flame for any reason, turn off the heat immediately. *DO NOT PICK UP THE PAN*—air currents may blow the flames

Batter-Frying

You can batter-fry many vegetarian foods. Some of my favorites are small fresh mushrooms (including shiitakes and wild mushrooms), textured soy protein chunks, and strips of tofu and seitan (particularly Seitan "Seafood," p. 45). I also like strips of unpeeled small Asian eggplant or peeled large eggplant that have been salted, left to drain for 30 minutes, then washed well and dried well. All of these foods can then be added right at the end of a stir-fry instead of fried meat, chicken, or seafood. They can also be served with a sauce or dip as an appetizer.

Cut the food into whatever size you like. Make sure the food is as dry as possible. If it is quite juicy, you might like to coat it with plain flour first so that the batter clings to it better. Follow the directions for deep-frying (pp. 172-173).

Pan-Frying

This is a method of making foods crispy without using a lot of oil. The food can be coated with Seasoned Flour (p. 49) or left plain. Use a large heavy skillet at medium heat. Heat 1 or 2 tablespoons of oil in the skillet. Add the food in a single layer and cook on medium heat until the bottom is golden and crispy. Turn the food over and cook the other side the same way. A good example of this method using a coating is the crispy slices of Breast of Tofu "Chicken" (p. 43). Strips of eggplant or zucchini are good panfried this way as an alternative to grilling or deep-frying.

Oven-Frying Tofu, Textured Soy Protein, and Seitan

This is the modern low-fat alternative method of frying. It can be very satisfactory for some things, but you must be the judge of the results. It is an excellent way to "fry" tofu that is to be used in stews, stir-fries, etc. It can also be used for browning seitan and reconstituted tex-

toward you. Drop a lid over the pan if the oil in the pan is burning. Sprinkle baking soda around it, or even in it. (You should always have a box of baking soda near the stove for this purpose.) *Never* throw water on a grease fire—it will only spread the flame. When the fire is out, open the windows to air out the harmful smoke, and don't clean up anything until it has cooled off.

SO HOW DO YOU DEEP-FRY?

I'll reiterate this important caution—once you have begun frying, you need to pay close attention to it, so don't try to do two things at once. Plan not to have any distractions. If you have little children, someone else should be nearby to deal with their needs.

Have the foods cut, dried, and arranged close at hand. Have your batter ready. The food itself should be at room temperature so that it doesn't lower the temperature of the oil. The batter should be cold. You can coat foods with flour, Seasoned flour (p. 49), cornstarch, or water chestnut flour all at once and arrange them on waxed paper-lined plates or cookie sheets. Shake excess flour, starch or batter off of foods before placing in the hot oil.

Have cookie sheets or roasting pans lined with several layers of paper towels ready to receive the food. If you want to keep the food hot after frying, preheat the oven to 250°F. Keep the pot or wok lid close by in case of fire (see special tips for safety p. 171-172).

Preheat the oil to the required temperature after you have all your food prepared. This takes about 15 to 20 minutes. Put the thermometer in place in the *cold* oil before heating. If you put a cold thermometer in hot oil, it will break. If you forget to do this, run hot water over the thermometer, and dry it thoroughly before placing in the oil. The proper temperature is essential. If the heat is too low, the food absorbs too much oil; if the temperature is too high, the outside will brown before the middle is cooked and the oil may be damaged by burning. Most foods are fried between 350°F and 375°F. Of course this is for sea level. Reduce the frying temperature by 5% to 10% for altitudes 1,000 to 5,000 feet above sea level, and 10% to 15% for altitudes over 5,000 feet.

Don't fill your pot more than half full of oil. A wok need only be filled with oil about 2 inches deep.

Dip a basket, skimmer, or slotted spoon into the oil before placing the food to be fried in it. This prevents the food from sticking to the implement.

Place the food in the oil in a single layer—don't crowd the pan. They may stick together if you try to cook too much at once, and the temperature may drop.

If you are using a pot with a frying basket, place the food in a single layer in the basket and lower the basket into the hot oil. If it bubbles up too much, raise the basket and wait a few seconds before lowering it into the oil again.

If you don't have a basket, lower one or two pieces of food at a time into the oil with tongs, a slotted spoon, or wire skimmer. Don't drop foods into the batter, lower them slowly. You want to avoid being splashed with hot oil.

When the food looks golden or brown enough for your taste, remove it with the basket, tongs, slotted spoon, or skimmer, and place it on the paper towel-lined pans. To keep the food warm, place the pans in an oven that has been preheated to 250°F. Don't leave the food too long in the oven. Ideally, fried foods should be eaten right away. See "twice-frying" (p. 170) for a better method of frying foods ahead of time.

Let the temperature return to the correct level between batches.

Every so often, skim the oil with the wire skimmer or a slotted spoon and remove any bits of food and loosened batter, which will burn if left in the pan.

SPECIAL TIPS FOR DEEP FRYING IN A WOK

Use a flat-bottomed wok, if possible. If that's not possible, place your round-bottomed wok inside the metal wok ring that comes with it, to steady it. If you are using an electric range, you may have to move the wok off of the burner to lower the temperature quickly. Have an extra wok ring handy to set the wok down on, and make sure to have oven mitts close by.

This is a good purpose for which to use that electric wok that has been sitting in your bottom cupboard. An electric wok is not very good for stir-frying, but, since the heat is controlled, it's excellent for deep-frying. You only need to have the oil at a depth of 2 inches in the wok.

tured soy protein chunks, cutlets and "brests." I use it for Italian-style "fried" vegetable "cutlets" or slices, but Chinese vegetables are rarely served in large slices, so it isn't really a suitable method for vegetables used in Chinese cuisine.

Tofu can be oven-fried with or without a coating. See the Oven-Fried Tofu on p. 175 for oven-frying without a coating. Seitan and soy protein should be coated with Seasoned Flour (p. 49). Preheat the oven to 400°F. Use dark cookie sheets; they brown foods better. Lightly oil the sheets before placing the food on them, leaving some space between the pieces. If you have an oil pump-sprayer, spray the tops lightly with oil. Use expeller-pressed Asian peanut oil for good flavor. Bake for about 10 minutes, or until the underside is nicely golden brown. Turn the pieces over and bake for 10 minutes more, or until the other side is golden brown. Use as you would deep-fried pieces.

CHINESE BATTER FOR DEEP-FRIED FOODS

Yield: ⅓ cup

The Chinese prefer a starch batter over a flour batter for its crunchy texture. This doesn't look like a very large amount, but it's thin, so it goes a long way.

Variations

You can add a clove of crushed garlic or a pinch of garlic granules, a bit of five-spice powder, or ½ tablespoon dulse or nori flakes for a "seafood" flavor. Use the dulse or nori with Seitan "Seafood," p. 45, or oyster mushrooms.

½ tablespoon powdered egg replacer
¼ cup cold water
2 tablespoons cornstarch or water chestnut flour
½ teaspoon salt
½ teaspoon baking powder
½ teaspoon powdered ginger

In a small, deep bowl, beat the egg replacer and water until it's quite frothy. Stir in the remaining ingredients.

Per tablespoon: Calories 13, Protein 1 g, Fat 0 g, Carbohydrates 3 g

HOMEMADE DEEP-FRIED TOFU

Fried tofu can be used as a snack, appetizer, or as part of a meal. Served with a dipping sauce, it is a common street-vendor food in China. It is tender and absorbent and so is also frequently used in soups, braised dishes, and casseroles. It can also be used in stir-fries such as

Use firm tofu. Pat it dry. For triangles, cut the block in half crosswise if the block is rectangular rather than square, then cut each half in half horizontally. Then cut each of the four resulting pieces into four triangles. For cubes, cut into ½ to 1-inch cubes, depending on your needs.

Place the tofu on clean tea towels while you heat the oil. See pp. 172-173 about deep-frying. Add several pieces of tofu at a time to the hot oil and fry, turning often, just until the tofu is golden or golden brown (according to your preference). Remove with a slotted spoon and drain on paper.

Reheat and crisp fried tofu by frying as above for a few seconds just until crisp and hot immediately before serving. You can also broil or grill the pieces about 3 inches from the source of the heat until crisped and heated—watch for scorching.

Before using in braised dishes, casseroles, or soups you might like to follow a method called dousing. This is supposed to make the tofu lighter and easier to digest, but it is an optional step. The fried tofu is placed in a colander, and boiling water is poured over one side and then the other. The tofu is allowed to drain for a few minutes. After the tofu has cooled, you can squeeze it to get as much oil and water out of it as you can.

Oven-Fried Tofu

This is an alternative to deep-frying tofu. Use firm tofu. Pat it dry. For triangles, cut the block in half crosswise if the block is rectangular rather than square, then cut each half in half horizontally. Then cut each of the four resulting pieces into four triangles. For cubes, cut into ½ to 1-inch cubes, depending on your needs.

Place the tofu on dark oiled cookie sheets. (Dark sheets brown foods better than shiny ones.) Oil the tops lightly, using an oil-spray mister or a brush. Use expeller-pressed Asian peanut oil for the best flavor. Bake at 500°F for 5 to 7 minutes per side, or until golden and puffy. These may be frozen for future use.

Crispy "Pork" with Sweet-and-Sour Sauce (pp. 132-133) or Pineapple Sweet and Sour (p. 133). It can be baked, broiled, or grilled with a barbecue sauce, or served plain with a barbecue or dipping sauce on the side, in place of pork or chicken. It freezes well.

If you live near a Chinese grocery store or tofu factory, you will be able to buy fried tofu for use in your recipes. Some supermarkets carry the Japanese variety of fried tofu cubes or triangles.

Fried Tofu with Dipping Sauce

Yield: 4 to 6 servings as a snack

1 pound firm tofu, cut into triangles and deep-fried (see pp. 174-175)

Dipping Sauce:
5 tablespoons light soy sauce
3 tablespoons rice, cider, or white wine vinegar
2 tablespoons chopped fresh cilantro
1 teaspoon chili oil

Deep-fry the tofu pieces until golden brown as directed in the recipe. Drain on paper. Serve hot or at room temperature with the Dipping Sauce.

This is a common snack sold by street vendors. For a low-fat variation, use Oven-Fried Tofu instead of the deep-fried tofu.

Per serving: Calories 138, Protein 8 g, Fat 10 g, Carbohydrates 4 g

Spicy Deep-Fried "Pork"

Yield: 4 servings

Depending on your relationship with fat, you can either really deep-fry the coated reconstituted textured soy protein chunks or oven-fry them. Either way, this dish is delectable.

1½ cups reconstituted textured soy protein chunks (pp. 50-51)
Seasoned Flour (p. 49)
1 tablespoon oil
1 large green or red bell pepper, cut into 1-inch squares
1 cup chopped green onions
1 tablespoon fermented black beans, mashed with a fork
1 tablespoon dry sherry
½ tablespoon grated fresh ginger
½ teaspoon chili garlic paste
1 teaspoon roasted sesame oil

Coat the textured soy protein in the seasoned flour. Either deep-fry in hot oil until golden all over (see pp. 172-173), and drain on paper, or oven-fry (p. 172).

Heat a large wok or heavy skillet over high heat. When very hot, add the oil. When the oil is hot, add the bell pepper and stir-fry until wilted. Remove from the pan.

Place the other ingredients in the pan, except the sesame oil. Stir-fry for 1 minute, adding a few drops of water or broth if necessary to prevent sticking. Add the peppers and sesame oil, and serve immediately.

Per serving: Calories 109, Protein 8 g, Fat 4 g, Carbohydrates 9 g

Dry Garlic "Ribs"

Yield: 4 servings

2 cups reconstituted textured soy protein chunks (see pp. 50-51), well drained
2 tablespoons light soy sauce
2 tablespoons cornstarch
1 tablespoon maple syrup
Freshly ground black pepper, to taste
1 tablespoon oil
2 tablespoons minced garlic
1 tablespoon roasted sesame oil

Mix the soy protein chunks with the soy sauce, cornstarch, maple syrup, and black pepper. Heat the oil in a large skillet over high heat. Add the soy protein and the garlic, and stir-fry for several minutes. Scrape the mixture onto a cookie sheet, and brown under the broiler, 3 to 4 inches from the heat. Turn the pieces and broil the other side. Serve immediately.

Per serving: Calories 151, Protein 11 g, Fat 7 g, Carbohydrates 13 g

This delicious but simple recipe uses textured soy protein chunks instead of sweet-and-sour Chinese pork ribs.

Lemon "Chicken"

Yield: 4 servings

12 to 14 ounces extra-firm tofu, cut into 16 slices and marinated in Breast of Tofu "Chicken" marinade (p. 43) for at least 8 hours
2 tablespoons dry sherry
1 tablespoon light soy sauce
2 tablespoons oil
¼ cup cornstarch

This is one of the most beloved Chinese restaurant dishes. This version is not sweet.

Sauce:

½ cup vegetarian broth
¼ cup fresh lemon juice
2 tablespoons roasted sesame oil
1 teaspoon grated fresh ginger
1 teaspoon light unbleached sugar

Drain the marinated tofu, and marinate again for 10 minutes in the sherry and soy sauce. Heat the oil in a large heavy skillet over medium-high heat. Drain the marinade and save it.

Toss the tofu pieces in the cornstarch. Arrange the pieces in the pan in the hot oil, and fry until crisp and golden on both sides. Drain on paper. Wipe out the pan with a paper towel, and turn the heat to high. Add the sauce ingredients to the pan, and bring to a boil. Add the fried tofu pieces, and cook 2 to 3 minutes until a sauce is formed. Serve immediately.

Per serving: Calories 239, Protein 7 g, Fat 17 g, Carbohydrates 11 g

SWEET LEMON "CHICKEN"

Yield: 4 servings

This is a sweeter version, different, but just as delicious as Lemon "Chicken." If you prefer, oven-fry the "brests" (see p. 172).

12 ounces reconstituted textured soy protein (3¼ ounces dry)
  "chiken brest," cutlets or chunks cooked in chickeny broth
  (pp. 50-51)
2 tablespoons cornstarch
1 tablespoon dry sherry
½ tablespoon light soy sauce
Dash of white pepper
Flour, cornstarch, or water chestnut flour
Oil for frying

Sauce:

¼ cup cold vegetarian broth (it can be the "chickeny" broth in which you reconstituted the textured soy protein)

3 tablespoons light unbleached sugar

3 tablespoons fresh lemon juice

¼ teaspoon salt

½ tablespoon cornstarch

1 teaspoon roasted sesame oil

4 thin slices of lemon, cut in half

Drain and gently squeeze the soy protein pieces to remove the excess liquid. If you use the "brests," cut them into approximately 1-inch squares. Toss the soy protein pieces with the 2 tablespoons cornstarch, sherry, light soy sauce, and white pepper.

Dredge the soy protein pieces in the flour to coat. Heat the oil in a large wok or heavy skillet, and fry the textured soy protein until golden brown (see pp. 174-175). Remove and drain on paper towels. Keep warm in a 250°F oven.

Remove all but 1 tablespoon of the oil from the wok or skillet. Combine the sauce ingredients, add to the skillet, and stir over high heat until thickened and bubbly. If it becomes too thick, add a little more broth. Place the fried "chicken" on a heated plate, garnish with the lemon slices, and pour the sauce evenly over the top. Serve immediately.

Per serving: Calories 317, Protein 48 g, Fat 0 g, Carbohydrates 28 g

Variation
Orange Sauce "Chicken"

We enjoyed a similar dish in one of our favorite Vancouver, B.C., Chinese Buddhist vegetarian restaurants, the Bo Kong.

For the sauce, omit the lemon juice and use ¼ cup freshly squeezed orange juice. Reduce the sugar to 1 tablespoon, and garnish with thinly sliced oranges.

Chapter XIV

SWEETS

There is a general opinion in the West that the Chinese have few sweets. That is not really true, but it is true that they have few desserts as we know them. The Chinese rarely eat sweets right after a meal; they generally eat them at tea time and enjoy them in a bakery or confectioner's shop.

Sweets in China are often made from ingredients that we Westerners find strange—glutinous rice flour dumplings, sweet red bean fillings, and soups, even white "wood ear" fungus in a sugary soup. Others may be sweet versions of common savory foods, such as sweet filled steamed buns, crepes, fried wontons, or pastries. Some famous Chinese desserts, such as Peking Glazed Apples, requiring many steps (including deep-frying, dipping in molten sugar which is then spun into threads and plunged into ice water) are best left to talented chefs in restaurants.

Since this is a homestyle cookbook, I've chosen a small representation of sweets that any cook could easily make and which fit a Westerner's idea of dessert.

The cookies are excellent with tea, rice wine, or dry sherry, but can also be served for dessert with fruit sorbet. They are not low in fat, but I have substituted oil and/or dairy-free margarine for the usual lard.

Steamed pears and other fruit in a simple syrup with wine are a favorite Chinese sweet, and any sort of refreshing fruit salad would also make an excellent ending to a Chinese meal. Tangerines, or mandarin oranges, and kiwis (Chinese gooseberries) make good additions to fruit salad. Fresh fruit of any kind in season is always appropriate, perhaps accompanied by some sugared nuts, a Chinese favorite.

WHEAT-FREE ALMOND COOKIES

Yield: about 3 dozen cookies

1 cup brown or white rice flour
½ cup light unbleached sugar, finely ground in a dry blender
2 cups finely ground blanched almonds
⅓ cup dairy-free margarine
About 36 toasted whole blanched almonds
Soymilk for brushing

Preheat the oven to 350°F. Sift the rice flour and sugar together into a medium bowl. Stir in the almonds and then work in the margarine. It should form a dough—if not, add water a few drops at a time. Press and roll the dough into small balls, and place them on oiled cookie sheets 3 inches apart.

Press a toasted almond on the top of each ball. Brush the cookies with soymilk. Bake for about 15 minutes, then remove carefully to racks and cool thoroughly before serving. After cooling, they can be stored in an airtight container for a couple of weeks, or they can be frozen.

Per cookie: Calories 96, Protein 2 g, Fat 7 g, Carbohydrates 8 g

Serve these with tea, rice wine, or dry sherry for some special friends. They are simple to make.

SESAME SEED COOKIES

Yield: 2½ dozen cookies

2¼ cups unbleached flour
½ cup light unbleached sugar, finely ground in a dry blender
1½ teaspoons baking powder
¼ teaspoon salt
½ cup expeller-pressed Asian peanut oil
½ cup soymilk
½ tablespoon powdered egg replacer
1 teaspoon vanilla
About 1 cup raw hulled sesame seeds for coating
Soymilk for brushing

These have been part of my (small) cookie repertoire for many years. They are not very sweet—a perfect accompaniment to tea, rice wine, or sherry.

Allergy Note

If you have a peanut allergy you can use any other oil instead.

Preheat the oven to 375°F.

Mix the flour, sugar, baking powder, and salt in a medium bowl. Mix the oil, soymilk, egg replacer, and vanilla in another bowl or beaker with a whisk, then pour into the dry ingredients. Mix into a smooth dough. Shape each rounded tablespoon of dough into an oval loaf shape. Roll in the sesame seeds to coat.

Place the cookies on oiled cookie sheets, brush with soymilk, and bake for 15 to 20 minutes, or just until golden on the bottom. Carefully remove to racks and cool thoroughly. These can be stored airtight for a couple of weeks, or frozen.

Per cookie: Calories 97, Protein 2 g, Fat 5 g, Carbohydrates 10 g

WALNUT COOKIES

Yield: 40 cookies

They love nuts in Sichuan province, especially walnuts. These very rich cookies go well with tea.

Dry Ingredients:

1 cup unbleached flour
¾ cup whole wheat pastry flour
1 teaspoon baking powder
½ teaspoon salt

Wet Ingredients:

1 cup dark unbleached sugar
⅞ cup dairy-free margarine
¼ cup soymilk
1 teaspoon vanilla extract

Other:

¼ cup minced walnuts
40 walnut halves
Soymilk for brushing

Mix the dry ingredients in a medium bowl. Beat the wet ingredients together in a food processor or in another bowl with an electric beater until fluffy. Add the dry ingredients to the wet, along with the minced walnuts, and stir well. Cover the dough and chill it for 1 hour to 2 days.

Preheat the oven to 350°F. Divide the dough into 4 equal pieces, then each piece into 10 equal slices. Roll each slice into a ball. Place the balls on 3 ungreased cookie sheets, at least 2 inches apart. Press a walnut half into each ball. Brush the cookies with soymilk.

Bake for 10 to 12 minutes, or until golden brown on the bottom. Cool on racks. When cool, store airtight.

Per cookie: Calories 89, Protein 1 g, Fat 5 g, Carbohydrates 9 g

STEAMED SPONGE CAKE

Yield: 12 servings

"Egg White" Mixture:

3 tablespoons EnerG Egg Replacer (this is the only brand that whips enough for this recipe)
¾ cup cold water

Dry Ingredients:

1½ cups white pastry flour
1½ teaspoons baking powder
½ teaspoon salt

Wet Ingredients:

1¼ cups light unbleached sugar
½ cup soymilk
2 tablespoons oil
¼ teaspoon vanilla extract
¼ teaspoon pure almond extract

The Chinese steamed sponge cake is a ubiquitous sweet in Chinese bakeries and tea houses. No doubt it has Western origins, but it is well entrenched in the Chinese cuisine of today. A recipe from an 18th century Chinese farmer's almanac described it as "Foreigner's Cake."

This vegan version is light and spongey. We like it with fruit on it, such as thawed frozen berries.

With dairy-free margarine or vegetable shortening, generously grease a small tube pan (9 inches across the top, 6 inches across the bottom, and 3 inches deep) or a special pan that makes 4 small tube cakes (4 inches across and 2 inches deep).

Place the egg replacer powder and water in a medium-sized deep mixing bowl. Beat with an electric beater, scraping the sides often at first, for about 10 minutes, or until the mixture looks like beaten egg whites that will hold a soft peak.

Mix the dry ingredients well in a medium bowl.

Blend the wet ingredients in a blender or food processor until the sugar is almost dissolved. Add this to the dry ingredients and mix briefly but well until the mixture is smooth, but without beating it.

Now scoop in the "egg white" mixture, and fold and turn the mixture carefully into the batter with a rubber spatula until it is homogenous, or until no big blobs of "egg white" remain and the mixture is a light, airy batter. *Do not stir it in.*

Scrape the batter into the prepared pan(s). Place the pan on a rack in a large pot above simmering water, or balance it on two chopsticks placed across the bottom of a large wok with simmering water in it. You can also use 4 chopsticks placed "tic-tac-toe" style. The water should not touch the cake pan. Cover the pot or wok tightly. (Do not cover the cake pan.) Cook over medium-high heat until a toothpick comes out clean when inserted in the center, and the cake is light and springy to the touch. This may take 1 hour. for the large pan, or 25 minutes for the smaller pans, but check often. (Since the cake contains baking powder, it will not fall like an angel cake unless you really give it a jolt.) Add boiling water to the large pot as necessary. The cake will not brown.

Place the pan on a cake rack for 5 minutes, then loosen the sides. Place a plate over the top, turn it over, and give the bottom of the pan a whack to loosen it. Serve hot or cooled with fruit.

Per serving: Calories 159, Protein 3 g, Fat 3 g, Carbohydrates 30 g

Mail-order sources for Marmite, and Vegemite, International Condiments and Seasonings, Vinegars, etc.

Cardullo's Gourmet Shop
6 Brattle St.
Cambridge, MA 02138

G.B. Ratto & Co.
821 Washington St.
Oakland, CA 94607
www.cardullos.com

ABC Vegetarian Foods
(meat analogs, agar, kosher gelatin, etc.)
Call this toll-free number to order,
or to find their nearest location.
1-800-765-6955 *(also good for Canada)*

The Mail Order Catalog for Healthy Eating
P.O. Box 180
Summertown, TN 38483
1-800-695-2241; Fax (931) 964-2291
www.healthy-eating.com
e-mail: askus@healthyeating.com

(catalog lists textured soy products of all sizes, dry mixes for seitan, nutritional yeast, and agar)

In Canada:

Choices Market
2627 W. 16th Ave.
Vancouver, B.C., Canada V6K 3C2
Phone: (604) 736-0009
Fax: (604) 736-0011

No catalog but will take phone or fax orders and ship COD anywhere in Canada. Prepaid and credit cards accepted. Discounts on volume buying. Friendly service.

Websites for mail-order Chinese or Asian Food

If you live in an area where it is difficult to find Chinese ingredients, such as vegetarian"oyster" sauce, canned vegetarian "roast duck," and other gluten products, the worldwide web can help.

All of these sites have mail-order catalogs for Chinese and Asian foods. The prices are reasonable and sometimes the shipping is free in the U.S. Some of the sites have recipes and other helpful information. If you don't own a computer, perhaps a friend, an internet cafe, or your local library can help.

www.welcome-to-china.com/ogs

www.asiafoods.com

www.easywok.com

www.gongshee.com

www.orientalpantry.com
(catalog lists Coin Tree Vegetable Mushroom Sauce, a vegetarian oyster sauce substitute)

Mailing Address:
423 Great Road (Route 2A)
Acton, MA 01720
Phone: 978-264-4576

www.quickspice.com
(catalog lists Lee Kum Kee Vegetarian Stir-Fry Sauce, a vegetarian oyster sauce substitute)

Index

Also by Bryanna Clark Grogan

20 Minutes to Dinner

Get in and out of the kitchen fast with tempting and nutritious meat-, egg-, and dairy-free recipes. 192 pp $12.95

The Almost No-Fat Cookbook

Dozens of recipes for winning your family over to healthful, low-fat eating. 192 pp $12.95

The Almost No-Fat Holiday Cookbook

Satisfying, festive meals that are heart-healthy and easy on the waistline. 192 pp $12.95

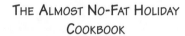

Nonna's Italian Kitchen

A tour of regional Italian dishes that reveals how Italian cooks work their culinary magic. All vegetarian, dairy- and egg-free. 256 pp $14.95

Soyfoods Cooking for a Positive Menopause

The latest information on why soyfoods work effectively to help women through menopause. Learn how to make delicious meals with soyfoods. 192 pp $12.95

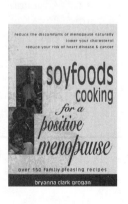

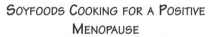

Purchase these cookbooks at your local natural foods store or book store, or you may order directly from:
Book Publishing Company
P.O. Box 99
Summertown, TN 38483
Please include $3 shipping per book